MANAGING THE HIGHER EDUCATION ENTERPRISE

MANAGING THE HIGHER EDUCATION ENTERPRISE

Nathaniel H. Karol

Coopers & Lybrand

Sigmund G. Ginsburg

University of Cincinnati

A RONALD PRESS PUBLICATION

JOHN WILEY & SONS, New York • Chichester • Brisbane • Toronto

Published by John Wiley & Sons, Inc.

Library of Congress Cataloging in Publication Data:

Karol, Nathaniel H
    Managing the higher education enterprise.

    "A Ronald Press publication."
    Includes index.
    1. Universities and colleges—United States—
Administration. I. Ginsburg, Sigmund G., joint
author. II. Title.

    LB2341.K34   378.73   80–12690
    ISBN 0–471–05022–9

Printed in the United States of America

10   9   8   7   6   5   4   3   2

To our wives and children
in grateful appreciation of their continued patience,
encouragement, and support

Foreword

After studying the role of presidents in 20 major American universities, Cohen and March, in *Leadership and Ambiguity,* concluded that a state of organized anarchy was the term that best described university culture. Neither the administrative, hierarchical model of the corporate world, nor the political model of democratic government with its checks and balances among the executive, legislative, and judicial branches would be appropriate. Where a continuously shifting membership body—the faculty and its committees—attempts to implement widely different methods to accomplish goals that are never fully identified or agreed on —conditions characteristic of the university—only anarchy, somewhat organized, prevails.

Cohen and March describe the university, only partially in caricature, as follows: "Teachers decide if, when, and what to teach. Students decide if, when, and what to learn. Legislators and donors decide if, when, and what to support." Decisions made within the university, they conclude, are a consequence of the system "but [are] intended by no one and decisively controlled by no one."

Such looseness in governance and management may indeed be the university's greatest strength even though its cost is great inefficiency. Orderliness, hierarchical authority, discipline, and widespread agreement do not contribute to the creativity, free inquiry, and pluralism that are the central characteristics of a good university. A university is not like a railroad whose goal is to run its trains on time, safely, and comfortably. The university's nature is to run its trains in scattered directions, simultaneously, with engineers who have minds of their own. There is nothing and should be nothing safe, on time, or comfortable about a university.

Nevertheless, as more and more tax dollars feed into higher education, both public and private, and as consumers of education give new interpretation to the phrase "caveat emptor" causing them to be more demanding and less trusting, universities are being asked to be less chaotic and more organized in their efforts to provide education for an increasing proportion of the population. In response, educators, particularly those on the administrative side, are developing a stronger interest in the practice of management. They hope to find a strategy of management subtle and flexible enough to preserve academic values while it also introduces greater effectiveness and more efficiency.

Our authors promise no miracles in the accomplishment of that goal. They systematically set down a number of significant questions that face anyone who hopes to lead a university in a way responsive to the new demands made on it. They then offer a variety of helpful answers.

In the complexity of university life no question has a single correct answer. What might be right for one institution might not be possible in another. Thoughtful readers will readily sort out the answers they can use.

The authors asked me to emphasize one point in my foreword: they make no pretense of being philosophers of education. They appropriately do not delve into educational programming or academic values. The values and goals of a university are determined by the faculty. Whatever these are, our authors say, they deserve a supportive and rational management framework.

Readers who have struggled with the problems of administering a university will note the authentic ring of what the authors say. Readers without the benefit of experience can be assured that the authors "have been there" and know in a very practical way what they are talking about.

TIMOTHY W. COSTELLO
President
Adelphi University
Garden City, New York

Preface

Higher education has long been a cornerstone of our free society, traditionally accorded a high place in our value structure. With the vital mission of equipping our citizens to function effectively in an increasingly complex society in which the state of knowledge is expanding at a geometric rate, higher education in our society should enjoy a reasonably secure position. But those who have closely followed trends in higher education have developed an increasing concern about the continued viability of many of our institutions and of the system of higher education as we have known it.

In recent years, we have witnessed the cost of education rising to prohibitive levels, and we have witnessed a startling attrition rate, particularly among independent institutions. We have witnessed a growing trend toward unionization among faculty, as well as other nonacademic employees, and growing schisms between faculty and administration.

We have also seen a variety of new developments, such as changes in the pattern of enrollments, changes in funding patterns and the imposition of a complex and demanding body of federal regulations. Institutions, by nature change resistant, have often found themselves not fully able to adapt or respond to these changes effectively.

Perhaps one of the most significant trends has been the change in the demand for the products of our higher education system—college graduates and PhDs. There are a number of reasons for the current state of disenchantment with higher education. But certainly, an important factor has to be that young people—and their parents—no longer are able to view a college education as the key to upward economic mobility and the good life.

During the administration of President Kennedy, and following the launching of Sputnik, federal policy was aimed at remedying the apparent decline in the quality of our education and the apparent technological lag which this superior Russian accomplishment seemed to signify.

Federal expenditures for graduate fellowships and traineeships rose from $31.7 million to a peak of $262.1 million in 1968–69. By 1972 the percentage of faculty with PhDs rose to 68%, as contrasted with 40% in 1955. In 1968 it was estimated that there were approximately two and a half academic jobs for every new PhD. By 1972 there were three new PhDs for every such job.

The situation grows worse. A recent study sponsored by the Mellon Foundation estimated that by 1990 the United States will have a surplus of 60,000 PhDs in the humanities alone, and this market condition is not confined to PhDs. According to a study by the U.S. Bureau of Labor Statistics conducted in 1978, one out of every four students with bachelor's degrees, as many as 2.7 million college graduates, will have to settle for a job that, in the past, generally has not required a college education. Critics have contended that our educational leaders are insufficiently conscious of these trends and their implications.

Consequently, those charged with the management of our higher education enterprise find themselves confronted not only with a myriad of practical problems, but also with changing attitudes reflected in part by a highly critical evaluation of institutions and their management by their multiple constituencies—trustees, faculty, students, state legislators, federal officials, alumni, community leaders, and the general public.

One can acknowledge that the institution of higher education has significant frailties and still assert that, despite its weaknesses and shortcomings, it remains one of our most valuable institutions. But that is beside the point. What is reflected by the current criticisms is that those who continue to value higher education are not necessarily willing to accept that we have to live with its defects.

The heightening of a critical attitude toward higher education also reflects itself in a diminished willingness to rely on educational administrators. Many constituencies are no longer willing to play a relatively benign and generally passive role in supporting the mission of higher education and in delegating broad discretion to institutional administrators in the financial stewardship of our higher education institutions. "Accountability" is the byword and the multiple constituents are concerned to know and understand how our higher education institutions marshall the resources to carry out their respective missions and how they manage and utilize those resources.

Given the time and the inclination, there is an abundance of written material to which these constituents can refer to gain a deeper understanding of the dynamics of college and university administration and its fiscal implications. The "Five Foot Shelf" included in this text contains an illustrative, but far from all-inclusive, compendium of some of this material, which ranges from the broadly philosophic to the technically detailed.

It is through the authors' perspectives, combining backgrounds in government administration, teaching, university administration, and consulting to colleges and universities, that this book hopes to make its contribution.

The book starts with two essential points of focus. The first is that higher education is a multi-billion dollar *enterprise*. The following few statistics may illustrate that point. In 1977 $42.9 billion was spent by all institutions of higher education, $28.9 billion by public institutions. Federal grants to higher education amounted to $9.6 billion ($4.8 billion to elementary and secondary education.) State appropriations for higher education operating expenses now exceed $15.3 billion. The total expenditures for education at all levels during 1976–77 amounted to 7.7 percent of the gross national product, and if one includes students at all levels, teachers, superintendents, principals, supervisors, and other instructional staff, but not support staff, nearly three out of every ten persons is *directly* involved in the educational process.

However unique its environment and the dynamics of its governance process, and however special and valuable its service, higher education is governed, *as is any other enterprise,* by the financial realities of income and outlay, and by the market realities of supply and demand. The second point of focus is that the multiple constituents of higher education, who are demanding increased accountability but, in many instances, have only a limited understanding of the complexities of university administration, need to develop a broad appreciation of the external issues and internal considerations that affect the condition of our educational institutions.

We have tried to discuss some of the important aspects of managing our post-secondary institutions in a manner that is not excessively technical. We have also tried to highlight some of the issues that provide a context for evaluating institutional operations. The term highlight is important. Each of these issues could receive extensive in-depth treatment. Although the constituents enumerated above will constitute the primary audience, many of those engaged in business management will, it is hoped, find that this helps to give them a perspective on their responsibilities as well.

The decision that one of the major functions of this book would be to highlight issues inevitably raised the question for the authors as to how the issues would be presented. It is, at least, theoretically possible to make a balanced presentation of all viewpoints while the authors remain inscrutably neutral.

The reader will not get very far into the text before discovering that the authors are quite scrutable. We have attempted to present opposing or contrasting views on the various issues discussed, but have made no pretense of neutrality. Our positions have been indicated explicitly in preference to letting our biases creep in through the manner in which the issues are presented.

If the reader finds some of the statements to be provocative, the reaction is intended. The authors believe that those associated with the management of our higher education enterprise cannot afford to be either passive or neutral. Higher education is in ferment. Its future viability depends upon strong, aggressive, innovative leadership.

NATHANIEL H. KAROL
SIGMUND G. GINSBURG

Chicago
Cincinnati
July 1980

Contents

Contents

MANAGING THE HIGHER EDUCATION ENTERPRISE

Chapter One

TRENDS AND ACCELERATING PROBLEMS

The labeling of some programs as "non-traditional" explicitly conveys that our institutions are tradition based and have tended to be change resistant. But this is no longer as true as it once was.

During the past half century we have witnessed technological advances (perhaps more dramatic and far reaching than the industrial revolution), major demographic changes, changes in the family structure, a greatly heightened social consciousness, and an increased emphasis on access to higher education for the economically and educationally disadvantaged.

An institution such as Higher Education could not survive in a society undergoing such radical changes unless it succeeded in adapting to those changes while striving to maintain its traditional values. Within this context, it is important that those concerned with the management of our educational enterprise have some appreciation of the specific ways in which societal changes are affecting higher education so that they may be in a position to better judge the effectiveness with which the specific institutions that are the subject of their concern are adapting to these changes.

The trends that will be briefly highlighted here are: Loss of Public Confidence in the Value and Utility of Higher Education; Changing Enrollment Patterns; Competition Among and Between Institutions and Sectors; The Rising Cost of Education to the Consumer and the Taxpayer; The Growth of the Community Colleges; Increasing Concern about Effective Management in Educational Institutions; and Erosion of Collegiality. These trends have been apparent over the last decade and appear likely to continue and, perhaps, accelerate in the next decade.

LOSS OF PUBLIC CONFIDENCE IN THE VALUE AND UTILITY OF HIGHER EDUCATION

This loss has been attributed to such factors as: campus unrest in the '60s; the perceived lowering of standards and requirements for admission and success in college; the proliferation of programs; the loss of uniqueness in holding a BA degree because of the large number of individuals attending college; the seemingly large number of individuals who have been disappointed in the quality of their educational experience; the exposure to the public of college graduates who are lacking in the basic skills that, it is believed, should have been acquired at the secondary level (but certainly at the collegiate level); the sense that teaching is just a job and nothing more; and the absence of a sufficient number of educational statesmen, leaders, innovators. Beyond these factors, there is a recognition that the social and economic argument that has often been blatantly or subtly advanced for going to college—you'll get a better job, have doors opened for you, lead a better life, meet good friends who will help you later in life—may not be totally or even partially accurate. At the very least, recent studies suggest that the gap between lifetime earnings of college graduates in contrast to non-college graduates appears to have narrowed considerably.

One recent study, in particular, suggests that we may have to re-examine some of our expectations in regard to higher education as an agency for social reform. The thrust of "open admissions" policies has been to open the doors of higher education to those who have historically been economically and educationally disadvantaged (generally members of minority groups), and to attempt through remedial courses, tutorial programs, special counseling and enlarged student financial aid, to ensure that the open admissions student is given every opportunity and encouragement to succeed and to achieve a degree.

For many of these disadvantaged students, despite attempts to ease their path to collegiate success, the handicap of inadequate academic preparation at the secondary school level is a most difficult one to overcome.

Moreover, there is a severe financial hardship involved for the economically disadvantaged to gain a higher education, despite the availability of financial aid. That they have been induced to pursue higher education under these circumstances is largely attributable to the fact that higher education is one of society's status symbols and that for some time there has been an impression that higher education represents the only sure path to upward economic and social mobility. This belief has been so widespread that in some instances students have been motivated to continue their education despite the handicap of low academic ability, as well as poor academic preparation. A recent study by Larry Leslie and Lowell Crary of the University of Arizona Center for the Study of Higher Education* suggests that we may have done a great disservice to these students in creating false expectations.

The study suggests that many low-income or disadvantaged students who do not perform well in high school might be hurting themselves financially if they forego four years of earned income for a college degree of increasingly questionable economic value. Those who are likely to see the greatest financial return on their college education, the study asserts, are high ability students who may recoup "two or three times or more" the financial return that low-ability students can expect.

The study, which used data from the National Longitudinal Study of the High School Class of 1972, based ability on students' high school grade averages or class rank. Study findings indicate that whether or not these are appropriate indices of true academic ability, they are reliable predictors of financial success. An alternative conclusion that this may support is that an educational thrust aimed at the disadvantaged must begin at a much earlier stage than college to be effective (a conclusion already reached by many governmental and educational leaders.) The adequacy of the sample may also be called into question. But taken at face value, the study leads to the conclusion that while *some* postsecondary educational training may have a financial payoff for low-income, low-ability students, extended study may not. To the extent that such a conclusion has validity, social concern for the disadvantaged might well also focus on removing the stigma associated with the lack of a degree and on fostering career opportunities for financial success that do not necessarily require advanced education. Stated differently, the sense of social justice and obligation that impels us to strive for equality of opportunity for the disadvantaged would seem to require that even more than the average student, the disadvantaged student should be provided with meaningful, realistic information on career opportunities, and their relationship to a postsecondary education.

* Larry Leslie and Lowell Crary, *The Private Cost of Postsecondary Education*, Topical Paper No. 13, University of Arizona Center for the Study of Higher Education, College of Education, September 1978.

Observers differ in the importance that they attach to each of the various factors presumed to have an influence on current attitudes toward education. Yet it is hard to dispute that the economics of today's environment—as reflected in both the diminishing number of promising career opportunities in proportion to the number of college graduates and in the rising cost of education—has aggravated the dichotomy between the concept of the liberal arts education as necessary to the full development of the individual and the career oriented concept of education.

Among the ingredients in today's environment that must be recognized as bearing on this dichotomy, two are perhaps the most critical. The exponential expansion of knowledge has meant that the well-educated individual will, under the best of circumstances, not be as comparatively well educated as his counterpart of fifty or even twenty-five years ago because the body of knowledge to be mastered is simply too large. A second point is that we cannot fail to recognize that the communications media (television in particular, despite the major defects in programming) constitute a major source of informal education.

The strong liberal arts institutions today continue to stress the traditional values of college and shy away from espousing and often attack the vocationalism and pre-professionalism approach that many admissions brochures stress. But, in fact, many institutions are stressing the job related aspects of the curriculum and the placement services available, in order to attract students. Even in fields of traditional study that have in the past attracted a large number of student majors, there is now an evident tendency toward building a coalition or joint major and minor with subject matter that appears to be more career oriented in order to maintain enrollments. Thus, as an example, we see less emphasis on political science and more on public administration and pre-law; English now involves a stress on communications and business writing; economics is more closely geared to management and business; philosophy geared to the policy-making sciences and public policy; and languages are geared to translation and business. Many colleges and graduate schools of arts and sciences seek various incentives such as scholarships, assistantships, combined, shortened, or accelerated programs in order to compete with the professional-school programs such as those in business, law, medicine, nursing, or social work. Striking an appropriate balance between the concepts of education as life preparation and education as career preparation is critical to our society. But it is, perhaps, even more critical to the mission assessment and survival of individual institutions.

CHANGING ENROLLMENT PATTERNS

Enrollment changes have occurred in the shift to career related depart-ments and schools, and, in response to apparent changes in employment opportunities, such as from elementary education teaching preparation to special education. Recent publicity on the surplus of teachers has also resulted in fewer students being attracted to schools of education. Further, as is well recognized, due to the slowing down of the United States birthrate, there will be fewer 17–21 year olds than in the great expansionary period of the '60s until sometime in the 1990s. Thus, most institutions have experienced or will experience declining enrollments from among new high school graduates. This has increased competition among institutions and induced many institutions to modify their ap-proaches (such as by adoption of more community oriented and "mid-life" programs) and marketing. The term marketing validly describes the increasingly aggressive efforts of respectable institutions to recruit new students. Declining enrollments have also resulted in lowering of standards of admission at some institutions and led to unemployment and underemployment of PhDs. Enrollment declines have also created concerns about tenure, promotion, and job security and led to excess space, particularly dormitory space. Projections of educational statistics published by the National Center for Educational Statistics reflect a total of 2,679,000 high school graduates in 1966–67 peaking to 3,149,000 ten years later and declining to 2,740,000 in 1986–87. Total college and university enrollments were at a level of 6,390,000 in 1966 and showed a steady but declining rate of increase projected to yield total enrollments of 12,903,000 in 1986. In this period, two year institutions are projected to increase from an enrollment level of 1,326,000 in 1966 and 3,883,000 in 1976 to 5,979,000 in 1986. Enrollments at four year institutions were 5,064,000 in 1966, 7,129,000 in 1976 and projected to decline to 6,924,000 in 1986. Graduate enrollments which were at 768,000 in 1966 and 1,333,000 in 1976 are projected to increase to 1,532,000 in 1986.

These statistics appear to reflect that, at least in the view of those compiling the projections, very substantial numbers of high school gradu-ates are expected to attend post secondary institutions, despite the cur-rent state of disillusionment regarding job prospects for college gradu-ates. But the statistical projections reflect two other interesting points. First, they suggest that the relative proportions of students enrolling at two year colleges and four year colleges are showing a marked trend toward two year institutions. This reflects a response by students to the apparent plethora of college graduates and emphasizes their inclination toward the career oriented and paraprofessional programs. This is also a response to the increased cost of education since two-year institutions are less costly; particularly since they are generally close to home.

The second point of interest is that the proportionate number of graduate students in relation to four year institution enrollments is expected to increase dramatically over 1966 levels by 1986. One interpretation of this statistic suggests that those who attend four year institutions tend, preponderantly, to be preparing for graduate and professional work recognizing that the bachelor's degree is, to an increasing extent, insufficient for career preparation. This statistic has particular meaning to the extent that four year institutions engage in mission reassessment and consider the possibility of specialization.

COMPETITION AMONG AND BETWEEN INSTITUTIONS AND SECTORS

Loss of public confidence and changing enrollments have created circumstances in which institutions have felt constrained to become increasingly competitive in order to maintain quality, provide salary increases, meet inflationary costs, replace or refurbish aging facilities and undertake new programs.

This competition has been between and among public and independent institutions; between the four year institutions and the universities; between four year institutions and community colleges; and between the various colleges and universities and the various proprietary "trade" or "vocational" schools, some of which are now authorized to grant associate degrees. Within a particular institution there is competition for students and resources among departments and schools and between traditional schools and non-traditional colleges for adults or evening students often with the latter more flexible, e.g., granting life learning credits. A number of business firms provide very satisfactory technical and broad training programs that are of direct value to employees and, in fact, can be accepted for college credits.

It should be understood that competition, when used in the context of this discussion, does not connote the same kind of aggressive activity that characterizes competition in the commercial marketplace. In the education sector competition still carries the more limited connotation of offering the same kinds of educational services as one or more institutions drawing from the same marketplace (this takes into consideration geographic location, the size of the institution, the range and quality of programs and tuition and fee levels, among other things.)

Although it is fair to say that most institutional administrators and their faculty have long maintained an awareness of "who the competition is," it is equally fair to say in general that they have not found it appropriate or necessary to make any particular use of this knowledge. In this connection, it might also be noted that too frequently the admissions office, which is ultimately concerned with marketing the institution to prospective students, is too remote from, rather than integrated with, the essential activities that relate to the mission and identity of the institution—as is development, the other marketing activity.

But signs of change are emerging. Increasing fiscal pressures and the heightened competition for students and funds are leading to a truer competition in which institutions are beginning to examine the reasons for the apparent success of their competitors, not necessarily with a view toward becoming more like them, but more broadly, in the interests of improving their own competitive position. This has not yet become a very sophisticated process. But, as an increasing number of institutions begin to approach competition more independently and aggressively, we can look to the model which combines market analysis with rigorous self-analysis, to be replicated.

RISING PRICE OF EDUCATION TO CONSUMERS AND TAXPAYERS

At many independent institutions the total cost of one year at college for the freshman entering in 1979 is approximately equal to about three or four years of college for the freshman entering in 1959. Depending upon the time frame chosen, a tremendous increase in prices charged can be demonstrated, although a more sophisticated analysis might show that the percentage increase has not significantly or may not at all have outpaced the rise in middle class income. There can be further comparisons between disposable income at two points in time, in relation to college costs or the net cost to a family of tuition after significantly expanded scholarship and loan programs have been developed and implemented. These programs have a more favorable impact on lower income families. There are also reasonable arguments to be made that, with the expansion of lower cost community college and public institutions, college is more accessible to more people at a lower average cost.

In the congressional debates of 1977–78 on tuition tax credit bills, it was claimed by the Congressional Budget Office that family income increased during 1967–76 at a faster rate (78.6% in the aggregate) than total student charges (76.7% in the aggregate.) However, research performed by the Congressional Research Service of the Library of Congress disclosed that during that nine year period federal income tax, Social Security tax, and state and local taxes more than doubled. As a result, disposable family income experienced an aggregate growth during the period of only 66.8%. Within the same time the consumer price index increased by 70.5%. Thus, rising student charges competed with the rising costs of other consumer expenses for disposable dollars that were increasing at a less rapid rate.

Clearly, the debate about college costs is more complex than the general figures on the considerable increases in tuition and fees, room and board costs would seem to reflect. It is, in any event, reasonably evident that for families with incomes in the $20,000 to $50,000 range (an income level still regarded as quite comfortable and which would make the children ineligible for *most* forms of student financial aid or eligible for only minimal amounts other than loans) the cost of sending children to independent institutions and even, in some cases, to public four year institutions, can constitute a very serious drain on savings, or cause a large debt burden on the family or the student. The problem becomes even worse when two or more children are in school at the same time.

Until recently, it has generally been the case that the variety of scholarship programs including no-need scholarships have had very little applicability to the family in the income range cited. (It is perhaps worth noting, in this connection, that nearly 17% of students from families with incomes of less than $12,000 were denied basic grants in 1978–79 because of "high family assets." In that same year dependent students from families earning less than $6000 annually got BEOG awards averaging $1,562 and totaling 29.9% of their college costs. Students from families with incomes below $12,000 comprise approximately 23% of the total number of private college students and in 1978–79 total financial aid awards (not merely BEOG) provided 70.9% of college expenses for students from families with income in the $6000 to $12,000 category. For students in the category of under $6000 family income this percentage increased slightly to 72.4%.) As discussed in the section on Student Financial Aid, two major federal programs, Basic Education Opportunity Grant (BEOG) and National Defense Student Loan (NDSL) have until recently been oriented primarily to families with incomes below $15,000 a year. Even in those cases, work and loans have often been part of the student package and the out-of-pocket costs may still be very burdensome. It is not uncommon for students to graduate from independent institutions with family or personal debts ranging from $5000 to $10,000 or more to cover the costs of education.

It can be reasonably argued that this is a very sound investment on the part of the student or family and a rate of return might even be calculated. A further argument is that the debt is paid off in inflated dollars. But for a 21 year old, the idea of starting graduate school or a job (which may be difficult to find) with a debt of $5,000 to $10,000 or more can be staggering. If one shares the view that the incurrence of a huge debt is not a desirable way to finance education (witness the large number of bankruptcies to avoid repayment of student loans until this was prohibited by law), the lifting of the income ceiling on eligibility for guaranteed student loans in late 1978 may be viewed as something less than a panacea. At the same time the taxpayer sees his taxes rising to support community colleges—the portion of the tax increase attributable to community colleges can be determined with relative ease and is often announced by county officials—support for public and independent institutions, in addition to other governmental services, also creates a rising tax burden. These are some of the ingredients that have created a climate of general taxpayer unrest. One manifestation of this unrest has been the voting down of school budgets.

GROWTH OF THE COMMUNITY COLLEGE

The most rapid growth sector in higher education has been the community college which, at its best, offers proximity, lower cost, emphasis on teaching (as contrasted with research and other activities not directly student related), and flexible curriculum, schedule, services, and approaches adapted to the needs, demands, and desires of the community. At its worst, the community college can be a vocational high school with low academic standards, offering no more than the illusion of post secondary education. But the growth of the community college and its ability in a buyer's market to attract good faculty and, at least in the past, to provide modern facilities, has posed a significant challenge to four year colleges and universities.

In order to gain students, these institutions have tried to attract transfer students from the community colleges, but more directly, they have tried to compete for freshmen. Tensions have been created within the four year colleges because some view the recruitment of community college students as a dilution of academic standards. One could probably generalize that the academic standards at community colleges are not high for a variety of reasons, but many students with high scholastic ability attend community colleges simply because they and their parents cannot afford the cost of other institutions, including the cost of living away from home.

With all institutions concerned about enrollment and the effects of an enrollment decline, it now appears that the competition between community colleges, universities, and four year institutions will intensify. Bodies such as State Post Secondary Coordinating Commissions are beginning to deliberate on whether such competition ought to be encouraged or whether appropriate allocation of resources would call for some greater degree of mission delineation.

INCREASING CONCERN ABOUT EFFECTIVE MANAGEMENT IN EDUCATIONAL INSTITUTIONS

There has emerged what has become known as the "Proposition 13 mentality." In its most aggravated form, this thinking is in the nature of a taxpayer revolt in which the taxpayer, responding to the general financial pressures to which he is subject, seeks substantial redress from his tax burden and, in so doing, questions the worth of the services which the tax dollars support. As this manifests itself in regard to higher education, it focuses in part on the quality of education, but even more pervasively on higher education management.

The traditional image of the higher education administrator is not unlike the conventionally unfavorable portrayal of civil service employees, i.e., people who are secure in their positions, isolated from reality, slothful in their work habits, and who generally "could not make it elsewhere." This uninformed view, in addition to its other inaccuracies, ignores the substantial and significant efforts to heighten the professionalism associated with higher education management by such organizations as the

American Council on Education and the National Association of College and University Business Officers, among others.

One of the significant results of this attitude is that it has contributed to a trend toward recruiting for educational managers from outside the educational system, e.g., Financial and Business Affairs Vice Presidents have been recruited from banking, insurance, and other segments of the profit sector. This effort has met with mixed success. Some of the recruits have brought a fresh and valuable perspective to higher education management. Others, accustomed to a more structured and disciplined environment, find themselves unable or unwilling to cope with the dynamics of university governance. In any event, we can expect to see a continued emphasis on higher education management and on the training and development of educational administrators.

EROSION OF COLLEGIALITY

It has been traditional at colleges and universities to have a sense of acting within a community with shared information, considerable consultation, decision-making among administration, faculty, and trustees, and in some institutions, a sense of the primacy of the faculty in all major decisions not only in strict academic matters, but also in terms of budgeting, construction, advertising, selection of administrative officers, and so on. In addition, there has been a sense of collegiality among and between institutions for sharing of information and ideas.

In recent years, however, there have been considerable external and internal pressures creating tensions which indisputably have weakened the concept of collegiality. Two of the major forces affecting collegiality, which we discuss in the following separate sections, are collective bargaining and the patterns and practices associated with federally sponsored research. Among the external and internal pressures the following are particularly important:

1. Enrollment changes at the institution and in its schools and departments caused by the changing population pool, and by economic and employment conditions;
2. Financial strains caused by the above and by the impact of governmental funding, impact of foundation and individual gifts, and by escalation of costs in all areas, including salary costs;

3. Collective bargaining pressures such as costs, emphasis on legalities, and, given the adversarial nature of the collective bargaining process, changes in the basic relationships;

4. More active role of trustees and governmental bodies; and

5. Resource allocation decisions at the institution as a result of 1–4, causing more conscious and more difficult choices to be made in regard to size of faculty and staff and allocations of space, equipment, supplies, research and travel funds. For example, if there are staff reductions to be made, how will they be accomplished?

There appears to be a trend toward potential conflict, competition, and controversy in the various relationships that previously were thought to be collegial. It is to be expected that a heightened atmosphere of insecurity and more restricted availability of resources to support the range of educational activities produces tensions and competition among the various segments of the institution. The competition would seem to be in the categories indicated below, and often at one institution several competitive pairings and various combinations and permutations are taking place at the same time. These categories are:

1. Faculty versus administration;
2. One or more colleges or schools versus other colleges or schools;
3. Liberal arts versus professional school;
4. Graduate versus undergraduate teaching or departments;
5. Teaching versus research;
6. Department versus department;
7. Tenured versus non-tenured faculty;
8. Sciences departments versus humanities departments;
9. Minorities and women versus white males;
10. Junior versus senior faculty;
11. Required subjects or core curriculum versus non-required subjects;
12. Students versus faculty/students versus administration;
13. Faculty versus Board of Trustees;
14. Administration versus trustees;
15. Trustees or administration versus State Education Department or regents or governor's office or legislature.

The effects of the decline of collegiality can also be listed:

A. Impact on the atmosphere on campus, cooperation, joint proposals, interdisciplinary approaches, and impact on the sense of community; and

B. In regard to cooperation with other institutions, there is some evidence of a tendency toward a diminution in the exchange of ideas, information, consortia approaches, joint research proposals, and referral of students and organizations to another institution (although many of these still take place). There is increased competition in recruitment for students, and thus increased costs attributable to advertising, publicity, and scholarship competition, particularly in the area of no-need scholarships. There is also increased competition among institutions (and even within institutions) for faculty, contacts with business, industry, foundations, government, individual donors. There is inherent in this competition the possibility and the reality of duplication of programs, seminars, and community service approaches.

The above are just a few of the trends affecting higher education today. It is important to note that there continue to be significant variations among institutions in the degree to which these tensions or competitive conflicts exist. Nonetheless because they add an important dimension of complexity to policy-making deliberations and, indeed, day to day administration, those associated with higher education management need to be alert to the potential for these competitive conflicts and sensitive to their implications and nuances.

Chapter Two

INFLUENCES ON HIGHER EDUCATION

A. THE ROLE OF GOVERNMENT

It is probably the case that the influence of government is felt more strongly by colleges and universities than by business and industry; through legislation, administrative regulations, court decisions, and the actions of the executive branch of government. The following are what might be considered some of the "usual" areas of governmental impact on society as a whole, including educational institutions:

Wages and hours;
Patents and copyrights;
Right to organize;
Taxation;
Anti-trust actions;
Affirmative action requirements;
Occupational safety and health regulations;
Retirement age and pension plan regulation;
Safe materials requirements;
Food and drugs;
Accountability for the use of government funds;
Regulation of utilities;
Requirements for competitive bidding;
Mortgages, interest rates, and loans;
Standards for construction and various business and industry practices;

Stockholder and consumer protection;

Requirements for safeguarding savings deposits;

And environmental regulations.

However, there are some very direct and major influences government has on universities, such as funding, approval of programs and degrees and chartering of the institution, affirmative action in regard to staff and students, access provision for the handicapped staff and students, graduate assistantships, research grants, regulation concerning experimentation with and use of human subjects, and animal care requirements, to highlight just a few. It should be noted at the outset that the role of government, as discussed here, refers to influences by both federal and state and local governments. Clearly, there are important distinctions as among state and local governments and the federal government. But from the perspective of the postsecondary institution, they combine to exert an increasing degree of constraint on the discretion and flexibility of institutional administration and increase the complexity of that administration immeasurably.

Funding

State funding formulas, based on the number of students are the major source of revenue for public institutions. (This is further discussed in the section on Financing Higher Education.) Various state subsidy programs for independent institutions, based on graduates or number of students, provide an increasingly important source of revenue. For both public and independent institutions, financial aid scholarships and loans by federal, state and local jurisdictions, and capital building and improvement programs on a grant or loan basis constitute important sources of funding. In addition, there is a variety of special grants, either one-time or continuing, that can mean the difference between starting or continuing a new program or relinquishing the program.

Governmental Approval

From the moment an institution makes application to be chartered to the time it seeks governmental funds or research grants, to the point that it contemplates the introduction of new programs or degrees in the interests of either innovation or expansion, one governmental agency or another, at one level or another, will need to be involved in the approval and decision-making process. Clearly, there is a governmental concern regarding the quality of programs, particularly when state funds, or certification or charter approval is involved. The appropriate state agency may also be concerned about a proliferation of programs in the state, which has the effect of draining state resources. This particular concern is just now beginning to be manifested with some regularity. The state agency is also the final place where complaints, concerns or grievances about an institution or one of its components can be brought.

Affirmative Action

The government requires affirmative action as a response to a condition that appears to reflect past discriminatory practices. This requirement has a particular impact on educational institutions. In regard to students, both independent (whenever federal funds provide the necessary leverage) and public institutions must show evidence of equal access and attempts to stimulate increased minority enrollment. Because of the spotlight on educational institutions and the threat of withholding funds that for many institutions may constitute the margin of survival, colleges and universities may well be under greater compliance pressure in this area than most other enterprises. One can note in this connection, that in contrast to other more organized sectors of the economy, such as organized labor, higher education has never been highly effective in organizing a lobbying activity aimed at either achieving a more favorable allocation of resources or securing a more temperate application of a compliance requirement. There is some evidence of progress in this regard, but institutions have historically found it quite difficult to unite in a "common cause," in part because they view themselves as so different from each other.

The Supreme Court's *Bakke* decision* may well be of profound importance. Although its full meaning is unclear and much disputed, the decision appears to set limits on the appropriate form of affirmative action. Nonetheless, educational institutions will feel compelled to continue to improve the proportions of minority students and women that are admitted and graduated.

The government's requirements regarding affirmative action in employment have great impact on educational organizations because the

*Regents of University of California vs. Bakke, Vol. 438, U.S. Reports, p. 265, June 1978.

government uses its leverage in this area much as it does in connection with an affirmative action program as applied to admissions. Thus, while striving to avoid what may technically be termed a quota, plans have been adopted by institutions to reach goals, commitments, or guidelines aimed at increasing the number of minorities and women employed at various levels and in tenured positions in faculty, administrative, and support ranks. Universities are very much in competition with each other for well qualified minority group members and women. Pirating of such employees by one institution from another is not uncommon. For those possessing specialized qualifications there may be a relative abundance of opportunities (in contrast to the generally bleak employment picture for females and minority group members). This can be viewed as a partial redressing of imbalances resulting from past discrimination and the operation of the traditional "old boy" networks that had effectively shut off opportunities, except for white males. It should also be noted that despite favorable improvements at many institutions, there are still significant problems ahead in terms of meeting the affirmative action goals established.

An inevitable byproduct of affirmative action is that many white males see it as a threat to their opportunities to achieve tenure or promotion, or even to obtain employment. They see a concerted effort to reverse imbalances resulting from past discriminatory practices as a form of reverse discrimination. For example, a vigorous affirmative action program at an institution might result in a circumstance in which a female sufficiently qualified but apparently less well qualified than some of her white male peers will receive preference in employment or tenure. In this context, qualifications, as traditionally measured, are defined to include such factors as length of service, number of degrees, number and kinds of publications, and teaching effectiveness.

Those concerned with affirmative action would view this as an appropriate and, in fact, necessary result if affirmative action is to achieve meaningful results. They would make the point that quality standards, whether pertaining to admission or to employment, should not be lowered. But they also believe that the testing of how and whether those standards are met needs to be modified, since continued utilization of the same criteria for qualification will necessarily perpetuate the long standing discriminatory and exclusionary situation. The woman's colleagues, denied an opportunity that under the "old standards" would be theirs, clearly have a different view. This then becomes a source of tension within the institution to which institutional administration must react with great sensitivity.

In this regard, as stated earlier, the Supreme Court decision in the *Bakke* case is potentially a momentous one for higher education and although related to admission of students could by analogy be regarded as having relevance for hiring, promotion, or tenure practices.

Some observers regard the *Bakke* decision as judicial statesmanship of the highest order, others have labeled it as judicial straddling. In essence, the Court ruled that institutions of higher learning can *consider* race in making their admissions decisions, although they may not specifically set aside a number of positions to be filled only by minority group members. In 1979 the number of minority freshmen medical students rose from 2228 in 1978 to 2463. Although this is a very nominal increase, the fact that the figure did not decrease may suggest that the anticipated "backlash" as a consequence of the *Bakke* decision with medical schools deemphasizing affirmative action, has not occurred. Justice Powell, speaking for the majority, stated that the California Supreme Court had "failed to recognize that the state had a substantial interest that legitimately may be served by a properly devised admissions program, involving the competitive consideration of race and ethnic origin." Justice Powell indicated what he would consider a "properly devised" program by favorably citing Harvard University's admissions procedures where "race or ethnic background may be deemed a 'plus' in a particular applicant's file, yet it does not insulate the individual from comparisons with all other candidates for the available seats."

If one seeks to determine the legality of the faculty preference case cited as an example above, the analogy of the *Bakke* case may offer some guidance. What that holding would appear to suggest is that there would be no impropriety in according preference to a female over her white male colleagues for promotion, provided that her status as a female was one of the weighted qualification factors as contrasted with setting aside certain positions exclusively for females. To continue the example, it remains unclear whether at some point the court might be prepared to hold that the disparity in traditional qualifications between the female faculty member and her colleages was such that in substance, sex was the only qualification factor used.

A counterbalancing consideration is that if affirmative action goals are to be achieved within any near term time frame, traditional factors will have to be accorded comparatively little weight because, by their nature, historical factors make them exclusionary.

Despite the ambiguities associated with the *Bakke* decision, institutions have begun to develop affirmative action plans and to revise existing plans in accordance with interpretations as to what the *Bakke* decision is believed to have called for. It is to be noted in this connection, that in 1979 the Supreme Court held in the Weber* case that employers may voluntarily give minority workers special treatment in hiring, training, and promotion and allowed even those employers with no proven history of racial bias to offer special preferences. Though the ruling was not specifically addressed to women, it is deemed to be applicable to them. This ruling would seem to diminish the likelihood that affirmative action programs will be inhibited by the *Bakke* decision. In any event, it is clear that pressures for affirmative action will continue and that they will continue to raise thorny issues in regard to the balancing of individual rights and societal goals.

Those concerned with institutional administration need to be sensitive to these issues. This means, for example, that it is likely that trustees will want to know more details about hiring, promotion, and tenure actions than had previously been provided to them. It means also that they must be sensitive to avoid an inadvertent exacerbation of the tensions an affirmative action program could produce and that there will be many more instances in which they must be alert to the necessity for legal advice.

Access Provision

An important thrust of government at the present time is a long over-due concern for the handicapped. The impact on education can be significant. As with all other institutions in society, education is expected to make more concerted attempts to employ the handicapped. But it is in providing access to hundreds of thousands of handicapped students, as well as handicapped employees, that educational institutions confront a major problem. The goal of government is to "main-stream" the handicapped. That is, it is the apparent goal of the provisions regarding elimination of barriers to the handicapped that *all* facilities will be made accessible to the handicapped, insofar as possible. The rationale, which has its parallel in the thinking reflected in the famous *Brown* case on discrimination, is that the full benefits of an education program are not derived unless students from diverse backgrounds are enabled to interact with each other in the learning process. This cannot be the case if the

* United Steel Workers *vs*. Brien F. Weber et al., 99 SCt, p. 2721, June 1979.

handicapped are provided with only limited access to facilities and are virtually segregated from the main-stream of academic life.

But the cost of compliance with federal requirements can be staggering, even if phased in over a number of years. It is relatively easy to deal with walkways and physical barriers on the grounds of an institution. The sizable costs involve elevators in buildings, ramps, toilet facilities, laboratories and various types of studios, gymnasium, infirmary and recreational facilities, the re-design of dormitory rooms and buildings, and so on. Although it is possible, if there are very few handicapped students, to track them and, in effect, schedule their courses in whatever buildings have ramps or elevators (not the optimum solution) there still are problems normally, in the gym, dorm, library, or student center. Some institutions have calculated the costs of compliance to be several million dollars and, depending on the number of handicapped students, at $50,000–$100,000 per student. This comes at a time when there is a substantially diminished availability of funds for major renovations or new construction and indeed for maintenance of physical plant. Hence, we have begun to see pressures on government by educational institutions to allow a long phase-in period and, more importantly, to make funds available on a grant basis, at the very least on a long-term loan basis at a minimal interest cost.

The issue of main-streaming is a very important one in terms of benefits to the handicapped and to society. But, cost considerations may impel some other solutions. One approach that could come about would be the designation of certain institutions in each area as primary institutions for various categories of handicapped individuals (analogous to the "magnet" school concept in the elementary and secondary school sector.) The argument can be made that, even though some travel or dormitory living might be required for the handicapped, on an overall cost benefit basis, in terms of providing first-class facilities, quality programs, and full attention to the special needs of the handicapped, it might be a far better approach than attempting to make fragmentary improvements at all institutions.

Graduate Assistantships

These programs provide special types of financial aid and research assistance to the institution and to particular programs, as well as to the individual student. Many students could not afford to seek graduate degrees without federally financed programs, and without such programs, the research capability and the production of PhDs would be seriously impacted.

Research Grants and Contracts

These grants are important to the country as well as to the individual institutions. They support both basic and applied research. Indirect cost reimbursement on grants and contracts can be an important income source (see discussion in Sponsored Activity.) But of greatest importance is the fact that the federal support helps the institutions to advance the frontiers of knowledge. In this area, as in others involving federal funds, institutions receiving federal largesse will subject themselves to federal compliance requirements associated with public policy objectives. Additionally, the research that is funded will correspond to current federal priorities. These could be either not fully in consonance with institutional priorities, or in specific conflict with institutional philosophies. For example, there was little resistance within institutions to acceptance of grants and contracts in furtherance of our space program—although many would have been inclined to accord expenditures for this program a lesser priority.

By contrast, there have been highly vociferous protests to acceptance of certain Department of Defense contracts by students and by some faculty members. This was particularly true in the turbulent '60s. Of major concern to financial administrators at many institutions is to avoid over-reliance on "soft money" (i.e., a transitory source of funding that cannot be relied on to continue at any given level), which should not be the basis for funding long-term commitments.

The above discussion has attempted to suggest the pervasiveness of governmental impact and influence on institutions. Institutional administrators must become aware of and responsive to governmental policies, procedures, requests for data, audits, regulations, etc. Appropriate officials must learn to deal effectively with the governmental process, including the budgetary, legislative and regulatory cycles and dynamics. Educational leaders must understand the political process and the political and public relations needs of governors, budget directors, various legislators and in turn their respective influences on government staff. University representatives are fully justified in being critical of many of the implementing regulations, policies and procedures promulgated by federal agencies with insufficient understanding of the environment to which they are to be applied and insufficient sensitivity to and concern for the implications, particularly the cost implications, of the requirements they impose.

But, university representatives often err seriously in reacting to these implementing actions by failing to fully recognize the congressionally imposed pressures, and the public policy considerations that give rise to the federal agency implementing actions. When institutional representatives focus on determining when federal objectives are compelling and how they can be achieved with minimal adverse impact or disruption to the institution, they can then concentrate their energies productively on attempting to bring about a reasonable and realistic implementation of the federal requirements in lieu of futilely resisting the requirements and creating a polarization that militates against achievement of workable accords.

Where that impact is significant and harmful, disruptive or burdensome, there are specific decisions to be made as to the appropriate institutional response. In some instances it will be appropriate, if not essential, for institutions to make common cause on a consequential issue. As noted earlier, higher education has not been notably successful in such attempts for a variety of reasons. For one thing, it is typically more difficult to achieve a consensus among educational leaders, as contrasted with other sectors of society, perhaps because educators are more likely to see and be concerned with a variety of nuances in any issue. It also appears more natural for those associated with education to "play devil's advocate" as contrasted with a joining of peers in a commonly agreed upon course of action.

It may also be observed that if the above mentioned tendencies are natural, it will require a sense of urgency to overcome them. As noted frequently, it is only in recent years that serious fiscal problems have imparted a sense of urgency to the management of college and university affairs. This heightened sense of concern is reflected in the focus on enrollments and student recruiting, and on the effectiveness of financial management, along with a new sense of the necessity to lobby effectively, both to insure that the federal budget process accords an appropriately high priority to postsecondary education programs, and to avoid government regulatory action that is deleterious or may constitute an inappropriate incursion on institutional prerogatives. If the term lobby is offensive to some, they may substitute another term. But the inescapable fact is that the balancing of priorities and the development of public policy is substantially influenced by various interest groups—women, minorities, labor, business, and so forth, that aggressively and articulately espouse their causes. In these difficult times, postsecondary leaders can hardly afford to refrain from doing likewise.

It cannot be too strongly emphasized that those associated with university administration and concerned with the financial health of the institution should be aware of the cost of government requirements. Derek Bok, President of Harvard, has written that at his institution, "compliance with federal regulations consumed over 60,000 hours of faculty time and cost almost $8.3 million in 1974–75 alone." Columbia's President William McGill noted that the Federal Register, where agencies publish their regulations, grew from 3450 pages in 1937 to over 60,000 pages in 1975 and that in 1977, almost 7500 new federal regulations were promulgated, all of which have impact on universities. Other universities have cited typical costs of compliance with federal regulations of $25,000–$75,000 to comply with Environmental Protection Agency requirements, hundreds of thousands of dollars in anticipation of, or in compliance with, Occupational Safety and Health requirements, several hundred thousand dollars for Buckley Amendment and Affirmative Action procedures, and potentially millions of dollars for physical modifications to provide access for the handicapped.

Some of the costs would need to be incurred at educational institutions in any event and certain costs are unavoidable (for example, Social Security and Unemployment Insurance costs are frequently included in compliance cost figures and that inclusion is highly questionable given the nature of those programs). However, it is indisputable that the cost of federal compliance requirements is substantial and there has been sufficient clamor raised regarding such costs to invoke a number of federal ameliorating actions, but the prospects for substantial improvements are not imminent. A variety of suggestions have been advanced from various sources to ease the burden of federal requirements. Some of them by the Federal Paperwork Commission, a body specifically established to examine ways of easing the burden of federal requirements. These include:

1. Legislative modifications to lessen the impact of Social Security and Unemployment Taxes on educational institutions;
2. Review of requests and rulings in regard to education to eliminate those that are unrealistic, poorly defined, unnecessary, etc.;
3. A more discriminating approach by government officials in establish-

ing policies and procedures to correct abuses (a host of laws, rulings and regulations have been promulgated and applied to all institutions because of the excesses or recalcitrance of very few);

4. An approach by the federal government which avoids, whenever possible, detailed specifications and monitoring of how things are accomplished, and instead emphasizes results.

A final, though very important point. As government, in one way or another, increases its funding and regulatory role over educational institutions (and the two are irrevocably linked), there is the danger that legitimate controls over expenditures, requests for information and supporting data, approval of master plans, programs, and degrees may transcend legitimate oversight and pass into academic control. We have been fortunate in the United States that this has been avoided, but it is not impossible to conceive that a governor, budget director, legislative committee, Commissioner of Education, Board of Regents, or middle level official could inadvertently or deliberately exceed the bounds of legitimate involvement.

Reactions to such incursion should be tempered by an evaluation of the act and whether it was simply misinformed or misguided, but there must be non-paranoid vigilance in regard to the academic freedom of institutions. The power to fund and regulate carries with it necessary and needed powers of the governmental agency to be involved, to approve, to monitor. This makes for a tightrope that government and its officials and education and its officials must walk so that there is a proper stewardship and responsibility in regard to governmental funding and regulation at the same time that there is proper recognition of the areas in which institutional freedom, prerogatives, and flexibility must be preserved as an essential means of preserving the values inherent to our educational system.

B. STUDENT CONSUMERISM

Much attention has been focused on student unrest in the '60s, in part because that unrest was one manifestation of a period of trauma in our society. Student political activism, far from being new, can virtually be regarded as traditional to higher education. University students have historically been early participants in radical social and political movements, often with the encouragement, if not the leadership, of their professors.

But student consumerism is a relatively new phenomenon and, as with student activism, one manifestation of a broader societal condition, but with its own special characteristics. Many thoughtful observers are inclined to believe that the consumerism that surfaced in the '70s is not merely a passing fad, but reflective of some fundamental societal changes. The general emphasis on consumer rights, full disclosure, etc. that has come to be known popularly as Naderism, is linked to the taxpayer's revolt, frequently referred to as the Proposition 13 mentality (because of the first dramatic manifestation in the state of California).

The concerns dealing with deceptive information about products and services, and the perhaps even more fundamental questioning as to whether the price of those products or services is commensurate with their value, may be viewed as a reflection of the attitude that the free market economy is not providing an adequate degree of protection for consumer interests.

To fully appreciate the extent to which student consumerism is contributing to the tensions associated with higher education management today, it is important to understand that student consumerism does not have the same historic or traditional roots as consumerism in general. In its earliest origins, the university was characterized by the coming together of distinguished scholars who, virtually by sufferance, permitted young aspiring scholars to "sit at their feet." Vestiges of that tradition can be found in the attitudes of some faculty members today—an attitude clearly difficult to reconcile with a circumstance in which student representatives frequently participate in trustee meetings and, more rarely, have voting rights.

The resistance to according a voice to students in the affairs of the institution is generally predicated on such arguments as that the interest on the part of any given student body is a transient one, in contrast to the faculty and administration who may be presumed to have a longer term stake in the institution. It is also observed that since students come to the institution to learn (if not necessarily to be taught) they can hardly be in a position to offer meaningful advice on what is to be taught and how.

Nonetheless, student influences are becoming increasingly pervasive, stimulated by a state of serious malaise. As noted elsewhere, the circumstance in which college graduates are finding it increasingly difficult to obtain career positions commensurate with their education (and, in many instances finding it difficult to obtain any kind of job!) has had an impact on enrollment trends and on attrition rates. This circumstance has also led students to conclude that their institutions are insufficiently flexible or responsive to their needs and that the faculty is excessively absorbed with their own needs and pursuits and insufficiently attentive to the needs of students.

In 1976 the New York State Education Department issued an advisory memorandum to all postsecondary institutions warning them of four basic problems related to students. These were:

1. Unclear and inconsistently administered procedures for redress of student complaints;
2. Weaknesses in full, timely, and accurate disclosure of information pertinent to decisions concerning students;
3. Unethical practices in advertising and recruitment; and
4. Varying tuition refund policies, some not as fair, equitable, and fully disclosed as they should be.

This listing was not, nor did it purport to be, an exhaustive listing. Some would even disagree as to the universality of the four basic problems and would substitute others as more important. It is important, however, that the State Education Department deemed the four sources of student discontent sufficiently significant to highlight them to all postsecondary institutions (public and independent), within the state. Other manifestations of student consumerism are readily apparent.

Student influences are increasingly being felt in such areas as faculty and program evaluation, the "quality of academic life" as related to such factors as counseling, housing, recreational facilities (and policy), food and parking services and facilities, and the influences and constraints on student behavior. Students have involved themselves in collective bargaining disputes, in decisions regarding the investment of endowment funds, and in decisions regarding tuition and fee increases. Indirectly, through the willingness or refusal to reside in dormitories, students have had an important influence on capital expansion and the use of facilities.

In addition to the factors already identified, there are two significant factors contributing to a heightened influence on the part of students. More stringent financial circumstances at least in part caused by declining enrollments, have increased the competition among institutions to secure and retain students. An additional and reinforcing factor is the federal government's Basic Education Opportunity Grant (BEOG) program (see discussion on student financial aid) which has had a major influence in enabling students to "shop around." Stated differently, it is clearly the case that although competition for openings at the most prestigious institutions remains keen, we are now seeing a buyer's market for students. Not surprisingly, this coincides with a plethora of candidates for faculty positions and can be expected to heighten faculty responsiveness to student and institutional needs. It is, consequently, evident that, although to some degree the support for a heightened student influence by trustees and administrators is a reflection of a changed philosophy, the primary impetus is pragmatic and financial.

At a minimum, student consumerism, abetted by federal and state regulation, is resulting in the imposition of increased administrative and financial burdens in relation to information dissemination. Interestingly, these requirements go in two directions. On the one hand, institutions are now required to exercise much greater care in safeguarding the privacy of information about students. On the other hand, a great deal of information regarding the institution is now being demanded for currently enrolled and prospective students.

Information is required regarding federal, state, and institutional student aid programs. This includes a description of application forms and procedures, methods used in selecting recipients and allocation of awards, award schedules and rights, and responsibilities of recipients. Information is also being required in regard to the cost of attending the institution, including tuition and fees, books and supplies, room and board and other living expenses, and refund policy as applied to those who drop out. Because of the implications for federally funded student financial aid—the Guaranteed Student Loan program in particular—the issue of refund policy has been a particularly abrasive one between the federal government and institutions. But many of the problems may have been put to rest by the promulgation of uniform guidelines for refund policy by the American Council on Education.

Pressures have also been created for improvements of information regarding the institutional programs, including the listing of degree, certificate, and diploma programs described in terms of both pre-requisites and requirements for completion. Also being requested is information regarding facilities, faculty, student retention and placement of graduates.

It does not seem likely, given the circumstances described above, that student influences will diminish. If indeed they are likely to increase, students will have a role in shaping fundamental institutional management policies such as tenure, collective bargaining, tuition and scholarship policy, and the budget process in general.

In the face of that prospect (more of a reality than a prospect for some institutions), the management of our higher education enterprise becomes more complex and there is an increased necessity to balance the diverse interests and perspectives of all constituents in a manner that is sufficiently sensitive to avoid the creation of untenable tensions. As is the case with faculty relations, the creation of a positive climate in which the administration and trustees are responsive to perceived needs can result in diminishing the feeling on the part of students that a pervasive involvement in the governance of the institution is essential to the protection of their interests.

Perhaps that observation is overly succinct. What it is intended to suggest is that student leaders do not seek a role in the governance of the institution because they want to run the institution. They are concerned, in a way that is unique and indigenous to these times, with the quality of their educational experience in the fullest sense and imbued with the sense that the time that they invest in higher education is of profound importance to them. Consequently, in keeping with the spirit of the times, they are not inclined to be passive or meek as consumers of educational services.

They would contend, for example, that although they may lack the ability to judge whether a professor is technically versed in his discipline and may lack the specific competence to judge his pedagogical techniques, they can make other substantive, albeit subjective, judgments. They can judge whether he is interesting, creative, stimulating, dedicated and involved. They can determine whether he is accessible and judge whether he is responsive. And these are judgments that they insist on making. On another level, they believe that one aspect of the uniqueness of the university environment is that collegiality extends to students and that, in contrast to other kinds of consumers, they can and should have some voice in the pricing of the service. In much the same way that aggressive faculties wish to participate in the examination of resource allocation alternatives before acceding to a determination regarding the size of the salary increase that the institution can afford, activist students desire a like participation before conceding to and accepting the necessity for a tuition increase.

Administrators and trustees who have difficulty in accepting the philosophic implications of student consumerism must nonetheless be sensitive to and prepared to deal with its pragmatic implications. The institution that fails to recognize the new way in which prospective students are making their acceptance decisions is likely to suffer more severely from enrollment declines than the more "market oriented" institution.

Chapter Three

FINANCING HIGHER EDUCATION—AN OVERVIEW

As noted in the earlier section on Student Consumerism, as recently as the '60s, the major focus of concern at colleges and universities was campus unrest. Students, often joined by militant faculty members, were vociferous in their expression of concern regarding such things as participation in research funded by the Department of Defense and investment of endowment funds in companies that pollute the environment, exploit underdeveloped countries or engage in other forms of "socially undesirable" activity.

The issue being raised was that of social responsibility. Should the great institutions of learning function as cloistered centers of scholarly endeavor, or should they be in the forefront on social issues of the day? It is an issue which has confronted universities throughout the world for hundreds of years and remains an issue in American institutions today—particularly as there is an increased emphasis on community orientation.

But the hard realities of survival caused the financing of higher education to supplant social responsibility as the central issue in the '70s. Indeed, the intensified community orientation, while it is impelled by other socially oriented factors, finds its main impetus in the necessity to increase the emphasis on non-traditional programs and continuing education to offset the decline in enrollments in traditional programs.

The dramatic attrition rate among small, independent institutions, coupled with the financial difficulties experienced by even the most amply endowed institutions, has caused those concerned with the management of higher education to focus more sharply on the sources of funding. In reviewing the annual statements and the proposed budget for the ensuing year, trustees are looking more carefully (or should be) at such questions as whether tuition income and endowment fund income have kept pace with rising costs, and whether these and other major sources of income have changed significantly as a proportion of total current revenue over the past five to ten years. The primary sources of income for colleges and universities are tuition and fees, federal funds, state and local government appropriations, endowment fund income, and gifts and contributions.

In general, independent institutions tend to rely on tuition and endowment fund income as the preponderant sources of funding support. By contrast, public institutions will generally have lower tuitions and rely most heavily on state funding. However, there are several points to be noted as qualifications to these generalities. First is that state funding is frequently related to FTE (full-time equivalent student enrollment). Consequently, public institutions and independents alike can be strongly affected by enrollment declines.

A second point is that, although the major independents are the most heavily endowed (some small, independent institutions are even more amply endowed proportionate to their size than Yale, Harvard, Columbia, and Emory, which has received $340,000,000 from a single donor), many of the major publics have been developing sizable endowments. Another point is that there is a growing trend, the Bundy plan in New York being the most notable example, toward state funding to independent institutions.

What is suggested by these rather significant qualifications is that, while the generalizations regarding the distinctions between financial support for independents and publics remain valid, they are becoming less valid. Bearing in mind the time honored maxim regarding the power that is associated with the purse strings, many thoughtful observers of the educational scene are concerned that the distinctions between public and independent institutions are becoming fuzzier.

As a final generalization on the subject of financing higher education, it is worth repeating that some institutions, both independent and public, have sought to avoid a dependence on "soft money" by establishing a practice or a tradition (rarely formalized as an explicit policy) that salary charges associated with tenured faculty will not be charged to federal grants and contracts. This practice is causing significant concern to a large number of research-oriented institutions because of newly revised principles of cost reimbursement, published in OMB Circular A-21 in March 1979. (See discussion on federally sponsored activity.)

The dollar consequences of this change can be quite significant for a major research-oriented institution. Because of this fact, it is appropriate that there be a reexamination of this practice, along with other long-standing institutional conventions, to determine whether it is still appropriate in the context of today's fiscal climate.

It has been argued that increasing faculty charges and indirect cost charges will diminish the funds available to support other expenses associated with federally sponsored research. One likely consequence of such an occurrence would be that, if awarding agencies find that the cost of funding projects has increased (or more accurately, that the cost to them has increased because their proportionate share has been more accurately identified), they will have to be more selective in the number of projects that are funded.

This assumes a limitation on the funds available to support research. Although, clearly such funds are not infinite, it is equally the case that the finite limits have not been conclusively established. Whether or not federal funds available to support research are increased is a function of the complex political process in which priority trade-off decisions are made. Perhaps institutions need to help awarding agencies to make a more persuasive case for increased federal support for research in lieu of acquiescing to the absorption of an increasing share of the costs of research when fiscal pressures make this increasingly difficult to do.

At particular points in time a specific circumstance may provide the impetus for substantially increasing support for research. (Examples of this are the launching of Sputnik and its impact on our space program, and the pledge during the Nixon administration to eradicate cancer.) But over the long-term those who are most profoundly concerned about the necessity to maintain an appropriate level of research activity must be certain that the case for support has been forcefully and persuasively made during the course of the budget development and appropriation process, buttressed by accurate information on the cost of research.

One important ingredient in any detailing of such costs is the identification of the cost impact of federal regulations (see discussion on the role of government). Thus far, this discussion has focused on the more global issue, i.e., the funding of research as a national priority. Indeed the rationale often advanced by institutional administration in pursuing a policy of restraint in seeking reimbursement for research related costs, is the global concern about the aggregate amount of funding available to support research. Financial exigency will necessarily dictate a shift of focus in which administrators give greater emphasis to the financial needs of their own institutions.

This should occasion a comprehensive and realistic reassessment of the costs and benefits associated with federally sponsored research. In this context the issue of dependence on "soft money" (and indeed the definition of what is "soft") needs to be reexamined.

Those institutions that believe that they have insulated themselves from a dependence on "soft money" by declining to charge the salaries of tenured faculty to federal grants and contracts, should examine the extent to which those grants and contracts fund equipment acquisitions, faculty travel, secretarial support, student financial aid (by providing support to lab assistants and research assistants who are graduate students), and other essential institutional expenditures; i.e., the presumed insulation from dependence on "soft money" is at best only partial. It is equally fallacious for faculty members to assume that they have avoided the possibility of having research priorities dictated by federal funding sources by persuading their institutions to refrain from charging their salaries to federally sponsored projects on which they work. Unless they are able to carry out the project entirely without federal support, they have not avoided subjecting their proposed research to federal priority judgments.

In any event, in discussing the sources of funding for higher education, it is important for those concerned with the financial health of a specific institution to be alert to changes in the relative proportions of the various funding sources over time, and to understand the reasons for those changes within the broader context of what is happening to those funding sources on a national basis. Have endowment fund contributions declined, or failed to maintain their historic rate of increase? How does this relate to national trends in charitable donations and donations to education in particular? Has the return on endowment diminished? How does this correspond to the experience of other institutions and to the economic conditions that impact on investment income?

An evaluation of income trends is crucial to effective management. But the implications of those trends cannot be fully understood, much less an appropriate course of action planned, in response to the trend that is observed without a broader understanding of the particular funding source and of what is happening to it nationally.

Development, or fund raising, as it pertains to the generation of endowment funds, and current fund revenue as well, and endowment fund management will be discussed in the next chapter. In the discussion that immediately follows other significant funding sources will be treated. Tuition, as a major source of income and an important matter for policy determination, warrants discussion along with a discussion on student financial aid. Also to be treated are state financing, including formula funding and state aid to independent institutions and other revenue generating activities.

STATE SUPPORT

State expenditures for higher education have become a significant source of support, not only for the public institutions but for private institutions, as well. Although as noted earlier, state support remains the primary source of funding for public institutions, it is interesting to note that changes in historical patterns have created a circumstance in which the increment of funding provided to public institutions from external sources, e.g., federal grants and contracts, gifts and contributions, has grown in size and significance coincident with a similar growth in size and significance of the increment of private institution funding provided by the states.

Generalizations regarding the magnitude, impact, methodologies, and underlying philosophies of state funding to higher education, must always be qualified by the acknowledgment of a wide variation among the states. Late in 1978 two studies were published which tend to confirm this variation while providing some interesting insights that have distinct implications for consumerism.

The first of these was the annual study by M. M. Chambers of Illinois State University. This study has traditionally involved an analytic comparison of appropriations to higher education by the various states. A second study, published virtually at the same time, was performed by D. Kent Halstead of the National Institute of Education. This latter study examined, for the first time, the tax capacity of the states and contrasted that capacity with actual tax effort and with national averages.

The combined results of these two studies were published in the October 16, 1978 issue of the Chronicle of Higher Education in the form of a state-by-state comparison of tax capacity, tax effort and appropriations for higher education which is reprinted below. The relationships depicted are not fully what might have been anticipated.

Previously, there had been a tendency to regard the aggregate state expenditures for higher education as a measure of the extent to which support for higher education was a high priority in a given state. But when the Halstead figures are combined with the former measure, one derives a somewhat different perspective.

For example, it is revealed that New York ranks *nineteenth* in tax capacity (the amount of tax per person that it could collect at the national average rates); *first* in the amount of taxes per person actually collected; and *twenty-seventh* in appropriations per person for higher education. This suggests among other things, that since higher education is one of the major tax supported services New York would perhaps have been a more logical setting for the first "taxpayer revolt" than California. By contrast to New York, California's figures show a ranking of *ninth* in tax capacity; *second* in tax effort; and *fourth* in appropriations for higher education.

It is to be anticipated that this new form of comparative evaluation will now be repeated on an annual basis. An examination of changes in the relationships of the three elements of comparison over time is apt to be very revealing, particularly if it can be compiled with some analysis of the forces within the states that may have brought about those changes.

FORMULA FUNDING

A formula approach to financing higher education has become increasingly popular among the states. A major virtue from the perspective of state legislators is that this objective, virtually mechanical approach avoids political controversy and provides an element of continuity in the funding approach from year to year and among the institutions. It provides what has been termed a "decision rule"* that establishes the areas of discretion and the limits of debate.

Some 25 states now budget by formula. Perhaps the most common attribute is that the majority of the formulas are related to enrollment. What this immediately suggests is that rigid adherence to the formula (and the use of formulas tends to generate rigidity) automatically results in diminished funding when enrollments decline. As noted in a later discussion on cost analysis, both variable and semi-variable costs are subject to downside rigidity. Hence, a decline in enrollment is apt to produce an incremental reduction in funding which exceeds the amount of

*Helsinger, Richard J., Jr. *State Budgeting for Higher Education: The Uses of Formulas* (Berkeley: University of California Center for Research and Development in Higher Education), 1976.

cost reduction that can realistically be anticipated from the reduced number of students. Moreover, the institution is virtually precluded from tapping other potential funding sources to make up this funding gap. For example, states will tend to restrict the ability of public institutions to increase tuition rates on the theory that they are giving appropriate consideration to the amount of tuition needed when considering funding sources and budgetary needs in the course of the appropriation process. In any event, a tuition increase in the face of declining enrollments may not be a very practical approach to funding.

As in many other aspects of state support to higher education funding formulas are subject to wide variation. Although enrollment is a key variable, other measures are employed where deemed appropriate; such as, the number of students, faculty and academic programs to determine basic needs; and gross square footage and population to determine plant operation needs.

The greatest virtue of formula funding, its standardized or automatic features, is also its greatest defect. A formula approach is not compatible with a discriminating recognition of differences among institutions and programs in the important area of quality, as well as in other aspects. Furthermore, to the extent that appropriations largely derived by means of the application of a formula are a critical component in the financing of an institution, institutional strategies will necessarily be oriented toward optimizing the results produced by the formula. Although the consequences may be less than salutary, it is reasonable to predict that the formula funding approach will continue to be used and, paradoxically, as issues related to funding become more complex, the application of a formula approach is likely to become more extensive.

PUBLIC AND PRIVATE EDUCATION

It is appropriate to discuss public and private education within the broader context of a discussion on the financing of higher education because financial pressures have created an alarming attrition rate among independent institutions and the decline in the number of independents is exacerbated by the growing competition from the publics that are able to charge significantly lower tuition rates.

It is possible to make a judgment that the efficient delivery of higher education services to meet the needs of our population, as we currently identify those needs, would call for a lesser number of institutions. But a value judgment can also be made that the quality and strength of our educational system also calls for sustaining private institutions as a vital component of that system.

The table reprinted on pages 40–41, which lists private colleges closed or shifted to public control from the spring of 1970 to the fall of 1978, provides one perspective on the attrition rate among independents.

Still another perspective on the plight of the independents is provided by a study prepared by the National Association of State Colleges and Universities* which concluded that the proportion of institutions in a precarious position increased in 1976–77 and that a representative sampling reflected that 34% of the institutions were losing ground financially.†

Until World War II, private education was considered the dominant force in higher education. Following the war, there was a major expansion in college and university enrollments stimulated largely by the GI bill, but also by the baby boom and by the emphasis on access to higher education for the economically disadvantaged. This expansion saw a much greater growth in the number of public institutions and in enrollments in public institutions. Political pressures by local communities resulted in establishment of an increasing number of community colleges or branch campuses of state institutions.

These institutions, because of their convenience and their lower cost proved particularly attractive to families with modest incomes. As pressures for "open admissions" policies mounted, these institutions became the principal vehicle for educating the economically and educationally disadvantaged. As noted above, increasing financial pressures on the private institutions, by contrast to the relative financial stability of the publics, has contributed to a circumstance in which public institutions are becoming increasingly predominant. It is to be noted, however, that assertions regarding the decline of the private sector are disputed by some experts. Russell I. Thackery, who served as Executive Director of the National Association of State University and Land Grant Colleges from 1945 to 1969, has asserted that the number of accredited private institutions has increased every year since 1970. This is in direct contradiction to the assertion by the National Institute of Independent Colleges and

---

* Fourth Annual Report on Financial and Education Trends in the Independent Sector of American Higher Education.
† Ibid.

Private-College Openings, Closings, and Mergers, 1970-78

Closings

	Type	Men's, women's, coed	Affiliation
Alaska			
Alaska Methodist U. (reopened)	4-year	Coed	United Meth.
Arizona			
C. Del Ray	4-year	Coed	Independent
Prescott C.	4-year	Coed	Independent
California			
Ambassador C.	4-year	Coed	Wld. Ch. God
California Concordia C.	2-year	Coed	Lutheran
Lone Mountain C.	4-year	Coed	Rom. Catholic
Santa Barbara Art Inst.	Special	Coed	Independent
Tahoe C.	4-year	Coed	Independent
U. Without Walls–Berkeley	4-year	Coed	Independent
Connecticut			
C. of Notre Dame of Wilton	4-year	Women	Rom. Catholic
Longview C.	2-year	Coed	Rom. Catholic
Silvermine C. of Art	Special	Coed	Independent
District of Columbia			
Dunbarton C. of Holy Cross	4-year	Women	Rom. Catholic
Immaculata C.	2-year	Women	Rom. Catholic
St. Joseph's Seminary (coll. div)	Special	Men	Rom. Catholic
St. Paul's C.	Special	Men	Rom. Catholic
Webster Jr. C.	2-year	Coed	Independent
Florida			
C. of Orlando	2-year	Coed	Independent
St. Joseph C. of Florida	2-year	Coed	Rom. Catholic
Georgia			
Norman C.	2-year	Coed	Baptist
Illinois			
Chicago Technical C.	4-year	Coed	Independent
Maryknoll C.	Special	Coed	Rom. Catholic
Monticello C.	2-year	Women	Independent
St. Dominic C.	4-year	Coed	Rom. Catholic
Tolentine C.	Special	Coed	Rom. Catholic
Winston Churchill C.	2-year	Coed	Independent
Indiana			
Concordia Sr. C.	4-year	Coed	Lutheran
Iowa			
Midwestern C.	4-year	Coed	Independent

	Type	Men's, women's, coed	Affiliation
New York—Continued			
Finch C.	4-year	Women	Independent
Immaculate Conception Sem.	Special	Men	Rom. Catholic
LaSalette Seminary	Special	Men	Rom. Catholic
Mills C. of Education	Special	Women	Independent
Our Lady of Hope Mission Sem.	Special	Men	Rom. Catholic
Packer Collegiate Inst.	2-year	Coed	Independent
Passionist Monastic Seminary	Special	Men	Rom. Catholic
Rogers C.	Special	Coed	Rom. Catholic
St. Clare C.	Special	Women	Rom. Catholic
St. John Vianney Seminary	Special	Men	Rom. Catholic
Verrazano C.	4-year	Coed	Independent
Woodstock C.	Special	Men	Rom. Catholic
North Carolina			
Kernersville Wesleyan C.	2-year	Coed	Protestant
Kittrell C.	2-year	Coed	African Meth. Episcopal
North Dakota			
Assumption C.	2-year	Coed	Rom. Catholic
Ohio			
C. of the Dayton Art Inst.	4-year	Coed	Independent
Mary Manse C.	2-year	Women	Rom. Catholic
St. John C. of Cleveland	4-year	Men	Rom. Catholic
Oklahoma			
American Christian C.	4-year	Coed	Protestant
Oregon			
Mount Angel C.	2-year	Coed	Independent
Pennsylvania			
Cushing Jr. C.	2-year	Coed	Independent
Penn Hall Jr. C.	2-year	Coed	Am. Baptist
Rhode Island			
Sacred Heart Jr. C.	Special	Women	Rom. Catholic
Tennessee			
Catholic Teachers C.	4-year	Women	Rom. Catholic
Mount St. Joseph C.	Special	Women	Rom. Catholic
Sem. of Our Lady of Providence	Special	Men	Rom. Catholic
Siena C.	4-year	Coed	Rom. Catholic
Texas			
Allen Academy	2-year	Coed	Independent
Dominican C.	2-year	Women	Rom. Catholic

	Type	Men's, women's, coed	Affiliation
Illinois			
Brisk Rabbinical C.	Special	Men	Independent
Daniel Hale Williams U.	4-year	Coed	Independent
Morrison Inst. of Technology	2-year	Coed	Independent
Massachusetts			
Cntl. New England C. of Tech.	4-year	Coed	Independent
Laboure Jr. C.	2-year	Coed	Rom. Catholic
Montserrat Sch. of Visual Art	Special	Coed	Independent
Wentworth C. of Technology (merged with Wentworth Inst.)	4-year	Coed	Independent
Michigan			
Lewis Business C.	2-year	Coed	Independent
Thomas M. Cooley Law Sch.	Special	Coed	Independent
Minnesota			
Mayo Medical Sch.	Special	Coed	Independent
Midwestern Sch. of Law (merged with Hamline U.)	Special	Coed	Independent
Mississippi			
Wesley C. (originally Westminster C.)	4-year	Coed	Cong. Meth.
Missouri			
Assem. of God Graduate Sch.	Special	Coed	Assem. God
Cardinal Newman C.	4-year	Coed	Rom. Catholic
Christ Seminary–Seminex (originally Concordia Sem. in Exile)	Special	Coed	Independent
New York			
Bais Yaakov Seminary	Special	Women	Independent
Boricua C.	2-year	Coed	Independent
Christ the King Seminary	Special	Coed	Rom. Catholic
Hadar Hatorah Rabbinical Sem.	Special	Coed	Independent
Touro C.	4-year	Coed	Independent
Verrazano C. (now closed)	Special	Women	Independent
North Carolina			
Hamilton C. (originally Biscayne Southern C.)	2-year	Coed	Independent
Ohio			
Chatfield C.			
Oklahoma			
Am. Christian C. (now closed)	4-year	Coed	Protestant
South Carolina			
Sherman C. of Chiropractic	Special	Coed	Independent

Continued on Following Page

Institution	Type	Men's, women's, coed	Affiliation
St. Mary's C. Seminary	Special	Coed	Independent
	4-year	Coed	Protestant
Maine			
Bliss C.	2-year	Coed	Independent
Northern Cons. of Music	Special	Coed	Independent
Ricker C.	4-year	Coed	Rom. Catholic
Maryland			
Bay C. of Maryland	2-year	Coed	Independent
Mount Providence Jr. C.	2-year	Women	Rom. Catholic
Ocean City C.	2-year	Coed	Independent
St. Joseph C.	4-year	Women	Rom. Catholic
Xaverian C.	Special	Men	Rom. Catholic
Massachusetts			
Bryant-McIntosh Jr. C.	2-year	Coed	Independent
Cambridge Jr. C.	2-year	Coed	Independent
Cardinal Cushing C.	4-year	Women	Rom. Catholic
Garland Jr. C.	2-year	Women	Independent
Mount Alvernia C.	2-year	Women	Rom. Catholic
Northampton Jr. C.	2-year	Coed	Independent
Oblate C. and Seminary	Special	Men	Rom. Catholic
Regina Coeli C.	2-year	Women	Rom. Catholic
St. Stephen's C.	Special	Men	Rom. Catholic
Stevens C.	2-year	Coed	Independent
Michigan			
De Lima Jr. C.	2-year	Coed	Rom. Catholic
Mackinac C.	4-year	Coed	Independent
Minnesota			
Corbett C.	2-year	Coed	Independent
Lea C.	4-year	Coed	Independent
Mississippi			
Gulf Park Jr. C.	2-year	Women	Independent
Saints C.	2-year	Coed	Church of God in Christ
Missouri			
Marillac C.	Special	Women	Rom. Catholic
Notre Dame C.	4-year	Coed	Rom. Catholic
Nebraska			
Hiram Scott C.	4-year	Coed	Independent
John F. Kennedy C.	4-year	Coed	Independent
John J. Pershing C.	4-year	Coed	Independent
New Hampshire			
Belknap C.	4-year	Coed	Independent
Canaan C.	4-year	Coed	Independent
Franconia C.	4-year	Coed	Independent
Mount St. Mary C.	4-year	Women	Rom. Catholic
St. Anthony C.	Special	Men	Rom. Catholic
New Jersey			
Alphonsus C.	2-year	Coed	Independent
Englewood Cliffs C.	2-year	Women	Rom. Catholic
Mount St. Mary C.	2-year	Women	Rom. Catholic
St. Joseph's C.	Special	Men	Rom. Catholic
Salesian C.	4-year	Women	Rom. Catholic
Shelton C.	4-year	Coed	Other
Tombrock C.	2-year	Women	Rom. Catholic
Walsh C.	2-year	Women	Independent
New Mexico			
C. of Artesia	4-year	Coed	Independent
New York			
Bennett C.	2-year	Women	Independent
Brentwood C.	Special	Women	Rom. Catholic
Briarcliff C.	4-year	Women	Independent
Stratford C.	4-year	Coed	Independent
Sullins C.	2-year	Coed	Independent
Washington			
Suplician Sem. of the Northwest	4-year	Coed	Rom. Catholic
West Virginia			
Greenbrier C.	2-year	Coed	Independent
Wisconsin			
C. of Racine	2-year	Women	Rom. Catholic
Layton Sch. of Art and Design	2-year	Coed	Independent
Mount St. Paul C.	4-year	Men	Rom. Catholic
St. Columban's C. and Seminary	Special	Men	Rom. Catholic
St. Lawrence Seminary	Special	Men	Rom. Catholic

Openings

Institution	Type	Men's, women's, coed	Affiliation
Alaska			
Inupiat U. of the Arctic	4-year	Coed	Independent
Arizona			
C. Del Ray (now closed)	2-year	Coed	Independent
C. of Ganado	2-year	Coed	Independent
Prescott Center C.	4-year	Coed	Independent
California			
American Acad. of Dramatic Arts–West	2-year	Coed	Independent
Christ C. Irvine	2-year	Women	Lutheran
Christian Heritage C.	4-year	Coed	Independent
Colegio De La Tierra	2-year	Coed	Independent
D-Q U.	2-year	Coed	Independent
Fielding Inst.	Special	Coed	Independent
Maharishi Intl. U. (now in Iowa)	4-year	Coed	Independent
Melodyland Sch. of Theology	4-year	Coed	Christian Ch.
National U.	4-year	Coed	Independent
New C. of California	4-year	Coed	Independent
Nyingma Inst.	Special	Coed	Independent
Rand Graduate Inst. for Policy Studies	Special	Coed	Independent
Rosemead Graduate Sch. of Psychology (merged with Biola C.)	Special	Coed	Independent
Santa Barbara Art Inst. (now closed)	Special	Coed	Independent
U. Without Walls–Berkeley (now closed)	4-year	Coed	Independent
Windsor U.	4-year	Coed	Independent
World U. West	4-year	Coed	Independent
District of Columbia			
Antioch Sch. of Law	4-year	Coed	Independent
Campus Free C.	2-year	Women	Independent
Washington International C.	4-year	Coed	Independent
Florida			
Henda C.	4-year	Coed	Independent
Talmudic C. of Florida	Special	Women	Rom. Catholic
U. of Sarasota	4-year	Women	Women
Virginia			
Liberty Baptist C. (originally Lynchburg Baptist C.)	4-year	Coed	Independent
Washington			
City C.	4-year	Coed	Independent
Prometheus C.	4-year	Coed	Independent
West Virginia			
Greenbrier C. of Osteo. Med. (now public)	Special	Coed	Independent
Puerto Rico			
Colegio Universitario Del Turabo	4-year	Coed	Independent

Shifts to Public Control

Institution	Type	Men's, women's, coed	Affiliation
Alabama			
Athens C. (Athens State C.)	4-year	Coed	United Meth.
Arizona			
Navajo C. C.	2-year	Coed	Independent
Florida			
New College (U. of South Florida)	4-year	Coed	Independent
Georgia			
Gordon Military C. (Gordon Jr. C.)	2-year	Coed	Independent
Indiana			
Fort Wayne Art Inst. (Purdue U.-Indiana U. at Ft. Wayne)	4-year	Coed	Independent
Maryland			
U. of Baltimore	4-year	Coed	Independent
Michigan			
Michigan C. of Osteopathic Med. (Michigan State U.)	Special	Coed	Independent
New York			
Voorhees Technical Inst. (New York City C. C.)	2-year	Coed	Independent
North Carolina			
Mitchell C.	2-year	Coed	Independent
Ohio			
Salmon P. Chase C. of Law (Northern Kentucky State C.)	Special	Coed	Independent
Western C. (Miami U.)	4-year	Coed	Rom. Catholic
South Carolina			
C. of Charleston	4-year	Coed	Independent
Palmer C. (Trident Technical C.)	2-year	Coed	Independent
Texas			
South Texas Jr. C. (U. of Houston)	2-year	Coed	Independent
West Virginia			
Texas C. of Osteopathic Med.	4-year	Coed	Independent
W. Va. Sch. of Osteopathic Med.	Special	Coed	Independent

Universities that between 1970 and 1978, 129 private colleges and branch campuses had been closed, while only 64 had been founded.

As noted in other chapters of this book, in today's economy, financial considerations are a major factor in determining enrollments. Private institutions, because of the necessity to place greater reliance on tuition income as a source of financing, have tuition rates that sometimes exceed the rates of public institutions in the same geographic area by a factor of four or more. This is not only a deterrant to many low income families, but the level of these tuition rates is often such that the student financial aid support that can be made available, as a result of federal funding, is insufficient and students are compelled to attend lower cost public institutions.

Proponents of private institutions (which are now frequently termed independents to connote a lack of affiliation or control and to avoid an inference of exclusivity) point out with some cogency, that the cost to educate a given student at a private institution may not necessarily be higher than at a public institution. But the cost *charged* to the student is higher because more of the cost at a public institution is borne by tax dollars. (As will be noted in the discussion on cost analysis, this suggests an important caveat in regard to cost comparisons among institutions.)

It is also true that families that elect to send their children to private institutions, and have the means to do so, are simultaneously providing funding support to the private institution through tuition payments and to the public institution through their tax dollars.

At times the rivalry between public and private institutions within a state is a bitter one. Administrators at private institutions view with envy the more stable and abundant financing available to the publics and the comparative ease with which they can obtain capital funding for major renovations to and expansion of physical plant. Administrators at public institutions, in turn, view with envy the comparative flexibility and freedom to act of their private counterparts.

Paradoxically, differences between the two kinds of institutions tend to diminish as the intensity of the rivalry increases. Some of the major public institutions have attained an academic stature that rivals even the most prestigious of the privates. In the competition for financing, the publics are increasingly competing for private sources of endowment funds and, in turn, the privates are increasingly being supported by state funds.

In the portion of this section dealing with state financing, the point is made that controls inevitably follow financing support provided from tax dollars. The public policy dilemma that confronts us as a society is how to temper the rivalry between publics and privates, and how to carve out an appropriate role for each and to preserve the essential distinctions between them. As state funding becomes more significant and as the states begin to address the issue of redundancy of resources in a more aggressive and systematic way, it will be difficult to avoid a degree of control that will make the designation of private institutions as independent an empty one.

Public and private institutions each serve a vital and unique function. One of the major challenges confronting our society is to find the means to financially sustain both.

STATE SUPPORT FOR PRIVATE INSTITUTIONS

With the growth of public institutions, coupled with rising costs and declining enrollments, private institutions have been compelled to lobby for a portion of the state support for higher education. The success of their efforts is partially reflected in the chart below, reprinted from the July 31, 1978 issue of the Chronicle of Higher Education.

Although the concept of state aid to private institutions is not a recent phenomenon (New York provided aid to what is now Columbia University but was then Kings College, in the 18th century) it is only in recent years that it has become a substantial and fundamental part of the funding structure for higher education.

In New York, the Bundy plan, instituted in 1969, was the forerunner of many other state plans, although the details of the model have not been fully replicated. This plan provides funding directly to private institutions, amounting in the 1978–79 year to $68 million. It uses a formula based on the level and number of degrees granted, whereas many of the newer plans are strictly capitation plans. As originally enacted, the formula was computed by multiplying by four hundred dollars the number of earned bachelor's and master's degrees and by twenty-four hundred dollars the number of earned doctorate degrees. In 1979 Bundy aid to private institutions was increased by 30% and the state has taken over the entire support of City University's four year campuses.

Currently, some 43 states make public funds available in some form to private institutions. By far the most frequent form is through aid to

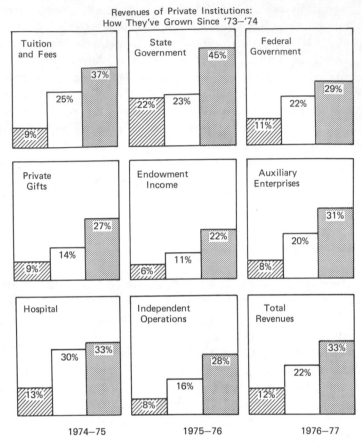

Revenues of Private Institutions:
How They've Grown Since '73–'74

Tuition and Fees	State Government	Federal Government
Private Gifts	Endowment Income	Auxiliary Enterprises
Hospital	Independent Operations	Total Revenues

1974–75   1975–76   1976–77

SOURCE: W. John Minter and Howard R. Bowen   Chronicle Chart by Susan Brown

students at both public and private institutions. The states spent some $746 million on comprehensive student aid in 1977–78, more than half of which went to students in private institutions. In addition, 13 states provide tuition equalization grants or grants specifically earmarked for students in private institutions and ten states provide direct aid to private institutions. Other forms of state aid include contracts for services, special funds for the disadvantaged and minorities, special subventions and student programs (including grants and scholarships in medical, dental, nursing, and health education fields) facilities assistance, authorities to provide tax exempt bonds, and other miscellaneous programs.

Institutional administrators recognize that, as with federal assistance, state aid carries with it the spectre of control. But it is also recognized that current financial circumstances leave the private institutions with no viable alternative. State control is in a very real sense more pervasive than federal control since it goes beyond accountability and implementation of public policy goals related to minorities, the handicapped, and so on. It also gets involved with program effectiveness.

There are already in evidence, signs that the states are beginning to exert their influence in a direction that is viewed as essential to sustain our higher education system at a price that we can afford and that our citizenry is willing to pay. Some 28 legislatures have set up postaudit oversight activities. Some 20 states have established performance audit units that report either to the legislatures or to the governor and at least 11 of these have made studies of higher education. Additionally, Higher Education Commissions and other state coordinating bodies are beginning to look at public and private postsecondary institutions as a single entity or body of resources and to evaluate resource needs in relation to student demands. This assessment inevitably leads to evaluation of contemplated new programs (or physical expansion plans), and to the conclusion that they are not needed. Some private institutions around the country have already "voluntarily" abandoned expansion plans when presented with such a conclusion by state officials.

Twenty states with statewide coordinating agencies place the responsibility for program approval with that agency. In the past the exercise of this responsibility has been confined to new programs, but there is a trend in the direction of extending this review to existing programs with a focus on quality, efficiency, reduction of duplication, and assessment of results. Florida, Kansas, Louisiana, New Jersey, New York, Washington, and Wisconsin have undertaken major reviews of graduate programs, including recommendations for discontinuance of nonproductive, qualitatively marginal, and duplicative programs. In Wisconsin program review has been extended to all levels of the university system.

The next step in this process will be viewed as far more onerous by institutions and, hence, is apt to meet with more vigorous resistance from both public and private institutions. This will involve the development of a comprehensive long-range plan for the state which projects future enrollments, examines total human and physical resources, determines attrition rates, and seeks to eliminate costly redundancy by planned phaseouts of courses, departments, and even schools within specific institutions. Such an approach will require, among other things, establishment of more uniform admission and retention standards and a carefully designed program of articulation among institutions.

While it is recognized that the resistance and political impediments to the exercise of that kind of control function by the state are formidable, the economic circumstances that are likely to bring such a control process about are equally compelling. Institutions resent, and properly resist, efforts to control, as exemplified by the medical schools that declined to accept federal capitation grants rather than yield to federal efforts to modify their admissions policy in respect to foreign transfer students.

But to extend that illustration, only a minority of the medical schools resisted. Resistance to state controls, which can be expected to increase, can only come from a position of strength, and the increasing importance of state financial support to private institutions constitutes a powerful source of leverage.

The increasing significance of state aid, particularly to the private institutions, is reflected not only in direct aid to institutions but as indicated earlier, also in the form of aid to students, comparable to the federal BEOG program. Some additional statistics illustrate the growing magnitude of this form of assistance. In 1977–78 Pennsylvania distributed about $71 million to 121,000 students, Illinois $78 million to 95,000 students, and California $79 million to 59,000 students. Although the average amounts of such aid would not appear sufficient to offset the substantial gap between public and private tuitions, in New York some observers see a close correlation between the initiation of the Tuition Assistance Plan (TAP) and a shifting of enrollments in favor of the privates.

The trend in New York was that in 1960 the private institutions had enrolled 62% of New York's students and by 1974 that share had dropped to 35%. (The figures are somewhat misleading because with the establishment of open enrollment the student population of the City University of New York expanded dramatically, to a peak of 250,000 students in 1974.) Following the institution of TAP between 1974 and 1977, private undergraduate enrollments increased by 16% while public enrollments increased by only 4%.

The TAP program, while problem ridden (by the spring of 1978 over 2000 students had failed to receive their TAP awards for the 1976–77 school year), is by far the largest of the state programs. The 1977–78 year saw awards of $208 million to approximately 355,000 students. The program is administered by the Higher Education Services Corporation, created specifically for that purpose. It is, unlike the federal **BEOG**, not subject to an appropriation ceiling, but is open ended. It awards grants on the basis of net family income in a range that tapers in 1978–79 from a maximum of $1800 for a family with an income below $2750 to $200 for an undergraduate whose family income falls between $18,000 and $20,000.

While this and similar programs in other states have been criticized as being inadequate, these programs clearly represent a substantial contribution to the support for higher education and are likely to grow in importance. A projection of their trends and potential impact on total resources available to students must obviously be an important component in the identification of the target population, the administration of student recruitment programs and the establishment of tuition policies.

TUITION

Tuition is one of the major sources of "hard money" and of unrestricted money. According to statistics published by the United States Office of Education, on the average about 36.8% of a private institution's current revenue funds come from tuition and fees as contrasted with 12.8% for public institutions. (Some individual institutions will find these figures quite low.) Tuition is also, within limits, one of the major funding sources over which the institution can exert control. It is possible, through careful attention and aggressive investment policy, within the limits of prudence, to increase endowment fund income. State funding programs, particularly those that are formula based, offer some opportunity for knowledgeable optimizing. It is to be presumed that improved concentration and effectiveness in fund raising will yield some results, in the form of increased annual contributions. But in the case of tuition, the institution can *decide* to levy a tuition increase, and inflationary cost increases provide a ready rationale for tuition increases.

But, this observation is not intended to imply that institutions have complete flexibility in regard to establishing tuition rates. Tuition policy is one of the areas that is apt to receive considerable attention from trustees because tuition is an important source of income and because tuition policy has many ramifications.

Because of its high degree of sensitivity tuition policy will necessarily be influenced heavily by precedent or tradition; i.e., all other things being equal, it will be easier for an institution that has had a practice of raising tuition rates regularly to institute an increase than for one that has been less frequent in its increases. The purpose of a tuition increase will frequently be to maintain the contribution of tuition to current fund income at its customary level or proportionality. A tuition increase aimed at compensating for anticipated shortfalls in other income sources will generally be more difficult to sustain.

Market conditions will also have an influence on tuition. We do not usually find significant disparities among the tuition and fee schedules of institutions that compete for the same students and those institutions confronted by decline in enrollments may be particularly loathe to risk compounding the situation with a tuition increase. Public institutions will find that the state may inhibit tuition increases. Considerable political capital may be gained by the legislature that proclaims publicly that it has avoided the necessity for a tuition increase by providing increased funding—when, in fact, the increase provided may be inadequate.

A key consideration in the formulation of tuition policy is the availability of student financial aid from both internal and external sources. Despite the limitations of cost analysis, as currently applied in higher education, it is possible for institutions to conclude in some circumstances that the incremental benefits associated with sustaining or increasing the level of enrollment make it desirable for the institution to fund or increase the funding for student financial aid. Such a decision is more apt to be made when an analysis of fund raising potential suggests that there is strong potential for securing increased scholarship funds. Internally funded student financial aid, in the form of "no need" scholarships, will also be viewed as a means of maintaining a diverse student body or attracting academic high achievers.

The availability of external sources of student financial aid, (federal, state, and other), and the relationship between that aid and the current level of tuition creates an area of potential leverage that is another component of tuition policy considerations. The example is cited elsewhere of postsecondary institutions in Puerto Rico that have experienced a very dramatic expansion in enrollments during the past several years with 80% of their students receiving full support from the federal BEOG program and from the campus based programs that are federally funded. The example is not fully generalizable because the students, in this case, come predominantly from low income families and the tuition levels at these institutions are relatively low in contrast to those of most institutions in the states. Nonetheless, the extent to which tuition is financed by student financial aid provided by external sources can significantly influence the ease with which tuition increases can be instituted.

Mention should be made of a tuition plan which has initially shown signs of being far more successful than would have been imagined. In the fall of 1978, Washington University instituted a "Tuition Stabilization Plan." It provided, in essence, that students who were willing to prepay four years tuition (an amount of $17,200 at the then current tuition levels) would avoid the prospect of a tuition increase during the four year period. The University also announced its willingness to make loans to cover the advance payment for periods of four to eight years at nine percent interest.

The plan has something for everyone. For the parents, in lieu of paying increased tuition rates which constitute a pure out-of-pocket cost, interest on the loan is paid and that interest is tax deductible. For the University, if they use an internal source for funding the loan, such as endowment loan funds, they presumably can draw down the full amount of the loan from such funds and, hence, they have, in effect, the present use of four years of tuition payments and a healthy return on the funds used for loans. Reports that many other institutions are considering adoption of a similar plan attest to its attractiveness. This also suggests that similarly innovative plans will likely be developed to meet tuition income needs without excessively burdening students and their parents.

The feasibility of a differential pricing policy is another potential component of tuition policy considerations. The strength of given schools and programs and the degree of student demand could give rise to a less uniform approach to tuition. Pricing based on quality of product and market demand—widely accepted commercial concepts—raises problems in the complex university environment and it should be particularly noted that limited experimentation with differential pricing has not produced very satisfactory results. But given the pressures on institutions in today's environment it is clear that this and other possible options cannot be summarily dismissed.

STUDENT FINANCIAL AID

Student Financial Aid embracing considerations such as the need for assistance, the sources for providing it, the basis on which it is provided, and the manner in which it is administered, is a critical aspect of higher education administration.

We have observed earlier that enrollment trends both in general and in relation to specific institutions are clearly influenced, at least in part, by tuition rates and other related costs of education. We have also noted that much publicity has been given, over recent years, to the fact that the financial burdens of higher education are becoming increasingly heavy and difficult for parents to bear.

In the period from 1968 to 1978, the cost of a public school education has risen 74% and that of a private school 77%. From 1970 to 1978 tuition at Harvard University increased by 85%. In the same period MIT increased its tuition by 88% and Boston University by 141%. While the growth in gross incomes has slightly exceeded the average tuition increases, net disposable incomes have lagged somewhat behind.

It is interesting to note that during the same ten year period referred to above enrollment increased, despite the increased financial burdens. During that period, census data showed that the number of whites in higher education increased 50% and for blacks the figures more than tripled. But this is not to say that increasing costs did not impact on the pattern of enrollments. Many students attended public institutions who otherwise would have attended private institutions, others sought two-year degrees in lieu of bachelor's degrees, or at least took their first two years at a junior or community college and still others studied only part time.

The important relationship between student financial aid and tuition has already been referred to. Figures on the proportion of total tuition payments funded by the various forms of student financial aid, federal, state, and institutional, are not readily available. But, the magnitude of financial aid funds being provided by the United States Office of Education is one indication of the importance of student aid funding, both to the students and as an indirect source of support to institutions. The chart that follows reflects the Higher Education Budget for the United States Office of Education.

What the chart clearly reflects is that support for higher education from the United States Office of Education is predominantly concentrated in the area of student assistance and its proportion is increasing. The wide range of federally supported student financial aid programs includes such programs as Fellowships to Graduate and Professional Students, Nursing Scholarship Program, Social Security Student Benefits and Veterans Education Benefits, among others. Although the latter two are

Higher Education Budget/U.S. Office of Education
(in thousands of dollars)

	1978	1979	CHANGE
Student Assistance:			
Basic Grants	$2,160,000	$2,177,000	+$ 17,000
Supplemental Grants	270,093	270,093	—
Work Study	435,000	450,000	+ 15,000
Direct Loans	325,660	304,400	— 21,260
Incentive Grants for State Scholarships	63,750	76,750	+ 13,000
Student Loan Insurance Fund	530,163	750,814	+ 220,651
Health Professions Insurance Fund	—	6,500	+ 6,500
Subtotal, Student Assistance	3,784,666	4,035,557	+ 250,891
Institutional Assistance:			
Educational Information Centers	2,000	—	— 2,000
Strengthening Developing Institutions	120,000	120,000	—
Language Training and Area Studies	18,000	18,000	—
University Community Services	18,000	—	— 18,000
Land Grant Colleges	2,700	2,700	—
State Postsecondary Education Commissions	3,500	—	— 3,500
Veterans' Cost of Instruction	23,750	19,000	— 4,750
Cooperative Education	15,000	4,000	— 11,000
Construction:			
Annual Interest Grants	4,000	29,000	+ 25,000
Model Intercultural Centers	5,000	—	— 5,000
Renovation Grants	—	50,000	+ 50,000
Wayne Morse Chair of Law and Politics	500	—	— 500
College Library Resources	9,975	—	— 9,975
Library Training and Demonstrations	3,000	—	— 3,000
College Instructional Equipment	7,500	—	— 7,500
Higher Education Facilities Loan and Insurance Fund	3,013	3,340	+ 327
Subtotal, Institutional Assistance	235,938	246,040	+ 10,102
Other Higher Education Programs:			
Special Programs for Disadvantaged	115,000	115,000	—
Graduate/Professional Opportunities	3,250	8,000	+ 4,750
Legal Training for Disadvantaged	1,000	1,000	—
Law School Clinical Experiences	1,000	—	— 1,000
Public Service Fellowships	4,000	—	— 4,000
Mining Fellowships	4,500	—	— 4,500
College Teacher Fellowships	—	—	—
Subtotal, Other Programs	128,750	124,000	— 4,750
Total, Higher Education	$4,149,354	$4,405,597	+$256,243

[Chart courtesy of *Higher Education and National Affairs*]

major programs that are quite significant to some institutions, the Veterans Education Benefits program has peaked and programs with the most widespread impact are the Basic Educational Opportunity Grants program and the Guaranteed Student Loan program. The three major federally supported campus based programs (i.e., awards are made through the institution rather than directly to the student): Supplemental Educational Opportunity Grants program, College Work-Study program and the National Direct Student Loan program are also quite significant.

The Basic Educational Opportunity Grant (BEOG) program is intended to provide the basic underpinning for federally sponsored student financial aid support. It was first authorized by the Education Amendments of 1972 to the Higher Education Act of 1965 and began with an appropriation of $122,100,000 in 1973 which has since grown to $2,177,000,000 in 1979.

Basic grant assistance is available to all eligible undergraduate students (generally limited to *four years of undergraduate studies*—this has significance for the educationally disadvantaged whose period of study may be extended by the necessity for remedial work) enrolled in an eligible institution on at least a half-time basis. The maximum award in the 1978–79 academic year was $1000, less expected family contribution but not to exceed one-half the cost of attendance. In late 1978 Congress raised the income ceiling for this program from $15,000 to $25,000.

The manner in which the program functions mechanically is that students submit applications to an Office of Education contractor for determination of expected family contribution. After this calculation is made, students apply to the institution of their choice, submitting an eligibility report provided by the contractor. Institutions are provided with Office of Education criteria for determining cost of attendance and a payment schedule. This enables the institution to determine the amount of the basic grant and then to put together the total student aid package. The institution bills the federal government for the award amount and acts as the disbursing agent.

It is worth noting that in the 1976–77 fiscal year, 67% of the BEOG funding went to students attending public institutions and 25% to students at private institutions (the balance was to students at proprietary institutions.) The number of public and private institutions participating is surprisingly similar—1,818 publics and 1,891 privates. Thus, despite the apparent correlation in New York between the advent of the TAP program and a redressing of the enrollment balance in favor of the privates, it would seem that the BEOG program has not had this impact and, even in combination with other segments of the student aid package, is apparently insufficient to bridge the gap in cost between the privates and the publics. This may also suggest that if a private institution is seeking to bolster its enrollments by recruiting low income students, it may have to place greater emphasis in its fund raising on tapping private sources for scholarship funds.

However, it is to be noted that some of our more prestigious and most costly institutions, that have established liberal scholarship policies, are finding it increasingly costly and difficult to sustain those policies. The comments on leverage should be recalled here.

The Supplemental Educational Opportunity Grant (SEOG), one of the three so-called campus based programs, supplanted the Educational Opportunity Grant program in 1973. It is intended for students of exceptional financial need and provides for a total award over four years, not to exceed $4,000 with annual awards limited to $1,500 or one-half of the total amount of student aid provided by the institution from public or private scholarships. Award recipients must "maintain satisfactory progress"—one of several aspects of administration that has posed problems for some institutions. The SEOG appropriation for 1979 exceeds $270,-000,000.

The College Work Study (CWS) program provides grants to institutions covering 80% of the wages paid to students working on campus or off campus in public or nonprofit organizations. Eligibility in this instance is influenced not only by financial need, but also by class schedule, health, and academic progress. This is the second major component of the campus based package with a 1979 appropriation of $450,000,000.

The third component of the campus based package is the National Direct Student Loan program. This provides for long-term, low interest loans with 90% of the funds for such loans to be provided by the federal government and 10% by the institution. (At the inception of this program it was contemplated that repayments over time would build up a rotating fund sufficient to avoid or substantially diminish the necessity for continued federal funding. Largely because of severe default problems and declarations of bankruptcy by graduates to avoid repayment—now declared illegal—that expectation was not realized.) For 1979 the appropriation for this program is $304,400,000.

Eligible students may borrow up to $2500 for a two-year program,

$5,000 for a four-year program and $10,000 for a program that includes graduate study. Repayment, with three percent interest charged on the unpaid balance, begins nine months after a student leaves school.

All three campus based programs have distributions to the states made on a formula basis with institutions then receiving distribution through submission of what has been called a tripartite application which is subject to peer evaluation. The application process is by no means pro forma and many institutions receive less than they otherwise might because their application is inadequately supported. Need determination and the packaging of aid are also aspects of this program that pose administrative problems as will be expanded upon shortly.

The Guaranteed Student Loan program with a 1979 appropriation of $532,313,000 is of major significance, particularly since Congress, late in 1978, eliminated the income ceiling on this program. (This coupled with raising the income ceiling for the BEOG program to $25,000, is likely to have a more dramatic impact than the tuition tax credit for which these actions were substituted.) This program permits lenders (either commercial lenders or institutions acting as direct lenders), to make loans directly to students without the necessity for credit ratings. The loans are guaranteed with a subsidized interest payment, either by individual state agencies (reinsured by the federal government), or directly by the United States Office of Education. The significance of this program for institutions is not only that for many students this may be virtually the only program for which they are eligible—or from which they can derive significant support—but institutions will also want to carefully weigh the possibility of becoming direct lenders.

The federally funded student financial aid programs provide for an allowance to be given to institutions to offset the administrative costs associated with these programs. That allowance has generally been found to be inadequate particularly since it must first be used to provide consumer information to prospective students. Effective administration requires adequate linkages with the counseling function (generally located in the office of the Dean of Students), the Bursar, Registrar, Admissions and Accounting offices. The severe problems associated with administration of these programs have received substantial publicity.

Among the deficiencies identified during the course of audit reviews were the following:

- Awards in amounts exceeding computed financial need;
- Awards to ineligible students;

- Inadequate documentation in support of awards;
- Inadequate needs analysis;
- No evidence of continued attendance;
- Inadequate accounting for federal funds;
- Payroll record/procedure deficiencies;
- Poor coordination between student financial aid office and business office; and
- Inadequate collection procedures including failure to exercise "due diligence."

Another source of concern to federal officials has been the refund policy and how clearly it has been established, applicable to students who drop out.

Because of the concern with deficiencies in administration and because of the substantial loan default rate, the Department of Health, Education and Welfare published a revised set of audit guidelines pertaining to student aid programs in 1978 and is placing greater emphasis on performance of student financial aid audits by internal auditors and by public accounting firms because of the limited resources which it has available to perform such audits.

Emphasis has been placed on the discussion of student financial aid, for two reasons pertinent to those involved in higher education management. Student Financial Aid expenditures, in the aggregate, exceed federal Research and Development expenditures as the most substantial source of federal support to higher education, and the prospects, at least in the near term, are for continued growth.

Federal grant and contract programs sponsored by the Department of Health, Education and Welfare, the National Science Foundation, the Department of Defense, the Department of Energy, and other major agencies do, however, represent a very major source of funding support to higher education. Federal R&D obligations were an estimated $26.5 billion in the President's 1978 budget to Congress, reflecting an annual growth rate of 5.2% since 1968. Estimates are that about 12% of this total currently is awarded to colleges and universities. Although there has been considerable dialogue on the failure of the federal government to reimburse institutions for the full cost of research and on the growing cost of federal compliance there has, as yet, been no definitive analysis on the question of the net contribution which federal R&D expenditures make to the financing of higher education.

Moreover, as institutional administrators analyze potential sources of financing for higher education, the federal government is the most viable and realistic source for increased support. It is clear that federal policies will call for that support to be provided preponderantly in the form of aid to students. A second very pertinent consideration is that the administrative demands associated with federal student aid programs and the generally poor performance record by institutions in administering these programs would suggest that this should be one of the particular areas of focus by trustees and other concerned constituents.

OTHER REVENUE GENERATING ACTIVITIES

As suggested in several of the chapters, an acceleration of costs that has outpaced revenue increases has occasioned a critical focus on cost-revenue relationships. One response has been to seek to develop the less traditional sources of revenue. Illustrative of the kinds of less traditional revenue generating activities that are now being more vigorously pursued are the following:

1. A variety of non-credit courses, seminars, workshops, lectures, focusing on particular interests or skills such as photography, gardening, interior decorating, music appreciation, piano lessons, bridge, physical fitness, dieting, cooking, wine tasting, speed reading, etc.;
2. Topics of the day, lectures, and discussion bringing well informed individuals to the campus to discuss issues in the news;
3. Renting of athletic facilities, rooms, and other facilities; for example, several institutions rent their athletic facilities to professional teams for training. Governmental entities have used university facilities and staff to run training programs;
4. Providing consulting, research, technical testing, and management services for business and industry;
5. Providing various clinics for the community dealing in reading, speech and hearing, counseling, and job counseling;
6. Establishing and running exclusively, or in partnership with another organization, various activities such as tennis, soccer, or bridge camps or weekends, preparation for post-collegiate careers, preparation for medical or law school examinations;

7. Providing computer service bureau functions such as programming, keypunch, and renting of time on the computer to business and industry;

8. Soliciting contributions to the institution of boats, equipment, books, art works, which can be used by the institution, rented, leased, or sold;

9. Sponsoring garage sales, bakeoffs, car-washes, marathon runs, amusement rides, walk-a-thons, bike-a-thons, raffles—all for the purpose of generating funds;

10. Sponsoring benefit performances, faculty-student games and contests, faculty shows, etc.;

11. Investing in various business enterprises and providing some management or technical skills;

12. Seeking commercial applications of various research efforts, patenting when necessary and selling the manufacturing or license rights or setting up a corporation to manufacture the product;

13. Utilizing the skills of faculty and students in particular areas to provide services and products such as films, various types of art work, advertising, scenery design, writing, translating and interpreting, market research;

14. Successful intercollegiate athletic teams have traditionally been regarded as a source of income, frequently at least sufficient to pay for the cost of the institution's entire athletic program (and still regarded as an important stimulus to alumni contributions.) But some institutions have diminished their emphasis on, or have eliminated, intercollegiate athletics, either on philosophic grounds or because they found that they were experiencing a heavy cost of subsidization. As with any activity that may be loosely categorized as auxiliary, it is important to examine the economics. The existence of a university press is far less prevalent than was the case 20 years ago. Food service is another illustration. Some institutions have found that they can adequately serve the needs of students, faculty, and other staff with a university operated food service that is at least self-sustaining. Other institutions have found it appropriate to contract out their food service operation.

Some of the revenue generating activities enumerated previously may well be regarded as remote from the mission of the institution and some constituents may regard them as inappropriate. The image which these activities may create is an important factor for institutions to consider before embarking on such activities. Another caveat to be observed concerns the concept of unrelated business income. So long as revenue generating activities not germane to the mission of the institution are relatively modest, the most serious exposure of the institution is the possibility that that unrelated income will be taxed. The more serious consequence is that such activities will become so extensive as to threaten the tax exempt status of the institution.

Subject to that important caveat, it is to be anticipated that as institutions confront limitations on the potential for increasing traditional sources of funding support, they will continue to turn to less traditional revenue generating activities.

Chapter Four
ENDOWMENT FUND MANAGEMENT

At the end of 1977 higher education institutions had an aggregate endowment of $16.3 billion. Various surveys of endowment funds and their use have disclosed wide variations in the extent to which institutions depend on endowment fund income to support current operations ranging from three percent to fifty-three percent. This wide variation suggests that the critical first question to be asked at any institution is "What is the function of the endowment at our institution?" It is only within the context of that question that an intelligent and explicit policy for endowment fund management can be formulated.

As suggested in the chapter on Development Activity, endowment fund management begins with the fund raising process. Appealing to the special interests of donors, while avoiding restrictions on donations, to the fullest extent possible, is part of the art of fund raising. It is also to be noted in this connection that a surprising number of restrictions are self-imposed; i.e., imposed not by the donor but by the trustees or even by the administration.

There are three basic classifications for endowment funds. "True" endowments involve restrictions on the purpose for which income is to be used or on the manner of use. Endowment fund income may also be unrestricted as to use and finally, there is the category of funds functioning as endowment. This latter classification applies to gifts or other funds, with respect to which a decision has been made, generally by the trustees, but on occasion, by the administration, to set them aside as part of the endowment because they are not needed for current purposes.

There should be a periodic examination to verify that funds included in the endowment are properly classified. This examination should also be the occasion for determining whether funds functioning as endowment should continue to be so treated. The occasion may arise when special circumstances create the need for additional funds to meet current expenditure requirements. Under such circumstances the potential utilization of some portion of the funds functioning as endowment would be one of the alternatives to consider.

The circumstances referred to above would not only be special, but generally unpredictable. One operating definition of a true endowment fund is that it is a perpetual pool of capital with no *predictable* need to utilize principal. This understanding of the nature of a true endowment fund has significant implications in regard to endowment fund management. The absence of any predictable likelihood that capital will be utilized, means that factors such as liquidity and volatility become irrelevant. It should perhaps be stated, at this early juncture, that although many discussions on endowment fund management assume an investment in securities, there are a range of other opportunities for securing a return on invested capital; e.g., real estate, oil and gas properties, going business, etc., none of which are ignored by the imaginative and aggressive endowment fund manager.

However well conceived and articulated, endowment fund policy, as it relates to the need for current income, should be re-examined periodically, not only within the context of changing internal conditions, but also giving consideration to the external economic environment and its impact on investment opportunities.

In 1967, the Ford Foundation commissioned a study on problems in endowment management. A primary point of emphasis in the report, resulting from that study, was that by unduly stressing current income and failing to establish the clear-cut objective of maximum long-term total return, institutions and their endowment fund managers had failed to insulate their endowment funds against the inroads of inflation and a shrinking dollar.

Among the major recommendations contained in the report were that:

- Trustees should not themselves attempt to manage their endowment portfolios, but should instead utilize professional managers;
- All funds that may have to be converted to cash within the near future (a period up to five years) should be removed from the endowment portfolio and invested separately in prime short-term obligations; and
- A plan should be adopted in which, each year, transfers are made from endowment to operating funds in an aggregate amount equal to five

percent of the three-year moving average market value of the fund, whether or not that amount is provided by interest or dividends.

Concurrent with the report mentioned above, the Ford Foundation sponsored another report entitled "The Law and the Lore of Endowment Funds" which was intended to support the total return concept advocated in the first report. The thrust of this report was to indicate that, generally, there is no legal impediment to utilizing a prudent portion of the appreciation on endowment funds. Many states passed the Uniform Management of Institutional Funds Act, which made such use possible. But there continues to be some variation in governing state laws.

These studies had a profound impact on college and university endowment fund management. Institutions hastened to adopt the "total return" concept, without necessarily giving full consideration to its applicability or lack of applicability to their circumstances, the external circumstances which provided a context for the Ford study recommendations and, most particularly, to what was required for effective implementation.

The experience of one institution is illustrative. A "total return" philosophy was adopted and the portfolio oriented heavily to industry leader, low yielding growth stocks. Unrestricted endowment fund principal was being utilized annually to produce the difference between the 6% return on the endowment needed to support the operating budget and the 2.6% return in interest and dividends actually being generated in current income by the endowment.

Unfortunately, the unrestricted endowment fund was being rapidly depleted by these drawdowns which did not represent amounts attributable to realized appreciation. Quite the contrary. The institution had not been *realizing* any gains, only losses. The growth oriented stocks were retained indefinitely in the portfolio, fluctuating widely in price over the years, but never liquidated. Securities would be sold only when the institution found itself in need of cash (and this never coincided with a high in the market) or when the investment manager lost confidence in a security whose value had plummeted.

The above scenario does not suggest that the total return concept is faulty or even that it was inappropriate for the particular institution whose experience was described. What it does suggest is the absence of a sufficient understanding of endowment fund management concepts and an ineffective implementation of investment goals.

As suggested earlier, every institution should carefully assess, and periodically reassess, the extent to which endowment fund income must be relied upon as a source of current revenue. This need will be balanced against the desire to preserve endowment fund capital in real dollar terms. There may also be the desire or the need to set aside funds to provide for some specifically identified future requirements.

This balancing of present and future needs is the basis for establishing endowment fund management policy. There are alternative investment policies that can be pursued to effectuate the endowment fund management policy. The investment policies relied upon should reflect a current assessment of the state of the economy and the nature of investment opportunities.

For example, an institution might conclude that a six percent annual income from the endowment fund is needed to support current operating expenditures. Its endowment fund management policy might, consequently, encompass a targeted objective of nine percent annual return and the three percent difference between the targeted return and the six percent would be an addition to endowment fund capital to offset inflationary erosion.

At a time when short-term yields, e.g. Treasury bills, are ten percent or higher, an appropriate alternative might be to temporarily maintain a portfolio that is highly income oriented. The increment of income above six percent would not be used, but would be transferred to endowment capital and invested.

A second viable alternative might be a long-term appreciation oriented approach which would be likely to involve the necessity to augment current income by liquidating securities and utilizing a portion of endowment fund capital to meet the need for six percent in current income.

Either approach can effect the same endowment management objective, if effectively implemented. But in the first illustration, use of the entire amount of endowment income earned for current needs would effectively result in a long-term depletion of the endowment. In the second illustration, long-term endowment depletion will also occur unless the portfolio, despite cyclical fluctuations, does in fact experience a long-term appreciation consistent with the targeted nine percent return.

In a 1976 study, statistics on about 150 college and university endowment funds reflected that portfolios were invested about 60% in common stocks, 30% in bonds, and ten percent in short-term investments. This suggests a thoughtful attempt to balance risks, current income yield, and long-term growth.

The preceding discussion raises an important question about the kind of information trustees need about the endowment fund in order to exercise prudence in making investment decisions or in support of decisions to utilize fund income, capital gains, or endowment principal. It has been suggested that the income account of the fund should reflect: interest received; dividends received; appreciation or loss in investments realized; appreciation gain or loss on investments during the period not realized; *and* an inflation loss factor to be deducted to maintain fund principal intact.

The inclusion of this last factor suggests a philosophy which says that the endowment fund must yield in current income and capital gains, an amount greater than that which is needed to support the current operating budget as a means of insulating the endowment fund from inflation. The alternative is to insure that development activity will produce a rate of growth in the endowment sufficient to offset the rate of inflation.

On several occasions in this discussion, emphasis has been placed on the *realization* of capital gains. Bearing in mind the illustrative scenario cited earlier, one can question whether a policy of investing in growth stocks is meaningful unless it encompasses an intent to liquidate the stock when a major portion of the growth potential is deemed to have been achieved with a concomitant substitution of a stock which is in an earlier growth stage.

These are not easy judgments to make, and this is one of the reasons that institutions engage outside investment managers. Utilization of outside managers is not necessarily the answer for every institution. But few institutions possess the necessary staff skills and informational resources and even the largest among the institutions make some use of outside professional investment managers to augment their internal skills.

If the trustees elect to use outside management for their endowment, they should consider the possibility of using more than one manager, so that explicit performance comparisons can be made. They should examine performance records in making their selection and seek to determine whether the investment manager has a particular investment philosophy and if so, whether it is one which is in consonance with their own.

The general principles that apply to the selection and utilization of consultants as discussed in the chapter on the Use of Consultants are applicable to the utilization of outside investment managers. Any outside expert must be afforded that degree of latitude which is necessary to effectively utilize his expertise. There is little point in paying for specialized expertise and then exerting a degree of control that unduly limits the discretion of the investment manager.

This means, for example, that trustees should eschew the practice of approving day-to-day transaction decisions. Beyond this, it also means that they should consider carefully the restrictions they seek to impose on the investment manager. On the other hand, it is essential that they establish an investment policy which makes clear to the investment manager the objectives to be achieved, secures his commitment to those objectives and measures his performance against them. In this latter connection, statistical performance measurement services, such as the A. G. Becker studies, are generally useful in investment management, but particularly valuable in assessing performance of outside managers.

Among the opportunities for enhancing endowment income, two which relate to securities should be considered: (1) lending of securities and (2) selling of options. Lending of securities is a transaction in which an institution temporarily gives up physical possession of securities in its portfolio in exchange for collateral which can produce short-term income. Typically, the lending institution causes the securities to be delivered to a broker who utilizes them to make delivery in completed transactions. The borrowing broker is required to return the securities upon notice and deposits with the lending institution collateral equal to or greater than the value of the borrowed securities. Ownership continues to reside in the lending institution and the institution is, consequently, entitled to any interest or dividends earned during the loan period.

Some firms specialize in serving as brokers between borrowers and lenders of securities. Smaller institutions with limited portfolios may find the net income derived from such a program, after broker fees and related expenses, to be insufficient to justify the administrative burdens. But many of the larger institutions have had such a program for years as a segment of their cash management program, and continue to find it profitable.

The selling of options is gaining more general acceptance as a hedging, rather than a speculative, technique and represents a legitimate opportunity for institutions to increase investment return. The growth of the options market has greatly facilitated options trading. At the same time, the process has become more complex, transaction costs can be high, and the opportunities for gain less spectacular. The institution that contemplates the use of this technique should not do so casually and should expect to utilize professional advice.

In considering these and other techniques, those charged with administration should be mindful of the issue of "unrelated income." Congress in 1950 imposed a tax on "operations of businesses which are clearly unrelated to the primary functions" of tax exempt institutions or organizations. Where extensive activity involving "unrelated business" income is engaged in (as noted in the earlier discussion on other revenue generating activities), there is the risk not only that the unrelated income will be taxed, but also that the institution may lose its tax exempt status. The two techniques referred to above have been explicitly found to be outside the definition of unrelated business income.

The subject of endowment fund management cannot fully be discussed without dealing with social responsibility as an aspect of investment policy. The various constituencies of colleges and universities, but most particularly students and faculties, have expressed the strong view that, although the primary purpose of endowment fund management is to secure the most favorable return to the university, institutions cannot ignore the uses to which such invested funds are put. It is wrong, they contend, to use university funds to support activities not in consonance with university policies and values.

Taken to its extreme, such an argument would preclude an investment in government securities when federal policies are considered by some to be particularly onerous. But it is not the purpose here to engage in a discussion as to the appropriateness of actively voting proxies or of avoiding investments in the shares of certain companies at a certain time because such companies are insufficiently mindful of ecology or support repressive foreign governments directly or indirectly, or give other evidence of not being socially responsible.

The key point is that the issue of social responsibility as a facet of investment policy did not disappear when the activism of the '60s receded. It continues to be a matter of widespread concern and cannot be ignored by trustees and administrators. Consequently, it is incumbent upon the institution that does not now have one, to adopt an explicit policy on social responsibility in investment.

Such a policy should clearly state the institution's posture on the extent to which social responsibility issues will or will not influence purchase and sale of securities and the mechanism to be used in giving effect to that influence. The voting of proxies should be similarly dealt with. If the trustees have established an endowment subcommittee, that body would be the appropriate one to initiate a policy on social responsibility in investment. As an aspect of the broader considerations involved in governance, it might be appropriate to recognize this as one of the areas of university activity that has special meaning for faculty and students and both ought, consequently, to be given an opportunity to make suggestions in regard to the policy that is to be established.

As noted earlier, there are wide variations among the practices of institutions in managing their endowment funds and pursuing appropriate investment policies. They vary in the extent and manner in which they utilize outside investment counsel, they vary in their emphasis on short-term or long-term considerations, they vary in the diversity of their investments and they vary in the nature of their investments.

But there is a discernible trend in the direction of making more wide-spread use of investment vehicles which at one time might have been considered quite unorthodox by college and university officials. A striking illustration is provided by a small institution* that has departed from endowment fund management norms with enormous success. The example is even more dramatic because the institution is not one of the major universities, but rather a small college with an enrollment of considerably less than 2000.

From 1973 to 1978 this college has doubled the book value of its endowment to $37.5 million (a valuation at market would reflect a value closer to $60 million with new contributions during that period accounting for only $5.4 million of the increase.) Stated in its most conservative terms, there has been an average investment return during the period of 16.2% annually. By contrast, the median total return for 150 endowment funds charted by the A. G. Becker Company during that period was 1.7% annually.

The trustees departed from the conventional wisdom in a number of ways. As noted earlier, the highly influential study sponsored by the Ford Foundation contained as one of its major recommendations the statement that trustees should not attempt to manage the endowment fund themselves. At this college that caveat was ignored and the Finance Committee retained total control without relinquishing any aspect of day-to-day control of the endowment either to a bank, outside portfolio manager, or even a professional in-house manager.

The conventional wisdom also calls for diversity in investments. An

---

*With one or two possible exceptions, the authors have concluded that where circumstances at particular institutions are referred to, the illustration is not strengthened by citing the name of the institution.

examination of the formal investment policies adopted by institutions would disclose that one of the most common features is a limitation on the concentration in any one security, as well as in any one form of investment. This accords with the age-old maxim regarding placing all of one's eggs in one basket. The college in this illustration has very deliberately departed from this policy and, in fact, has concentrated its investments in a very few highly successful vehicles.

A key tenet of the college's investment policy is to seek out an undervalued company and invest in it heavily. The departure from tradition also manifests itself in the selection of investment vehicles as exemplified by the purchase from the AVCO Corporation of its WDTN television station in Dayton. It might be noted, relative to the issue of unrelated business income, that a separate company was formed to run the TV station and that company pays taxes on earnings.

Other institutions both large and small, have also exhibited a tendency to depart from some of the more cherished traditions of conservative endowment fund management. One major university, with a very substantial endowment engages profitably in arbitrage opportunities. A medium-size college, with an endowment of $11.2 million has pursued at least one aspect of the approach described above, ferreting out undervalued companies among second tier stocks, and has succeeded in achieving a total return averaging nine percent annually over a 10-year period. Another large institution has effectively used a small portion of its endowment funds (about four percent) for both venture capital and commodities. Still another institution counts a shopping center among its diversified investments.

A key ingredient in all of the illustrations cited is not that the institutions adopted approaches that were non-traditional or unorthodox, but rather that they adopted thoughtfully conceived approaches that were deemed appropriate for *their* circumstances. The bold approach adopted by the college in the first illustration might well have spelled disaster for another institution whose trustees were less astute investment managers *or* could not devote the necessary time and attention to the affairs of their institution.

Endowment fund management is an area that presents one of the more significant opportunities for trustees to utilize their business acumen in making a contribution to managing the financial affairs of the institution. But it demands a thoughtful assessment of their own capabilities, as well as all of the other factors discussed which bear on the development of specific policies and practices related to the needs and circumstances of the particular institution. There is both a moral imperative and a legal consideration in terms of the fiduciary responsibilities of trustees (see Chapter 8).

In legal terms, it is unquestionably true that for many years the "prudent man" test would be deemed to have been satisfied when trustees pursued a highly conservative policy aimed at avoiding risk of loss. Such an attitude is still likely to be found in many of the courts today. But one can speculate that the time is not far off when a court will define prudence in different terms and will question the stewardship of the trustee who fails to take reasonable business risks to generate an improved return on the endowment when the institution is starved for income.

Quite aside from legalities, the example of the college, which has been able to increase the proportion of the operating budget funded by the endowment from 11% to 20%, is compellingly attractive to the concerned trustee. The trustee who is not content with a passive role, will have to give serious consideration to whether a departure from orthodox methods is appropriate when endowment fund management is considered within the context of that institution's overall financial circumstances.

Chapter Five

DEVELOPMENT ACTIVITY

Development is a euphemism for fund raising. But it also connotes that, contrary to some popular beliefs, success in fund raising is not merely due to the activities of a charismatic president or a championship football team and requires a great deal of thought, organization and development.

It is also big business. In 1975–76, when voluntary support of American colleges and universities rose by 11% (the largest annual increase in a decade), more than $2.4 billion were received from businesses, foundations, and individuals. Among the major recipients were Harvard University, $59,025,806; University of California, $57,480,517; Stanford University, $41,759,938; Yale University, $37,724,243; University of Rochester, $33,577,123; University of Pennsylvania, $31,676,698; Columbia University, $30,122,556; University of Minnesota, $127,105,899; Case-Western Reserve University, $26,637,746; and University of Chicago, $26,614,127. Recalling the discussion on the diminishing difference between public and private or independent institutions in the section on Financing Higher Education, it is interesting to note that among these leading recipients are one quasi-public and two clearly public institutions.

There are, in fact, at least three major kinds of fund raising campaigns that take place at an institution, each of them quite distinct. There is the major campaign, the ongoing annual givers campaign, and the efforts to obtain funding from federal and private foundation sources. All should be part of a carefully orchestrated plan and the activities associated with them made known to all of those who are concerned with the governance of the institution.

THE CAPITAL CAMPAIGN

The major capital campaign can produce a very substantial influx of funds within a relatively short time frame (capital campaigns can be initially planned to extend over several years and will, at times, be subsequently extended beyond the time initially contemplated because of failure to meet campaign goals). The capital campaign is usually, but not necessarily, related to a specific objective or set of objectives and, in many instances, may coincide with some special event that tends to enhance its appeal and give focus to the campaign. Its major thrust is a targeted sum of money to be obtained largely through one-time major gifts. It can be anticipated that a small fraction of the donors will produce in excess of 60% of the total dollars, and most of this will come, or be pledged, in the first six months of the campaign.

The launching of a capital campaign is not to be taken lightly. It demands a very intensive activity and extensive commitments from many people. To some extent, it conflicts with the ongoing givers campaign, although, when used properly, it can be a source for identifying staunch regular donors.

A major capital campaign should be preceded by a market analysis that seeks to determine an appropriate campaign goal, as well as whether the campaign is likely to succeed or not. The answer might be negative simply because the timing (e.g., the current status of the economy) may not be right. In this connection it is also not unusual for institutions to defer the formal announcement of a campaign until they have secured sufficient pledges to serve both as a stimulus to the campaign and to insure its likely success.

In some instances, institutions engage consulting firms that specialize in this kind of market analysis to assist them in making an advance assessment before launching a campaign. Among the considerations involved in determining whether to use such assistance are the size of the campaign and the nature and availability of university resources. The general guidelines outlined in the discussion on the use of consultants are equally applicable here.

However, the use of consulting assistance in the development area is sufficiently widespread to warrant a few additional words. In this area, perhaps more than in most others, it is imperative to determine before hiring a consultant, what it is that the consultant is to do. What they cannot do is reasonably clear. Consultants should not be expected to identify specific prospects, nor should they be expected to raise funds. In fact, internal development staff does not truly raise funds, but instead facilitates the process by which the President and other key figures who personify the institution raise funds.

Some institutions need counsel to help them develop new approaches to fund raising. Others need an objective, comprehensive and systematic analysis of their potential and the identification of new sources of support. A facet of this takes the form of individualized prospect research or the preparation of campaign promotional and communication materials. Consultants can assist an institution to establish a properly functioning development organization (including recruitment and training of key personnel), or they can accelerate the learning process of existing staff members. Finally, consultants frequently play a significant role in the management of a major capital campaign or in the management of a significant fund raising event associated either with a capital campaign or with an ongoing program.

ANNUAL GIVERS CAMPAIGN

The ongoing annual givers program is frequently thought of as an alumni plan. While, undoubtedly, alumni constitute a natural and primary source of repetitive giving, there are many other "friends" of the institution that can be regarded as potential repetitive donors. Statistics suggest that any donor who makes a substantial gift (substantial should be defined for these purposes in relation to the donor's means), can be counted upon to make repeat donations as many as six to eight times. But these are not automatic.

An annual givers program is not normally conducted with the same degree of intensity as a major capital campaign, but requires an equally high degree of organization. Both require a high degree of familiarity with tax and estate law, particularly if the institution is to make full utilization of deferred giving programs.

There are a variety of deferred giving techniques. Among them, the charitable remainder UNITRUST has considerable appeal to donors and to the donee institution. In general, the characteristics of these trusts are that:

● The donor irrevocably transfers money, property, or both to the trustee (either the institution itself or some other entity, frequently a bank), who invests and reinvests the assets as a separate fund;

- Donor (and/or other designated beneficiary) receives an amount each year determined by multiplying a fixed percent, say five percent, by the fair market value of the trust assets, valued each year. Any income not paid out is added to principal. If income is insufficient to pay the required amount, capital gains or principal make up the deficit;
- On the donor's death, death of other designated beneficiary, or expiration of the term of the trust, payments terminate and the then assets of the UNITRUST are the absolute property of the designated charitable remainderman.

Clearly, this type of giving enables the donor to continue to enjoy the benefits of the income from an amount he plans ultimately to donate, either for himself or a designated beneficiary. At the same time, he secures immediate tax advantages, relinquishes the burden and the risk of investing the funds in question, prevents the dissipation of the principal by family members who may be incapable of managing funds, and protects against the creditors of the donor and beneficiary. For the institution, this form of deferred giving provides certainty as to the gift and, in some instances, may provide an immediate income, over and above the return committed to the donor or beneficiary during the life of the trust.

However, institutions should be conscious of the administrative requirements associated with this type of program. They should also be aware that agreements governing this type of trust should not be entered into without benefit of legal advice, and those acting for the institution must be fully current on applicable state and federal law. Trustees, in particular, must be conscious of the fact that these trust agreements impose special fiduciary responsibilities.

FEDERAL AND PRIVATE SOURCES OF FUNDING

Pursuit of federal and private foundation sources of funding is frequently relegated to the research administration function because these sources are normally drawn upon most frequently to support faculty research. (See discussion on sponsored activity in Chapter Six.) Professional "grantsmen" may be found, both in full-time positions on many campuses, or in the ranks of outside consultants. Such individuals can, in some instances, play an important role. The art of proposal writing can be overstated and its needs can normally be readily accommodated within the institution; i.e., it is not difficult to find assistance within the institution if the preparation of an articulate grant proposal is truly a difficult chore for a faculty member. Normally, however, the difficulty in articulation is symptomatic of a faulty conceptualization of the project to be undertaken. The special value of "grantsmanship" assistance lies in connection with those funding sources, particularly private foundations, where the priorities and interests that will govern the award process are not fully discernible from published materials.

GENERAL OBSERVATIONS

There are a number of general observations that are applicable in varying degrees to all three of the types of fund raising activities touched on above. First, mission evaluation, in addition to being essential to the survival of the institution in the marketplace, is extremely relevant to fund raising. While some donors will undoubtedly support the institution because of sentimental association with it as an entity, support will come predominantly from those who identify with the institution's mission, or some aspect of it. This does not mean that an institution should gear its activities to the interests of potential donors. Quite to the contrary, it should be wary of undertaking commitments that are essentially incompatible with the nature and long-range goals of the institution simply because funding support for those commitments is available.

On the other hand, the self-evaluation that should be an ongoing process with any institution should, necessarily, include questions that are pertinent to fund raising. To what interests are we appealing when we ask donors for support? Which are our special attributes as an institution that can persuade prospective donors that we merit their support? Can we define the types of donor to whom our mission and programs would be most appealing? Have we done an adequate job of articulating for ourselves and for our prospective donors what our institution is all about?

An information system is essential to any effective and comprehensive fund raising program. At a minimum, such a system should: assist in monitoring payments against pledges; trigger congratulatory notes or cards to major donors on appropriate occasions and trigger repeat requests to past donors at appropriate intervals. In addition, a cataloging of donor interests that can be accessed on a timely basis can facilitate an intelligently targeted approach in the annual program. For example, donors who have an identified interest in a particular subject area can be viewed as potential supporters of an academic chair in that discipline area. A means of courting such donors is to invite their attendance at special lectures or colloquia related to the subject matter of their interest.

Developing sources for potentially significant or major donors requires extensive research beyond the review of alumni lists. Some very basic resources include:

Who's Who in America
Regional *Who's Who* and also local and national professional directories (for doctors, engineers, lawyers, et al.)
Poor's Directory and the *Directory of Directors*
Dun and Bradstreet's Directory of Corporate Executives
Social registers, where available
City and state directories of businesses and professional firms
The Foundation Directory

Other useful publications include *The Wall Street Journal, The New York Times, Business Week* and others. The aggressive and informed development staff will probably subscribe to a clipping service to maintain current information relative to its major donors, present and prospective.

Because donors have special interests, they will tend to condition their gifts in many ways. They will frequently designate a specific purpose for the gift. Or they may restrict the gift to the maintenance of the principal and the use of interest income only. Institutional representatives must be imaginative, forceful and persuasive to seek to minimize the conditions imposed by donors, because unrestricted funds quite obviously have the most utility for the institution. Since, as noted above, appeals for support must frequently be made on the basis of special interests, it is frequently not possible to obtain a completely unconditional donation. Under those circumstances a second desirable alternative is for the institution to seek donations in those areas which relieve the institution of current operating costs (or more precisely, provide income to support such costs). Scholarship support is one of the more obtainable forms of support and generates tuition income. Support for an academic chair provides important relief in the faculty salary area.

Development is one of three major funding sources (Endowment Fund

Management, and Student Recruitment being the other two) in higher education management that require particular focus in today's difficult financial climate. This is especially true of the smaller institutions, many of which are struggling for survival and many of which handle the three areas of activity cited in a less than fully effective way.

The smaller institutions generally cannot afford the investment for the highly skilled management required in these areas and paradoxically they are most in need of such skills. On the other hand, some small institutions have a proportionately large staff investment in these activities, relative to their overall resources. But it is an investment that is frequently not producing an adequate return.

Reporting relationships is a key element in determining the effectiveness of the development operation. Does the development officer report directly to the President? The President is frequently the chief fund raiser for the institution but rarely has the time to exercise meaningful supervision over the development office. Or does he report to someone who can assess his performance and guide him in the application of his specialized skills in the most productive manner?

Participation is another key ingredient to the effectiveness of a development officer and the programs he establishes. This has two facets.

First is the participation of the development officer. Is he afforded sufficient participation in the mainstream of the institution's activities to enable him to acquire the degree of familiarity and understanding that permits him to speak of the institution with conviction and persuasiveness? Although development officers are in a very real sense engaged in "selling" the institution to prospective donors, some development officers have little or no understanding of the product they are selling; i.e., they do not know the qualities that make the institution unique and give it its special identity. Relating back to the discussion on donor restriction, development officers are frequently not given a sufficient understanding of the various programs and the nuances of financing them to deal effectively with funding sources to secure funds in the way they can be used best.

Another facet of participation relates to those who participate in the development activity. Such participation should not be, but frequently is, confined largely to the development officer and the president. The president, as the principal, most prestigious, and often the most articulate spokesman for the institution, will necessarily be involved in fund raising activities, particularly in relation to major sources of funding. But Presidents tend to be overused, particularly when the development officer is lazy or unimaginative or the president has a particular predilection for fund raising.

Trustees should have a key role in the development activity. This does not mean that they should be selected on the basis of their donations (although such a practice is by no means unheard of). But it is not unreasonable to expect them to contribute in accordance with their means as a reflection of their interest in the institution. In the absence of this kind of example, support from donors more removed from the institution is much more difficult to obtain.

It is important to recognize that the trustees constitute the key link to the business community from which a major portion of the institution's contributions will be derived. With their wide and influential circle of contacts, trustees can be highly successful fund raisers for the institution, if stimulated to play this role and provided with sufficient information as to institutional needs.

It is in part for this reason that institutions frequently establish a trustee's subcommittee on development. Such a subcommittee will work closely with the development officer, will receive periodic reports on the various aspects of development activity, including collection of pledges, and will have a role in the formulation of development campaigns.

Generally, the faculty constitutes a major untapped source for participation in fund raising activity. Even in the area of seeking research support, an area most directly of interest to faculty members, many institutions lack a systematic program for stimulating faculty participation. This is even more true of other aspects of fund raising.

Yet, faculty have the motivation or can be motivated, to raise funds, if not for the general use of the institution, then for their specific departments. This is recognized at those institutions that employ the budgeting concept of "every tub on its own bottom" (see discussion on Budgeting in Chapter 8) where each department is encouraged to generate its own funds as a means of initiating new programs or sustaining program initiatives.

Faculty members also have the ability to be highly persuasive fund raisers, since they will be the most articulate spokesmen for the programs in which they are involved and because they are apt to have made lasting impressions on some former students who are now highly successful and may be viewed as sources for direct contributions and contacts to other potential donors. It should be noted in this connection that assistance in fund raising need not be confined to alumni. One institution (in fact a public institution) has been very successful in establishing a national network of "friends," none of them alumni, who are active and effective fund raisers for the institution.

In summary, the development activity is vital to the private institution and of growing importance to the publics. The competition for support among a wide range of eleemosynary institutions has become more keen, placing a high premium on effective fund raising. At least four key ingredients to effective fund raising are information, organization, participation, and mission evaluation.

Chapter Six

SPONSORED ACTIVITY

Sponsored activity, as defined in the federal cost principles for educational institutions contained in the Office of Management and Budget (OMB Circular A-21) encompasses organized research, which is sponsored by federal and non-federal agencies and organizations, as well as projects financed by external sources, which involve performance of work other than organized research and instruction. Illustrative projects or programs would include health service projects, community service programs, and agricultural extension services. Although for many years sponsored activity was of significance only to those approximately 200 major institutions that engaged in extensive organized research, the growth of community service programs has enlarged this group of institutions.

The emergence of the federal government as a major source of funding for university research activity can be traced to the accelerated demands of World War II, with increased impetus provided by the launching of the first Russian satellite, Sputnik, in 1957. The 20 year period commencing in 1946 saw the passage of the Public Service Act of 1946, which encouraged support of research investigations at scientific institutions; the authorization of the Office of Naval Research; the formation of the National Science Foundation and the growth of the extramural programs of the National Institutes of Health, culminating in 1967 in a level of federal R&D funding approximating $16 billion.

To those concerned with the financial and general well being of the educational enterprise, the increased reliance of the federal government on institutions of higher education as a resource for research and assistance in the implementation of national goals must be regarded as a mixed blessing. Unquestionably, federal funding has provided a stimulus to expanded research programs which have enriched the academic environment. Sponsored projects have also provided an important source of institutional support, funding the acquisition of hundreds of millions of dollars of scientific equipment, providing for substantial assistance in construction of new facilities, funding additional expenditures such as faculty travel and secretarial support and, through funding of research assistants, providing an important source of student financial aid.

However, the degree of reliance on federally funded projects as a source of support for faculty salaries (particularly at many medical schools) has contributed to the erosion of faculty collegiality and to the transfer of loyalties from the institution to the funding sources.

When the faculty member perceives future career advancement as related principally to publications and other externally oriented activities, when needed support services come primarily from federal agencies and federal program officers deal directly with faculty, it is small wonder that faculty members cease to identify with their institutions. The ready availability of federal funding has also induced institutions to take on activities which are not necessarily in full consonance with institutional goals and priorities. This tendency can be exacerbated when long-term commitments are made to programs or activities which are temporarily financed by external "seed money," but for which no long-term source of institutional funding has been identified.

Institutions have become increasingly aware that with federal funds comes federal regulation and the desire to use federal funding to implement public policy goals carrying with it a heavy administration burden and substantial cost. Additionally, and most importantly, there is the "accountability" requirement. Promoted in part by the pressures of the General Accounting Office, the House Government Operations Committee and other "watch dog" groups, federal agencies have moved increasingly to impose on institutional recipients of federal funding a degree of precision in accounting for and documenting costs far beyond that which has governed their internal activities. In fairness, it should be noted that there is a growing perception of need for greater accounting and costing precision for internal purposes.

Accountability must be understood within the context of the special stewardship requirements associated with the expenditure of public funds. Over the years numerous "horror cases" have arisen, involving the improper use of federal funds. At one point, there was a rash of cases in which costs were transferred from one project to another, either to avoid a cost overrun on the former, or to avoid having to return unexpended funds on the latter.

Although institutions have generally been guilty of loose practices, rather than of deliberate malfeasance, the general public, stimulated by sensationalism in news reporting, tends rarely to differentiate the two circumstances. The dilemma for those charged with management of the institution is that federal program officials deal primarily with their faculty counterparts, fostering the impression that the locus of the research is insignificant in relation to the question as to who is performing the research. However, grant and contract awards are made officially to the institution and it is the institution that is charged with insuring compliance with federal requirements.

Because faculty members see university administrators as having no meaningful role in securing federal grant and contract support, they perceive them as exclusively involved in enforcing onerous compliance requirements which "get in the way of research." This makes it particularly difficult for administrators to satisfy accountability requirements. The most controversial of the accountability requirements has been the requirement for "faculty effort reporting" or "personnel activity reporting" to support salary charges to federal grants and contracts.

Federal cost principles establish documentation requirements for costs associated with salaries and wages of faculty or professional personnel that are charged to sponsored agreements, either as a direct project charge or as part of one of the indirect supporting activities, the cost of which is partially allocated to sponsored projects. Those charges must be supported or documented either through a system of monitored workloads or a system of personnel activity reports.

The monitored workload system calls for the distribution of salaries and wages, based on budgeted or assigned workloads, revised periodically as required, to reflect any significant changes in workload distribution. Some of the principal categories of significant change would be: a material modification in teaching load, unanticipated addition or removal of administrative assignments, sabbatical leave, or beginning or ending work on a government agreement.

Personnel activity reports are intended to reflect an after-the-fact reporting at the end of each academic period, of the percentage of effort devoted by each employee to the various activities in which that employee was engaged. Under either of these two alternatives there is a requirement to account for 100% of the activities on behalf of the institution, whether direct or indirect.

These requirements have undergone modification on several occasions over the years. The most recent major modification was introduced in March 1979 after almost three years of extensive and heated debate. But, despite the extensive time devoted to developing the most recent cost principle revisions and, in particular, to the provisions regarding salary support, this area remains a source of tension between the institutions and the federal agencies and within the institution between faculty and administrators. The problem is a major one because salary support is by far the largest component of the costs of sponsored activity. It has involved cost disallowances or cost set asides ranging up to $27 million and more by federal auditors and has provoked bitter and emotional disagreements. The controversy stems from reasons that are practical, emotional, and philosophic.

A very practical consideration that rarely surfaces in the arguments concerning faculty effort reporting is that institutions rely on a number of different sources of funding support for their budgets. In the case of some major institutions, and particularly their medical schools, federally sponsored activity has been a significant source of support for faculty salaries. Consequently, a change in the budgeted activity on which federal salary support was based (i.e., a circumstance where the faculty member ultimately devotes less effort to a sponsored project than had been planned) could have a detrimental financial impact on the institution by causing a reduction in an important source of funding.

An aspect of the faculty salary support problem related to, but separate from, the question of documentation is that many institutions, both public and private, have had a policy or a practice of declining to charge salaries; sometimes medical school faculty will be charged while arts and sciences will not be. This difference reflects that there are more substantive differences among different departments within universities resulting from both internal and external factors than many outside the university environment realize.

There are a variety of reasons for the practice of declining to charge faculty salaries to grants and contracts. Faculty members prefer not to have their salaries related to "soft money"; they also feel that if their salaries are not charged to federally sponsored projects, they need not be influenced by federal priorities in the pursuit of their own research interests. This is hardly a valid assumption if they must depend on federal support for other project related expenses. Finally, some institutions adhere to the philosophic belief that it is improper to charge the salaries of tenured faculty to federally sponsored projects.

But whatever the reasons for this practice, it is now being reassessed by most of the institutions that have engaged in it. An appropriate reason for reassessment would have been the recognition that the institution can no longer afford to voluntarily relinquish substantial sums of potential revenue. But the reassessment has been stimulated by another circumstance.

Revisions to the federal cost principles in March 1979 have made explicit that the base of organized research to be used in distributing indirect costs must include all costs associated with organized research including salary costs voluntarily absorbed by the institution. Federal agency officials are interpreting this to mean first, that although the institutions formerly did not consider it necessary to document the amount of effort the tenured faculty devoted to sponsored projects, that is now required. Second, it is asserted that the institution must not only absorb the salary costs but must also absorb the related indirect costs.

These interpretations are being contested. But they tend to illustrate what can occur when, in the formulation of policy, government officials fail to give adequate consideration to the incentives created by their policies. Institutions that were formerly inclined to absorb costs that they could legitimately have charged to the government are penalized by being required to absorb even more costs than they intended. The result is that many of them may elect to change their practice and pass the costs on to the government. Government costs will thus have increased with no substantive improvement in research or in the stewardship of federal funds.

The controversy over documentation requirements, particularly as related to salary support, most frequently centers on the differences between the normal practices of most institutions and what federal officials think they ought to be. There are some genuine difficulties in budgeting in advance for some activities, such as committee assignments, as required by the monitored workload system. More generally, colleges and universities have traditionally been more loose in their contractual relations with their professional employees than many other enterprises. Consequently, the articulation of faculty responsibilities at the outset of the academic year in a very explicit and reasonably detailed manner, would represent a radical departure from the normal practices of most institutions. Ironically, the strongest influence on articulating faculty assignments and responsibilities with greater explicitness seems to come from the activities of faculty unions. (See chapter on Collective Bargaining.)

An important consideration is that, although other professionals, such as accountants and attorneys, are accustomed to the discipline of accounting for their time, faculty members, who for many years have functioned with a very substantial degree of latitude and flexibility, are not accustomed to account for their time and are highly resistant to such an accounting. (This is a generality that applies with varying intensity to different disciplines; e.g., university spokesmen have pointed out that engineering faculty have far less difficulty in accommodating to effort reporting than do arts and sciences faculty.)

They make the philosophic argument that the interrelatedness of their activities makes it impractical and unrealistic to attempt to allocate or apportion their efforts. The classic case cited is that of the senior faculty member at a teaching hospital who, in treating a research patient, while observed by interns, is simultaneously engaged in teaching, research, and patient care.

Institutional administrators, frustrated by government compliance efforts on the one hand and faculty resistance on the other, have at times contended that documentation for faculty salary charges to federal grants and contracts is unnecessary. The ultimate test, they say, is "did the government get what it paid for—i.e., was the research or other activity for which the granting agency provided support effectively accomplished?"

Such a contention begs the question. The predominant form of support for federally sponsored activity, whether the grant or contract instrument is used, is a cost reimbursement arrangement. So long as this continues to be the major approach to support, federal granting agencies, in the fulfillment of the stewardship requirements associated with spending of federal funds, must take reasonable steps to assure themselves that the costs that have been reimbursed were actually incurred and are properly attributable to the project to which they were charged.

As taxpayers we can accept no less. There have undeniably been instances of genuine abuse in which substantial amounts of money were improperly paid. While these amounts constitute only a minor fraction of the total sums awarded to colleges and universities, they can be viewed within the proper perspective of exceptions only when institutions can effectively demonstrate that they have established adequate systems of control.

What appears to be principally needed is a careful and unemotional reassessment of whether present instruments, methods, and procedures for supporting research and other federally sponsored activities at institutions are appropriate. The significant changes that such a reassessment is likely to produce will not come quickly. But there are some hopeful signs. One of the sources of difficulty is that faculty members engaged in major projects will receive support from several funding sources, each desiring to account for its funds in a discrete way, while the faculty member tends to treat all the funds as one pool of fungible money. At this writing the National Science Foundation is experimenting with an approach that seeks to at least partly ameliorate this circumstance.

In the interim, until some solutions are found, both federal officials and university officials need to adopt a broader, more objective perspective than either party has evidenced in this highly emotional controversy. Federal officials need to recognize that in providing support for activities conducted at colleges and universities, they must avoid the imposition of requirements aimed explicitly or implicitly at changing the character of the institution. Institutional officials must in turn make an objective reassessment of the manner in which the institution conducts its affairs in the context of the major changes that have taken place. Both parties should find a common meeting ground in the identification of reasonable procedures and controls which are necessary for effective internal management and, hence, should be capable of satisfying external requirements.

Another important and highly controversial component of federally sponsored activity is the reimbursement of indirect costs. In accounting terms, the concept of indirect costs is a relatively simple one. Those costs which can be directly attributed to a particular project or activity, such as travel, salary, or fringe benefits of an individual who serves the project on a full time basis, are classified as direct. Those costs associated with services which benefit a number of activities, such as the services of the purchasing department, are classified as indirect. The key to whether a cost is classified as direct or indirect is the ease with which that cost can be identified with activities which it benefits and the amount of trouble and expense the institution is willing to incur to make such identification. In theory, all costs could be treated as direct.

Recovery of indirect costs has been a source of tension between faculty and university administrators. One principal reason for this is that as funding sources utilize the fixed price contract or program officials seek to stretch their funds, the impression is conveyed to the faculty that any increase in indirect costs will diminish the funds available to support the direct costs associated with their projects. Additionally, faculty members who believe their support services to be inadequate, such as those who are dissatisfied with the office space allocated to them and how it is maintained, unhappy with their secretarial support, or irritated by the time and difficulty involved in processing purchase requisitions, view the reimbursement by the federal government of the costs associated with those services to be more akin to a profit.

Concerns by faculty members and others who question indirect cost reimbursement have led to invidious comparisons; with those institutions having lower indirect cost rates being held forth as shining examples of efficiency. More often than not a comparatively low rate signifies underrecovery either through neglect or as a matter of deliberate policy, rather than efficiency in operations.

But comparisons of rates among institutions, though frequently made, should be avoided because they are apt to be misleading. There are some major variations in indirect cost calculation procedures, which make for a high degree of non-comparability. These include:

- Differences in whether given activities are charged directly to projects or treated as indirect costs;
- Variations in the base used to distribute research indirect costs to organized research projects;
- Determinations as to whether specific activities are to be assigned to one indirect cost pool or another. Because the various pools are distributed differently, this determination can significantly influence the rate and cost recovery;
- Selection of the appropriate unit of measure or base for allocating indirect cost pools to research;
- Results of audit and negotiation; and
- Variations in the way institutions organize activities.

In order to promote greater comparability, as an additional tool to assist them in evaluating the "reasonableness" of indirect cost rates, federal officials have been striving to impose requirements for greater uniformity in costing practices among institutions. These efforts are not likely to be fully successful. Significant variations in the way institutions organize their activities and in the precision with which they account for the costs of those activities, will continue to justify differences which make indirect cost rates among institutions non-comparable.

Indirect costs are recovered from the federal government by establishing a rate which is then applied to grants and other agreements with federal agencies. The rate is a ratio, expressed as a percentage, between indirect costs and a direct cost base—historically either direct salaries and wages or total direct costs excluding capital expenditures.

The rate is established through negotiation with a single cognizant federal agency that has been designated to act on behalf of all federal agencies in this capacity, generally because it provides more support to a particular institution than any other agency. Institutions are required to submit an indirect cost proposal annually to support the establishment of an indirect cost rate. The proposal and its supporting documentation may be subject to review by an auditor, a negotiator, or both, depending on the procedures employed by the cognizant federal agency.

Those institutions with relatively modest amounts of federal support for research and educational service (the current figure is $3 million or less) may use the so-called simplified method for submitting an indirect cost proposal. This method, which involves a formula approach, is far less burdensome to the institution, but has traditionally produced significantly less cost recovery.

The alternative to the abbreviated procedure is the so-called long form, which *must* be used by institutions with federal support in excess of $3 million, and *may* be used by institutions with less support. This requires the use of sound cost finding techniques involving an analysis of the research, instructional, and other activities conducted by an institution to determine the type and level of administrative and other services supporting them and the most appropriate unit(s) of measure for allocating the costs of these supporting services to the benefiting activities in reasonable proportion to the services rendered to them. The cost of the supporting services is then distributed by the use of work sheets to those activities serviced.

Indirect cost rate calculation and negotiation is a rather sophisticated process requiring skilled personnel who are familiar with the subtleties of federal procedures. It is fair to say that most institutions underrecover the costs associated with support of research and other sponsored activity. This underrecovery takes place at three levels.

The most readily perceived level of underrecovery results from an explicit waiver. This occurs when an institution deliberately accepts an indirect cost rate less than that which has been officially established on a particular grant or agreement. There are cogent and valid reasons for such a waiver in some instances, particularly when the project in question is deemed to be of special value to the institution. But more often than not, such waivers are not adequately controlled and not subject to critical scrutiny.

A second level of underrecovery occurs when an indirect cost rate is negotiated which is appreciably lower than the rate that had been calculated. This is generally attributed to "hard nosed" federal auditors and negotiators. It is indeed inevitable that among the multitude of federal personnel involved in this process, some will be intractable and unreasonable. But, success in negotiating a rate equal to or closely approximating the rate that had been calculated, is largely in the hands of the institution. It depends primarily on the cost finding techniques employed by the institution and the adequacy with which the institution supports or documents its costs.

Institutions have all too frequently negotiated rates that represent less than full recovery of allowable costs, reflecting their sensitivity to faculty concerns about "high" rates. Under such circumstances the institution makes a blanket waiver of revenue without ever fully determining how much income is being given up or why. A more prudent approach would regard the rate establishment process as a vehicle for establishing the institution's full entitlement. Waiver of reimbursement could then be handled on a case-by-case basis in the course of which the income relinquished can be weighed against the benefits to be obtained and the necessity for waiver of indirect costs can be verified.

The most subtle form of underrecovery results from the variations in permissible rate calculation procedures. The failure to utilize legitimate techniques which will have the effect of more accurately and equitably assigning costs appropriately attributable to sponsored activity contributes significantly to underrecovery of costs. However, this form of underrecovery is not likely to be detected by institutional management except by those skilled in the techniques of rate calculation.

Another important aspect of the indirect cost rate process that bears significantly on the extent to which costs are recovered is the manner in which rates are established. Indirect cost rates may be established as either provisional, final, predetermined, or fixed with a carry forward provision.

A provisional rate is a temporary rate, used by awarding agencies as a basis for estimating and funding the amount of indirect costs applicable to a grant or other agreement until actual indirect costs are determined and a final indirect cost rate established. Two major difficulties with this procedure are first, that when the final rate is established, a substantial amount of administrative effort may be entailed in adjusting the rate on each project.

Even more significant is the fact that the final rate may call for a refund on the part of the institution, if it is lower than the provisional rate. On the other hand, if the final actual rate is higher than the provisional rate—and this is more likely to be the case—the institution must seek to collect the difference from each supporting federal agency. Frequently, the funds to reimburse this difference may not be available, particularly since there may be an interval of two years or more between the establishment of the provisional rate and the determination of the final rate.

A second alternative is a predetermined fixed rate negotiated and agreed to for a specific future period. Since this rate is not subject to adjustment, it is appropriate for use only when there is reasonable assurance that the rate agreed to will approximate the institution's actual rate. This requires a degree of economic stability that has not been present in recent years and is not foreseeable in the predictable future. For example, energy costs impact materially on the indirect cost rate. Given the potential for fluctuations in these costs, it would be highly risky for institutional representatives to fix a rate based on an existing level of cost.

Because of the palpable shortcomings in both of the alternatives outlined above, a third alternative was developed and referred to as the fixed rate with carry forward. Under this procedure a rate is computed and fixed, for a specified future period, based on an estimate of that future period's level of operations. When the actual costs of that period are known, the difference between the estimated costs and the actual costs is carried forward as an adjustment to a subsequent period for which a rate is established.

This latter procedure is the *only* procedure that will insure full recovery of costs *based on the rate that has been established*. Nonetheless, because of the interval between the fixing of a rate for a period and the determination of the actual rate experienced, in an inflationary period, the cost difference may create a balloon of such significant impact on the rate that some institutions have waived a portion of the "carry forward" to avoid too large a rate increase.

This is an uncalled for relinquishment of funds which the institution is legitimately entitled to recover. The procedures contemplate, whether or not they are sufficiently explicit on this point, that the rate will be adjusted whenever a material fluctuation can be demonstrated. This will minimize the "balloon." The length of the interval between the close of the year and the establishment of the final rate is due to the workload of federal auditors and negotiators and their consequent inability to keep current. For additional discussion on this point, refer to Chapter 14 on Audit.

A surprising number of institutions continue to utilize the second alternative, namely the fixed predetermined rate. Since federal negotiators will be reluctant to agree to this alternative, unless they are reasonably certain that the actual rate will be equal to *or lower than* the predetermined rate, one may be assured, prima facie, that this procedure results in underrecovery. The majority of institutions utilizing this procedure are public institutions. Hence, this is additional evidence that unenlightened policies on the part of states in sharing indirect cost recoveries with public institutions, results in underrecovery of indirect costs to the detriment of both parties.

Public institutions encounter a special problem associated with indirect cost recoveries since technically the state, which funds all of the indirect costs which are being reimbursed, is entitled to the full recovery of such costs. In practice, states vary in their treatment of this source of revenue and the varying state policies bear a direct relationship to the aggressiveness of public institutions in seeking full recovery of indirect costs. Some states permit the institution to retain all recoveries. Others insist that all such recoveries be remitted to the state or be treated as a budgeted source of revenue to supplement the state appropriation.

In many instances this revenue is shared between the state and the institution, based on the recognition by state officials that such sharing can stimulate research and, hence, the growth of sponsored activity which will result in the financing of many costs which would otherwise be borne by the state and will also result in the growth of indirect cost revenues. The recognition of the benefits that can result from sharing a portion of indirect cost recoveries to be used as seed money to stimulate research has also prompted many private institutions to distribute a portion of recoveries to academic departments in proportion to the indirect costs which they generate.

Federal grant programs have, for many years, been governed by a cost sharing requirement, which is congressionally mandated. The congressional intent has never been clearly established, except that it is evident that the institution must bear *some* share of the costs associated with federally supported projects. Institutions must, consequently, be wary of attempts by federal agencies to impose a degree of cost sharing that is unwarranted. The implications of specific agency policies must also be examined with care. For example, where agency policies specify that costs shared by the institution must also bear their proportionate share of indirect costs, the institution might well look to share in another element of cost, perhaps indirect costs. Many institutions cost share to a much greater degree than is legally required. For example, institutions that, as a matter of policy, do not charge the salaries of tenured faculty to federal grants are cost sharing those salaries. Nonetheless, some institutions in this category also engage in additional cost sharing.

Although, as noted, federal agencies will vary in their implementation of the cost sharing requirement despite continuing efforts to achieve greater consistency in this and other areas of federal grant administration policy, there is a tendency to look to historical patterns of institutional cost sharing—formal and informal—and to seek to establish those patterns as a level for continued cost sharing. But institutions cannot afford, in today's changed financial circumstances, to sustain historical levels of cost sharing and, consequently, should be actively engaged in an assessment of the costs they can and should bear.

The special requirements associated with federally sponsored activities have caused many research oriented institutions to set up special units to administer grants and contracts. At times, these units also act as information sources and assist faculty in identifying opportunities for outside funding. Public institutions have, in many instances, established these units as separate corporate entities, often called Research Foundations. This has been a device for avoiding the application of state regulations (e.g., in regard to purchasing) which may inhibit effective support of research activities. The important considerations to be balanced are the necessity for creating mechanisms which facilitate research activity, while avoiding a loss of institutional control.

As a postscript to the foregoing, reference has been made several times to the fact that in March 1979 OMB Circular A-21, the cost principles governing reimbursement under federal grants and contracts, was significantly revised. This event warrants more than a passing reference.

The specific impetus for the modification was the testimony of the Office of Management and Budget (OMB) officials in an appropriation hearing. At that hearing, in which imposition of a statutory ceiling on indirect cost reimbursement was being considered, OMB officials, in arguing against the imposition of the ceiling, committed to "tighten" the cost principles.

The cost principles revision is of significant importance to sponsored project administration, in part because of its salutary effect in stimulating improved accountability; and in part because of its adverse effect in increasing the burdens and the costs of sponsored project administration.

But possibly of even greater significance is the nature of the process in which the cost principle changes were promulgated and the climate that governed those changes. The changes were developed over a period of almost three years during which there was much heated and rancorous discussion among university and government representatives. This is reflective of a pervasive and highly disturbing change in the federal/university relationship.

For many years, commencing in 1946, as referred to in the introductory portion of this chapter, the federal/university relationship in the pursuit of research and related activities was conceived of by both parties as one of mutuality. A contribution to sustaining our institutions of higher learning as a vital national asset was explicitly recognized as an objective of federal policy. The essential research role of our institutions in helping to expand the frontiers of knowledge was also recognized.

By contrast, this past decade has been marked by a pronounced deterioration in this relationship. The former partners have taken on the appearances of adversaries, with neither exhibiting a willingness to understand the imperatives and constraints that govern the behavior of the other. It will take a high degree of statesmanship on the part of both parties to restore the relationship to its former healthy state.

Chapter Seven

ORGANIZATION AND GOVERNANCE

Developing an organizational structure for an institution involves the art and science of organizational analysis but also a good measure of personality and tradition. Despite organizational principles and the contribution of the newer theorists, it is not uncommon, because of a new president or upon the retirement or departure of a powerful administrator, for the structure to be rearranged to meet the president's operating style and the personalities and capabilities of particular individuals.

There are probably as many definitions of organizing as there are writers in the field. To choose one definition (Harvey Sherman's in *It All Depends*,* except for an insertion of the word "efficiently"), we can define organizing as "the process of grouping activities and responsibilities and establishing relationships, formal and informal, that will enable people to work together most effectively and efficiently in determining and accomplishing the objectives of an enterprise."

PRINCIPLES OF ORGANIZATION

In deciding upon an organizational structure, the president and business officers should know something about organizational theory. Some of the classical principles are:

Objectives: An organization should have a clearly defined objective (or objectives).

Authority: (scalar principle—chain of command) The organization must have a supreme authority and clear lines of authority should run from

---

**It All Depends,* by Harvey Sherman, University of Alabama Press, 1966.

that individual (or group) down through the various levels of hierarchy of the organization.

Responsibility: Authority should be commensurate with responsibility.

Specialization: To the extent possible, the work of a person or unit should be confined to a single function or a group of related functions and these functions should be grouped under one head.

Efficiency: Objectives should be attained at the lowest possible cost (human, monetary, or other resource costs).

Unity of Command: Each individual should be accountable to only one superior.

Coordination: The organization must provide for a method or mechanism for coordinating all efforts toward common goals or objectives.

Span of Control: There is a limit to the number of immediate subordinates where work is interrelated, that one individual can supervise. Many writers have come up with set numbers for this limit, 6-8-10. But an appropriate limit depends on a number of factors such as the nature of the organization, how rapidly decisions must be made, the capabilities, personality, style of the superior and of the subordinates, and like considerations.

Short Chain of Command: There should be as few levels of supervision as possible between the chief executive or supreme authority and the lowest organizational unit.

Delegation: Decisions should be made at the lowest level having the competence to make the decision.

Balance: There must be continued concern that there is a reasonable balance in the size of the various units within the organization, between attempting to standardize policies and procedures and insuring flexibility and ability to react, and between centralization and decentralization of decision-making.

Accountability: Authority may be delegated but responsibility may not and accountability for all actions within a span of responsibility must be established.

Although these principles have value, as Herbert Simon has said, they are like proverbs. Consequently, one can have a good principle that contradicts another. For example, a short chain of command will frequently be contradictory to or inconsistent with a small span of control.

The newer organizational theorists provide approaches that can be broadly classified into the 1) human relations or behavioral science focus, 2) the decision-making focus, 3) the biological focus, 4) the mathematical focus, or 5) the systems focus.

Whatever principles, approaches, or focus is used or combination of principles and approaches, the goal is to structure the organization for planning, decision-making, implementing decisions, coordinating, controlling, and communicating. But often, the structure, hierarchy, policies, and procedures that follow from this kind of systematic approach to organization are considered to be in conflict with collegiality and the committee discussions that characterize faculty decision-making. Thus, any semblance of a rigid or formalistic structure tends to be called into question by the faculty as being non-academic. Administrators who attempt to introduce a great degree of order and efficiency into the decision-making process will be accused of treating the institution as a business rather than as a college. (One clear manifestation of the general lack of success in introducing business-like techniques into institutional decision-making is the length of time that decisions usually require in the college and university environment, except in those rare instances where the president functions as an authoritarian. But a judgment on the effectiveness of the decision-making process should not only consider the time consumed by the process, but also its end product—the quality of the decisions.)

In examining the efficacy of the current organization of an educational institution, the following should be considered:

1. The effects of time and growth;
2. The impact of external influences;
3. The need for organizational balance;
4. Changes in key personnel and the caliber of present staff;
5. Possible new objectives or changes in emphasis in the future;
6. The need for reasonably rapid reactions to changing times and needs;
7. The size of the institution and whether it is public, independent, or part of a multi-campus system. Size considerations include number of students and the mix between full-time and part-time, graduate and undergraduate; the size of the faculty and the mix between part-time and full-time, graduate and undergraduate faculty, number of colleges and schools and number and type of professional schools, size of non-faculty staff, endowment (restricted and unrestricted); number of

buildings and types of buildings and number of areas; type of auxiliary enterprises and their scope, and size of the budget;

8. Signs of potential or possible organizational problems (these may be caused by poor organization planning and design, by reasons other than organizational problems, or by a combination of organizational and substantive reasons). Some of the more frequently encountered signs versus symptoms are:

   a) difficulty in arriving at sound decisions in a timely fashion;

   b) unrest, back-biting, high turnover, absenteeism, poor morale;

   c) poor communications, many rumors;

   d) imbalance in the assignment of responsibilities and work;

   e) difficulty in determining accountability and responsibility;

   f) inadequate development of staff;

   g) lack of concern or interest about the structure—a desire to simply copy someone else's chart, or a belief that it is all a matter of the right people and the right attitude, or conversely, that organization has nothing to do with people problems;

   h) a sense of drift and lack of accomplishment—ineffectual performance

It should also be noted that colleges and universities face the traditional problem of relating line activities effectively to staff activities. In business there is considerable emphasis on achieving an effective blending of line and staff functions to further the goals of the enterprise with the expectation that the results can be measured by the "bottom line."

In education, in part because of the natural resistance to central authority—already alluded to—and also because academics tend to view those associated with administration as self-perpetuating impediments, the traditional conflict between line (those who contribute *directly* to the achievement of the organization's mission) and staff (those who contribute *indirectly* to the achievement of the organization's mission) rages with more vehemence than in industry. The tensions and antagonisms are between faculty and administration and between academic administration and nonacademic or business affairs administration, business affairs, and student affairs. As noted elsewhere, if one seeks reasons why those associated with business administration are not more effective in their roles, a frequent cause is that they lack authority and support from authority and are often made to feel that their functions are ancillary, insignificant, or even unnecessary. The hope continues to be that the staff, those not directly involved with the central objectives of the educational enterprise—teaching, learning, research, public and community service—will see themselves and be seen as supportive and facilitating achievement of the central missions of the institutions.

Beyond the identification of potential problem areas in the organization, there is need to recognize the impact of personality and style. Depending upon the power and personality of the Chief Executive, his length of service, his relationship with the Board, his manner of selection, and the history and present circumstances of the institution, the structure of the organization may be completely, moderately, or minimally controlled by him. Thus some Presidents may like a very rigid hierarchy with few individuals reporting to them, others may like a much looser and informal organization.

Within the context of this overview, it should be possible to focus in more detail on the organization chart for an educational enterprise. But, it should be further noted that often an organization chart is out of date by the time it is issued or very soon thereafter. It tends to show things the way they were, or the way they are supposed to be, rather than the way they are. It cannot disclose informal relationships and the true power relationships, and in an attempt to clarify, explain, and be complete, various enhancements are sometimes introduced that serve to confuse rather than elucidate. It is, in any event, true of any organization, particularly in the educational environment, that power structure and decision-making mechanisms cannot be fully discerned from an organizational chart.

The simplest way to begin to focus on the matter of organizing might be to list all distinct activities and functions that are currently performed or can be expected to be performed in the foreseeable future. Once these are listed, the task is to group them in some logical way that will facilitate planning, decision and policy-making, carrying out of activities, communication, and coordination.

Many institutions have found that the best starting point is three broad groupings—academic affairs, student affairs, and business affairs. But even so broad and basic a structural arrangement is subject to variation. To restate what has been noted above, in somewhat different terms, differences in leadership style are nowhere more graphically demonstrated than through the interpersonal relationships used to effectuate the various aspects of the institution's mission. Consequently, if the formal organization means anything to the institution's leadership and if it bears any relationship to the realities of the way the institution actually functions, it will inevitably and indelibly bear the imprimatur of the President and his principal subordinates.

The following simple chart depicts some typical functions, that are grouped under each of the three major organizational divisions, although several of the functions can readily be transferred to other groupings:

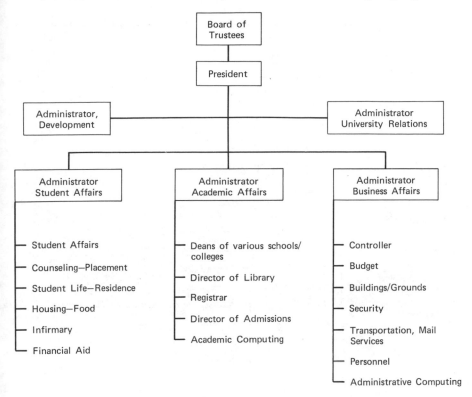

Depending upon the size and complexity of the institution and the factors previously cited, the titles used may include Chancellor, Vice Chancellor, Dean, Vice President, Senior Vice President, Provost, Executive Vice President, or Director. There may also be a need for a number of assistants (administrative, executive, and special) for a variety of functions ranging from the traditional "assistant to," to assistants for affirmative action, community affairs, governmental liaison, minority affairs, and so forth.

In a large university one might find the following chart:

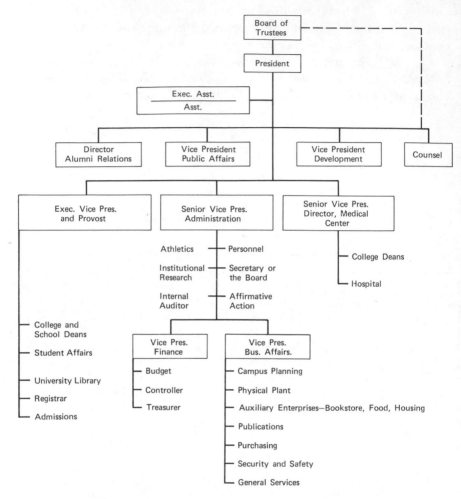

Two examples of organization charts have been presented, but there are dozens of combinations, permutations, different functions, broader or narrower groupings, more or fewer levels and senior officers, etc., that could be established from these two charts. Functions can be and have been readily transferable.

Some of the frequent organizational questions or concerns that an institution will face are:

1. Someone has to act in the President's absence and generally the Provost or Academic Vice President or the Chief Academic Officer, by

whatever title is second in command and performs this role subject to some very explicit limits. But, when the President is not away, should the other senior officials (Vice President or Senior Vice President) report through the Chief Academic Officer to the President or directly to the President? At some institutions the President is more of a public figure, spending much of his time away from the institution engaged in fund raising and other activities. Under those circumstances it has sometimes been expedient to establish the position of deputy president, generally designated Executive Vice President, with broad authority for internal management. Under this kind of arrangement all other Vice Presidents report to the President *through* this position.

2. What should be the organizational role of the Board of Trustees in interacting with officials other than the President, and in fact, how should the Board be organized? Should any functions, e.g., counsel, internal audit, report directly to the Board?

3. Should there be a combined position, Vice President for Finance and Administration (Business Affairs), or separate Vice Presidents? In the financial and business areas, should budgeting (Budget Director) be separated from accounting (Controller), with different officials in charge of each function, and should these two individuals report to the same superior or different individuals? How should long-range planning be related to budgeting? Recognizing that there is a vital necessity for a close working relationship between Business Affairs and Financial Affairs, should the two areas be combined or be under the direction of a single individual (Executive Vice President, Senior Vice President for Administration, Vice President for Financial and Business Affairs), or should there be a Vice President for each area reporting to an Executive Vice President or President?

4. Should the Professional School Deans, or Chief Official of a Medical Center have any special status or reporting relationship, or are they to be treated, organizationally as any other Dean?

5. Is there a need for a separate Dean of Student Affairs reporting directly to the President, or should the position (if there is one) report to the Dean of the College or the Chief Academic Officer?

6. What title should the development officer have and should he report to an Executive Vice President or Provost, the senior administrative officer, the President, the Board or some combination thereof?

7. The above question can also be posed in regard to the chief public

relations officer. (This is generally a lobbying position which may also be termed governmental relations officer and will almost always be found in a public institution.)

8. To whom should the counsel report (whether a full-time university employee or someone on retainer to the university): the President, the Chief Administrative Officer, the Board, the Chairman of the Board, or some combination thereof (assuming that the individual handles legal matters both for the Board of Trustees in the performance of its functions and for the Administration)?

9. Should the Internal or Operations Auditor report to the Vice President for Finance, the Senior Vice President for Administration, the President or the Board?

10. Should the individuals concerned with affirmative action and compliance with various governmental programs be assistants to high ranking officials (the President or Senior Vice Presidents) or Directors of small units, reporting to a senior administrative official? The final decision as to organizational placement and title may be due less to good organizational planning than to the political need to satisfy the agency imposing the requirement and/or the community at large. For example, the position of affirmative action officer may be placed in a direct reporting relationship to the President as a means of reflecting its importance when the President may have neither the time nor the inclination to exercise any effective supervision over the function.

11. Should housing, bookstore, food services, student center and auxiliary enterprises report to the chief business officer, the chief administrative officer, the chief student affairs officer, the Dean of the College? And if some of these services are contracted out, should there be a liaison person to the contractors and to whom should the liaison person report?

12. To whom should the Financial Aid Director report—the chief fiscal officer, the chief student affairs officer, the chief academic officer, or the admissions director?

13. To whom should the Admissions Director report—the chief student affairs officer, the chief academic officer, or the President?

14. Is it best to centralize the admissions, registration, counseling, placement, and fund raising functions or to have each major school or college have one or more of these functions directly under the Deans of the particular school or college?

15. Should there be small computer centers for each major school or college or should the computer resources be centralized? Should academic computing services and administrative computing services be centralized and if so to whom should the director of the computer center report—the Chief Administrative Officer, the Chief Academic Officer, or the Chief Fiscal Officer?

16. Should there be a combined Personnel Office for academic and non-academic personnel and to whom should it report—the Chief Administrative Officer or the Chief Academic Officer, or should there be separate offices? Should the person concerned with affirmative action, contract compliance, and the handicapped report to the Personnel Officer, the Chief Administrative Officer, the Chief Academic Officer, or to the President?

17. Should the Alumni Relations Director report to the President, the Chief Development Officer, or the Chief Administrative Officer?

18. Although more a governance and general management issue than a strictly organizational issue, how should the budgetary decisions be made and what is the role of the chief fiscal officer vis-á-vis the chief academic officer vis-á-vis individual Deans—vis-á-vis the President?

If one were to pose the foregoing series of questions to a representative sampling of trustees and institutional administrators, it is likely that there would be a wide range of responses. It is also likely that having asked each of these individuals what he considers the optimal organization arrangement, in each instance if one were to then inquire as to the degree of correspondence with that optimum at his own institution, one would again find many departures. This is in part because there will rarely be a full consensus within an institution in regard to the appropriate organizational relationships. It is also in part because, although a new leader will use organizational change as a symbolic means of asserting his presence, he also will be wary of attempting too radical an organizational change in what is recognized to be a change resistant environment. This is one of the reasons that he will resort to an informal organization.

The ultimate test of any organization is if it works. But there are at least two cardinal principles of organization that should be treated as virtually immutable: functional entities should ultimately report to those who are willing and able to exercise effective supervision over them; and where coordination between or among two or more functions is essential, it should be formally built into the operational structure so that it is virtually impossible for one of the functional units to act unilaterally.

It should be noted that in planning and implementing any organizational change, careful attention must be devoted to a full discussion with individuals affected by the changes and those who deal with the functions to be changed. It may well be that what appears logical in the planner's mind, just won't work in practice or that the negative impact on morale with consequent organizational disruption, resignations, leaving, etc. will vitiate the apparent value gained by an organizational structure that appears to be more rational or efficient.

Those planning the change must recognize that the reasons for the change, the advantages and the disadvantages, the other alternatives reviewed, all should be discussed with those involved. Employees are concerned about compensation as an important issue in job satisfaction but at certain levels, are even more concerned about status, titles, number of functions they supervise, number and levels of subordinates, to whom they report and how they compare with their peers, their place on the organization chart, etc. The sophisticated organizational analyst knows the dangers of "simply" moving a box around, up, or down on the chart, or putting in dotted lines, or reducing the number of functions reporting to an individual.

This discussion has attempted to indicate the complexities involved in organizing and the fact that organization structures do and should change in the face of different times and challenges. However, it should be recognized that the very considerable effort called for in planning and implementing organizational changes is very necessary. Highly talented individuals can probably perform in a satisfactory manner in poorly organized enterprises, and marginally talented people can probably perform in a satisfactory manner in very well organized institutions. But if the goal is, as it should be, to maximize and optimize effectiveness and efficiency, we need to organize educational institutions so that the highly talented can perform to their limits and the satisfactory performers can do a better than satisfactory job.

GOVERNANCE

The governance of an institution involves a complex set of relationships depending upon the nature of the institution, its size, history and traditions, present circumstances, and personalities involved.

Both public and independent institutions relate to: federal, state, and local government authorities; Boards of Trustees; faculty, student, and administrative associations and governing bodies; various accrediting bodies; alumni associations; and a host of documents that set forth aspects of governance including constitutions, charters, by-laws, plans, legislation, administrative regulation, procedures, etc.

The public institution has more involvement than the independent institution with state agencies such as the governor's office, education department, budget office, the legislature and its committees, state auditor and/or comptroller. However, it is also true that independent universities have significant contact with State Education Departments because of general regulations, registration of programs, etc. As various state funding programs for independent institutions are discussed, developed, implemented and enlarged, there is increasing contact with the same agencies dealt with by the public institutions. Community colleges have, in addition, contact with county legislatures and executive offices. Those institutions that are part of a multi-campus system also have governance and reporting relationships, and controls, imposed by a President/Chancellor, System Board, and various central administration offices.

While the focus of this chapter on governance is at the individual institution, the preceding discussion seeks to indicate that some major decisions as to policies, funding, controls, practices (and in collective bargaining situations—salaries, workload, etc.) may not be entirely within the scope of power of the particular institution. In the worst cases, from the individual institution's viewpoint, the individual institution's president may have little to say about some matters that will vitally affect the institution. At the very least, the forces external to the campus, be they governmental executive or legislative or central system administrators, make various demands on the institution and impact upon decision-making in regard to the allocation of resources. In addition they make various demands in regard to information, reporting, control, audits, and inspections. The institution must spend considerable time and energy in regard to the external forces or constituencies by waging an offensive campaign to secure maximum resources and autonomy and a defensive campaign when confronted by the normal tendency by central administrators and others to exercise oversight or control that limit local operations.

It should be noted in regard to the various governmental and central administration bodies and officials, that they are properly concerned about priorities for funding, a reasonable amount of accountability and ways of insuring adequate standards, systems of control, and adherence to policies.

Turning to the individual institution, the issue of governance can be approached by looking at the role of the Board of Trustees, the President, the Chief Academic Officer, the Chief Business Officer, the Chief Student Affairs Officer, the Office of the President, the Deans, and various faculty governing and consultative bodies, and student government bodies.

The Board of Trustees, generally, is the legally recognized governing body of the institution and as such is normally responsible for the broad objectives and policies of the institution. In addition to approving, and at times, initiating and developing major objectives, programs, policies, capital expenditures, building plans, fund drives, and the institution's budget, the Board is directly involved in hiring the President, reviewing his performance, and if necessary, firing the President. In addition, depending upon the particular institution, the Board may be the ultimate authority in regard to granting tenure and promotions, deciding particular grievances, and a variety of other matters.

The relationship between the Board and the President is a critical one. It is vital to both that there be full and frank discussions, good channels of communication, and that necessary data and information be readily available to the Board presented in a manner which is of use to the members. The President should seek to achieve a high degree of support from the Board and their confidence in his leadership. He can accomplish this through good communications, ready accessibility, sound analysis, presentations, and a demonstrated grasp and command of the educational and administrative issues and details involved in his function as Chief Executive Officer.

Board members are customarily individuals drawn from the business, legal, and other professions, public officials, community leaders, or alumni. A problem in the selection of members is how to insure a representative Board, yet one that has influence and impact on fund raising, governmental and community contacts, and educational and management sensitivity and acumen. Board members normally do not have detailed knowledge of educational problems and thus are more likely to be knowledgeable about business related problems such as budget, labor relations, capital expenditures, etc., rather than on academic matters such as tenure, degree programs, etc.

The President and his administrators consequently have an obligation to carefully explain to Board members the academic and educational issues and to assist them in becoming knowledgeable about academic matters. As the Board achieves a working knowledge of educational administration, augmenting their knowledge of general management, the Board has the means of truly helping the President to be more effective by providing him with a sounding board and another source of sound and informed judgment.

The President should also serve as a channel of communication between the various constituencies of the University: faculty; administrators; staff; students; alumni; the general community; and the Board. The President should share with the Board the various perspectives, needs, and concerns of these diverse groups and in turn explain and interpret Board actions to those groups. (The President is in trouble as an administrator and cannot effectively fulfill his responsibilities as Chief Executive Officer when there is frequent direct communication between the Board members and groups of the faculty, students, or other constituents.) However, he is also expected to serve as the implementor of Board policy, and the faculty may believe that a President has not adequately represented their concerns about such matters as tenure and compensation to the Board when in fact the President may have served to moderate Board action.

Depending on the size of the Board, it may be best to organize into several committees with committee meetings held monthly or as frequently as is necessary. The committees can serve for detailed analysis, review, and recommendations in regard to the areas of their responsibility. The Board organization could include such committees as: Academic Affairs, Finance, Investments, Building and Grounds, Development, Honors and Awards, Alumni Relations, Student Affairs, and Employee Relations/Collective Bargaining, and such ad hoc committees as may be appropriate. Establishment of an Executive Committee of the Board is generally advisable. It should be empowered to act for the Board except in matters of appointment and removal of a President.

There continue to be strongly differing views on whether it is preferable for the Board to make extensive use of committees. Some trustees are concerned that the committee approach is conducive to the full Board "rubber stamping" committee actions. This can and does occur but need not be a necessary consequence of a committee approach. In most instances time constraints and the variety of complex technical issues involved in university administration virtually demand a committee arrangement if the Board is to have a meaningful influence on the affairs of the institution. The committees, if they are sensitive to the prerogatives of the Board, can effectively serve to highlight and distill key issues and facilitate the Board's handling of them.

Boards will generally be asked to include student or faculty representatives as voting members and this has raised particular problems in regard to tuition increases, collective bargaining increases, and academic matters. A number of Boards have chosen to permit student and faculty representatives to attend meetings and voice their concerns, but not as voting members and not as participants in executive sessions.

The President

The President of each institution, depending upon his own strengths, weaknesses, and interests, the interests and concerns of the Board, and the nature and needs of the institution and its various constituencies (the needs and concerns of the institution, the Board and the President will change over time), may place primary emphasis in terms of the use of his time and talent on one or more of the following:

Academic matters: quality of education; curriculum improvement and development; faculty development, selection, promotion, tenure; program evaluation; new program development; and general academic planning.

Financial matters: budget planning and control; major academic and non-academic expenditures; investment decisions; and financial planning.

Fund raising: fund raising for the operating budget, for endowment, for new buildings or new programs.

External relations: relations with various levels and units of government; community and public relations; alumni relations; and professional associations.

Student affairs: recruitment and retention of students including marketing techniques and financial aid; and accessibility to students and parents and to high school principals and counselors.

General administration: ability to choose and retain outstanding subordinates, evaluate performance, establish goals, motivate staff, establish a sound managerial climate; and conduct good employee relations.

The President's priorities will determine what gets his detailed attention and also what his operating style might be. As noted earlier, if he is going to be off-campus a great deal of the time for fund raising, alumni relations, or other external relations functions, he may delegate a great deal to a Provost or Executive Vice President so that he is the planner, fund raiser, external relations individual, and his surrogate in charge of day to day operations. (In some organizations there may be the position of Chancellor who in effect is the outside person and the President the inside person and chief executive officer).

The President may choose to have a very tight organization structure with everything funneled through one, two, or three people. Or he may have a larger group of high level officials serving as a cabinet. The President may also find it helpful to have various types of advisory committees such as a combined Faculty-Student Council, or Faculty-Administrator-Student Council serve to recommend and review in various areas of institutional life. Although he may wish to spend his energy primarily on matters of academic quality and program—which is natural since most Presidents have followed a career path through the various professional academic ranks—financial concerns, fund raising, and external relations may at various times claim most of his attention.

Of primacy in considering the role and functioning of the President, is the question of leadership and the type of leadership style provided. That leadership expresses itself both in management skill and in inspirational and charismatic qualities that influence trustees, constituents, and subordinates. Particularly as institutions face greater stress due to a declining market, and thus face increasing competition and financial concerns, the leadership of the President will become an even more vital factor in determining the success of an institution.

The Chief Academic Officer

In general, the Chief Academic Officer acts as President in the absence of the President and serves as the individual directly concerned with the totality of the academic life of the institution. This will frequently include concern for the activities of all schools and colleges, the library, research activities, academic support services which depending upon the institution could include admissions, registrar, computer center and financial aid, and could even include student life. The most difficult aspects of this individual's job frequently include his relationship with strong deans of colleges or schools, the professional schools, and his role with the faculty, particularly faculty governing bodies. The Dean of Academic Affairs, Provost, Vice President (Senior Vice President or Executive Vice President) for Academic Affairs is often asked to "represent" the faculty and faculty concerns to the President, the "business" side of the house, to the Trustees, etc. In turn, he is asked to be an academic manager and not just an academic representative by the other constituencies, to be able to set priorities, allocate scarce resources and achieve understanding and consensus.

The Chief Business Officer

The Chief Business Officer will normally have under him various financial operations (Budget, Controller) and business operations (Personnel, Buildings and Grounds, Security, Purchasing, etc.) although in many large institutions there may be a Vice President for Financial Affairs and a Vice President for Administration or Business Affairs. Some institutions even have the budget formulation function combined with planning under the jurisdiction of a Vice President separate from the Vice President who has jurisdiction over accounting (budget implementation).

There are natural tensions between the academic and business organizations of an institution. This is due not only to the difference in perspectives, but also largely due to the difference in roles and constituency. Academic administration is concerned with program improvement and with creating an environment that is stimulating to students and faculty. Deans and other academic administrators will frequently find themselves in the posture of making demands for increased funding. They will also be vigorous and vociferous in denouncing controls and restrictions that "get in the way" of effective program performance.

Business administrators are facilitators. Their role is to assist in procuring, husbanding, and allocating resources to academic programs and to assist in their effective fulfillment through the provision of necessary support services. But theirs is the thankless job of acting as a catalyst for painful trade-off decisions among conflicting priorities. A part of their constituency are the external groups, such as state and federal agencies that seek to exert controls and insure accountability.

Business officials are too frequently viewed by faculty and academic administrators as overly absorbed in form, with too little appreciation of the mission and objectives of the institution. At the same time, external groups frequently see business administrators as functioning on the periphery of the institution too removed from any real authority to insure the necessary accountability.

This gap between "academics" and "business types" can be exacerbated by the fact that, as noted earlier, the president's background, interest, and sympathies are normally academically rather than administratively oriented. Hence, the business administrators will frequently perceive, *and be correct in their perception,* that they are outside the power structure. It is, consequently, a major responsibility of the president to avoid this isolation, to bring business administrators into the mainstream of the institution, and to provide them with both an audience and support so that they can serve him and the institution effectively.

The goal is to integrate the skills, outlook, knowledge of the financial/business side of the educational enterprise with the academic side so that revenues are allocated and services offered, in the most effective and efficient manner.

Chief Student Affairs Officer

The Chief Student Affairs Officer may include under his supervision some or all of the following:

Student Housing and Food Service;
Counseling;
Placement;
Student Center;
Student Organizations;
Financial Aid; and
Health Services.

Many of the concerns about this role are similar to those related to the role of the business officer. It is fair to say that for a long time this function was not held in high esteem. The growth in the importance of student financial aid, the rise in student consumerism and the increased competition for students have made the job of the individual, principally concerned with the totality of the student's academic experience, a far more important one. Institutions need to examine whether the staffing of this position is in consonance with this increased importance.

Office of the President

The Office of the President, headed by a Director, Assistant to, Executive Assistant to, or Administrative Assistant plays an important role in coordination, communication, scheduling, optimal use of the Chief Executive's time, and in follow through actions. Of importance in the success of such an activity, in serving as personal staff and general staff to the President, is the tact and diplomacy in dealing with individuals who by title, responsibility, and salary outrank them in the hierarchy. Thus, they must learn to deal sensitively with their role as eyes, ears, and occasionally as spokesmen for the Chief Executive.

Deans

The role of the Dean is a critical one in the academic enterprise. The Deans serve as both academic and administrative leaders of their respective schools and colleges and as spokesmen to and from the central administration for the interests of their units. Because the Dean is equivalent to a mini-President, responsible for a major component of the institution's academic offerings, many of the issues central to the organization and governance of the institution, and many of the rivalries among units within the institution come to focus and are resolved in the relationship between the Deans and the Central Administration.

The strong Dean (Medical School and Law School Deans generally fall into this category) is a major asset to the institution, but at the same time a source of administrative tensions. Such Deans believe that their enterprise is, or should be, self-contained. They are sometimes loathe to provide details regarding their operations to central administration. They normally want, and frequently have, their own support services. To the extent that such support services are provided centrally, the Deans will tend to be highly critical and, not infrequently, seek the flexibility to procure such services elsewhere. They contend that if their budgets are to be charged with the cost of services, they ought to have the ability to procure such services from whatever source can provide them in the most cost effective manner. This is a highly cogent argument, but one which ignores the issue of economics of scale and the various pressures, union, governmental, and other, which may result in an inability on the part of the institution to provide support services on a fully competitive basis. But this source of tension is a healthy one since institutions generally have focused insufficient attention on the cost efficiency of support services.

The adoption of the concept of "every tub on its own bottom," discussed more fully in the section on budget, originated, at least in part, in response to pressures from Deans of the more profitable schools, who urged that each unit be treated as self-sustaining and allowed to retain its "profits" for program enhancements and new program initiatives. Clearly, such an approach is less appealing to the liberal arts school and others that are likely to require a heavy subsidy from the institution if treated as self-contained cost centers.

It is in this critical area that the President, when confronted with strong academic leaders with their own powerful constituencies, urgently requires the active and knowledgeable support of the trustees in balancing the interests of consistency in such areas as job classification and compensation with other important interests. These would include the need to sustain programs which, although not paying their way, are endemic to the mission of the institution.

Faculty Committees

Faculty committees are an intrinsic element of the college and university governance structure. The concept of collegiality and peer review finds its most characteristic expression in the operation of these faculty committees, particularly in respect to such matters as tenure and promotion reviews. As in most other aspects of college and university administration, it is difficult to generalize about the role of faculty committees. At some institutions, faculty actions on tenure and promotion are virtually binding with institutional officers (Provost, Vice President for Academic Affairs, or President) exercising a role that is largely nominal. In other instances, the faculty role is a less conclusive one.

A model, that with qualifications can be labelled classic, involves an initial recommendation by a Faculty Committee on Personnel. If the recommendation is endorsed by an appropriate institutional officer, it will be approved. If the institutional official rejects the recommendation, the faculty committee or the faculty member will have the opportunity for appeal to the President or to the Board. Conversely, if the faculty committee acts negatively on the promotion or tenure proposal, the faculty member may appeal that decision to the President or to the Board. (Often appealing to the personnel committee and then the grievance committee as first steps in the process.)

In other environments, such procedures would be regarded as unduly cumbersome, time consuming, and a dilution of authority. But these procedures are at the heart of university governance. However, although those associated with colleges and universities would regard the process as an essential means of guaranteeing academic freedom, federal authorities, in their implementation of affirmative action requirements, have asserted that the process is not, in itself, a sufficient guarantee that qualifications will be fairly and equitably reviewed in connection with promotion and tenure actions. They tend to look for an explicit detailing of review criteria and an articulation of the reasons for failure to act affirmatively on particular candidates.

This demand for documentation is viewed by many academics as inconsistent with the nature and style of the collegiality system and the resulting conflict poses a serious issue for trustees and others responsible for university administration.

Students

As noted in the discussion on student consumerism, the question of student participation in decision-making is also an important governance issue. As also noted elsewhere, the involvement which students seek in governance is not normally predicated on a deep seated conviction that they should be part of the structure so much as it is a reflection of concerns about aspects of institutional life that impinge directly upon them; such as tuition increases, dormitory conditions, food service, parking, registrar and bursar procedures, counseling, job placement, security and safety, accessibility of faculty and staff, and general campus environment. It may be accurate to say that students are not generally equipped to make academic decisions or other key decisions related to governance, and equally accurate to observe that the student interest is a transient one, and that only a minority of activist students seek involvement in governance.

But these assertions are relics of a vanishing attitude and are advanced with increasingly less frequency. The more predominant attitude is that students should be given a voice in the governance process. As with the faculty, it is generally felt that this should be a non-voting participation. But the fact of participation has symbolic significance and also constitutes a means by which they can express their concerns directly to those engaged in policy making and can engage in a dialogue in regard to these concerns. As with the faculty, the desire for active participation in the governance process is less strong when students perceive that that process is sensitive and responsive to their needs and concerns.

Summary

In summary, while it is possible to have effective governance within the framework of a variety of organizational arrangements, the form of organization selected has considerable relevance to the effective management of the institution. The continued vitality of the institution, its ability to marshall its resources for optimum performance, and its adaptability to change are all also a reflection of the dynamics of the governance process, with particular reference to how the President relates to trustees and staff and how the Deans fit into the structure, and the nature of the participation afforded to faculty and students. At a time when the fabric of higher education was considered to be much stronger and less threatened by both internal and external forces, there was a greater inclination to accept existing organizational arrangements and governance relationships as given. However, when, in today's environment, colleges and universities are confronted with the necessity for painful reassessments in a variety of aspects, a re-examination of organizational and governance issues should be a part of that process.

Chapter Eight

MANAGING HUMAN RESOURCES

Managing scarce resources is a major aspect of educational administration currently, and promises to continue in importance in the foreseeable future. Generally discussions on higher education management center on financial resources, budgets, capital funds, endowments, cash flow, energy conservation, space utilization, or the use of executive time.

But more attention has to be given to the people side of university administration—how we manage the people who work for the institution —namely faculty, administrators, and staff. Too often the President's and Trustees' concerns over finances, curriculum, academic and student matters, leave too little time and attention to be directed to the needs and concerns of the individuals at all levels, from maintenance staff to Vice President, who work for the institution. Increasingly, universities and colleges will be concerned about productivity, motivation, results, creativity, entrepreneurship, attracting students, and financial support, all of which are related to the quality, performance, and dedication of those who serve the institution. We deal with faculty and faculty concerns in several sections of this book because of their overwhelming importance in carrying out the primary missions of the educational institution, but it has become increasingly important to be concerned about all staff at the institution as well as sound personnel practices applied both to faculty and the entire staff.

The concern, then, in this section is to deal with approaches toward insuring and improving the quality, performance, and dedication of those who serve the institution. Areas we will cover include: Recruitment and Selection; Position Responsibilities and Compensation; Performance Evaluation; Motivation; Civil Service Systems; and Other Aspects of Human Resource Management. We offer a general overview and touch lightly on some matters in these broad areas and provide a more detailed level of discussion in regard to some aspects that have not, in our view, received sufficient attention from higher management.

RECRUITMENT AND SELECTION

For middle and junior management and various support staff levels, the usual types of recruitment and selection procedures prevail—ads, word-of-mouth, resumes, interviews, and testing where appropriate. But at upper levels, the Search Committee or Advisory Committee is the traditional means of screening candidates. Then, usually three to five names of potential candidates are selected for presentation to the decision-maker(s)—President or Trustees—for final selection. From a potential candidate's perspective, a newspaper or professional journal ad may not be very revealing and may in fact be deceptive when a selection decision, usually in favor of an in house candidate, has in fact already been made. From the Search Committee's perspective, the goal is to identify a group of outstanding candidates through ads, nominations, and word-of-mouth so that they can present a number of candidates who are clearly qualified, with the hope that one among them will have the right chemistry with the decision-maker. Effective support to the Search Committee can be provided by the services of an executive recruitment service, or by various educational placement agencies, such as HEARS (Higher Education Referral Service).

A number of basic guidelines are generally observed in the search process. The chairman should be someone who is respected widely and has the interest, time, and skill to lead the process, meet deadlines, etc. A broad representation of individuals should serve, but too large a committee may be counterproductive. Frequently, there are one or two high level representatives who would work most closely with the candidate, such as one or two vice presidents if recruiting for a vice president, one or two faculty representatives, one or two students and one or two administrators.

Intelligent selection, particularly when a committee is involved heavily in the screening process, demands the establishment of clearly articulated qualification criteria, preferably weighted in accordance with importance. Criteria can be categorized as either essential or desirable. The applicant must have certain types of experience or attributes and, if possible, as many of the desirable experiences and attributes as possible. But, if an applicant lacks one or more of the essential characteristics, this would generally be grounds for elimination. The image of the institution is enhanced when basic courtesies to candidates are observed. It is amazing how frequently they are not! Receipt of resumes should be promptly acknowledged and applicants should be informed as to progress on a timely basis.

When a number of candidates are selected for interviews, the interview schedule should be carefully worked out so that the applicant's and the committee's time is maximized. Committees sometimes divide into small groups for initial screening, so that it is possible that not all the members will see all the candidates initially. A sufficient amount of time should be set aside with the person to whom the individual will report, as well as for a concluding meeting with the full committee. The committee, of course, has the objective of determining how the candidate will fit in and of determining how the candidate will react to various situations. A related and equally important goal is to inform the applicant about the institution and its dynamics and about issues and problems, and to make the institution and the position attractive to the candidate.

Industry has recognized that in job moves, whether or not relocation is involved, the spouse is very much affected and should be brought into the process and given an understanding of the new situation.

There are differing philosophies on whether a selection committee should present the ultimate decision-maker(s) with one preferred candidate or with several alternative candidates. Because interpersonal relationships are particularly sensitive in the academic environment, the latter course is generally preferred. But the committee should provide analytic comments on each candidate to give the selector the full benefit of the committee's evaluation.

An approach that has been utilized in selecting candidates at the executive level (President, Vice President and Dean) is to ask the candidate to make a presentation of some depth and scope regarding one or more key issues of concern to the institution. This approach attempts to avoid a circumstance in which the candidate responds briefly to a series of unrelated questions and conveys no coherent impression as to his philosophy, attitudes, and analytic abilities.

Once a position is filled, it is axiomatic that the art of management calls for drawing upon the strengths of the individual and providing maximum incentive and growth potential.

Too often a subordinate is unclear as to his responsibilities, authority, relationships to others, and as to the overall objectives, toward which his efforts should be directed. Further, he may be unclear as to the criteria and process which will be used in measuring and evaluating his performance and as to the reward structure. Whether or not the institution uses a formal management by objectives system, it is desirable to specify goals each year for the individual and the unit he may be supervising. Because the education environment does not involve "bottom line" measurements, it is important that there be other clear methods for setting goals and measuring performance.

Classification System

A classification system is normally the formal means by which relationships among positions are established and appropriate compensation levels created. Because such systems are customary with civil service systems, formal classification systems are more frequently encountered in public institutions than with private. Administrators at private institutions have sometimes expressed concern about the so-called rigidities of a formal classification system. But, particularly with the emphasis on equal employment opportunity, it is necessary to have a structure which compensates on a comparable basis for comparable work and uses objective, rather than subjective, bases for evaluation to the fullest possible extent.

Merit System

Similar considerations obtain in relation to merit systems which, though often discussed in management courses, are not frequently implemented in practice. Many administrators have flirted with the idea of introducing a merit system only to conclude that the tensions likely to be created would negate the value of the system. In lieu of a system, special increases may be selectively awarded on an ad hoc basis in instances where performance is considered to be superior.

It is to be noted that salary structures and merit systems, to the extent that they exist, need to be reviewed not only in relation to their internal consistency, but in relation to the structure of peer institutions and, for non-academic positions, compensation for comparable positions in industry in the area or region may also be relevant. The advent of faculty collective bargaining has created an impetus for faculty salary increases, but also has impeded attempts at extending the concept of differential salary scales in different schools or disciplines. Salary scale differences for medicine or law, as compared with the College of Arts and Sciences, tend generally to be accepted. There would be resistance, though, to establishing differentials for engineering or business school faculty who may be more difficult to attract. On the other hand, one quite frequently encounters a special increment for the star scholar—the "distinguished professor." Organized faculties have asked for "equalization" pay and use a variety of formulas in an attempt to equalize salaries across the board.

Attempts to compete for attractive candidates, academic or non-academic, often take the form of hiring within the salary range for the position, but at a level higher than the entry salary in the range. This seemingly sensitive accommodation between the requirements of a formalized structure and the flexibility required to meet a competitive situation is not without problems, because it does violence to the concept of experience increases which is built into most salary progression systems. For example, among administrators and support staff, hiring in above the entry salary level can produce a situation in which a Grade VII Counselor may very well be earning less than a newly hired Grade VI Accountant.

Whether as a result of civil service systems or classification and salary systems, or a union contract, the issue of appropriate compensation, comparative compensation, and competitive compensation will increasingly command attention. In large personnel offices, the wage and salary administrator, or the compensation specialist or benefits administrator are job titles that are relatively new. And, job titles themselves may be a problem. The executive secretary who finds someone else with the title administrative secretary, or administrative assistant, or senior administrative assistant, or assistant to may consider this a cause for great dissatisfaction. The concern about titles, where such small words as "to" appear or don't appear in one's title, is not limited to clerical or junior employees. Directors, Executive Directors, Associate and Assistant Vice Presidents, Vice Presidents and Senior Vice Presidents also are concerned about their titles.

In some excessively rigid systems, in order to justify a salary increase predicated on markedly superior performance of customary duties or perhaps the undertaking of additional duties, it is necessary at times to create new titles or narrow gradations within job categories. The end result may be too many grade levels with too few substantive differences between and among grades—the essential difference being the number of adjectives used in describing the position. Differentiations can and must be made between and among various jobs, but the process is not an easy one.

For many people occupying non-academic administrative positions within colleges and universities, the "Peter Principle" does not operate. They recognize when they have attained the position which calls for their highest level of competency. Under these circumstances, unless they are, by this time, close to retirement age they will seek a comparable position at another institution, perhaps a larger one, as the only realistic means of securing further salary increases.

Many institutions, particularly smaller ones, recognize this and realize that they can only expect to retain junior and middle management staff for a limited time. They accept this with relatively little concern. More often than not they have failed to establish the kind of internal career development system that would enable them to handle this natural attrition with minimal disruption. But there is considerable concern about retention of top level managers. Comparisons have become more frequent of late, which contrast compensation levels of senior college and university administrators with those at similar levels of responsibility in other organizational entities.

The fact that academic administrative salaries tend to be lower than in other environments has in the past been attributed to such factors as greater security, fewer demands, and no profit or loss responsibility. But these differences are diminishing and with the increasing financial pressures on higher education institutions, high quality leadership at senior levels is increasingly imperative. In some cases, institutions face the problem of highly talented senior administrators who will not and may not care to become president. Such individuals may have "topped out" at a relatively early age and while the compensation level may perhaps be considered comfortable, the absence of further opportunity for progression is a source of concern. How to sustain the drive and motivation of the very talented may become a significant problem, particularly in public institutions. Special fringe benefit packages, released time for consulting, sabbatical semesters, as well as increased salary levels may help to meet the problem.

Performance Evaluation

There is an evident trend, but not yet very strong, in the direction of establishing performance criteria. These criteria can be termed objectives, milestones, goals, or whatever seems most appropriate to the particular organization. They should be as specific and as objective as possible; e.g., percentage increase in number of applications and enrolled students; percentage decrease in the number of sections enrolling under ten students; percentage decrease in the number of days vehicles are out of service; percentage increase in the number of alumni contributing to the alumni fund and in the average gift; percentage increase in the number of square feet cleaned per maintenance person, etc.

It may be argued, with some cogency, that frequently the quantitative results cited above may have a greater correlation with other factors than with the individual whose performance is being measured. For example, success in fund raising may, at times, be only remotely related to the effectiveness of the Development Officer. But no attempt of objectively measuring the performance of an individual in charge of a particular unit can justifiably exclude consideration of the end results in the particular area of responsibility.

In addition to what might be described in quantitative terms, there are also factors that may be considered as qualitative factors in evaluating a professional's performance and in some instances, the criteria can apply to support staff as well. These qualitative aspects of performance also constitute criteria for evaluating candidates for middle to high level vacancies. Some of the traits to be considered are:

Intelligence—has broad and specific knowledge and can apply the knowledge; quick grasp of the general, as well as the technical; sharpness and clarity of thought and expression; ability to get to the heart of a matter; ability to learn from the past, deal with the present, anticipate the future.

Individual Confidence and Self-Knowledge—trust and confidence in one's own ability while recognizing situations where one doesn't know enough about a problem and thus takes steps to acquire the knowledge either personally or through staff assistance, ability to handle defeats and bounce back with confidence.

Integrity—his word and promise are good, holds to high standards of truth, honesty, and ethics, and expects the same of others.

Interpersonal Relations—ability to communicate and relate to people.

Innovation—ability to think beyond the traditional or pedestrian to see new approaches, better ways to do things; a willingness to "dream things that never were, and say, why not"; possesses a healthy dissatisfaction with the status quo.

Implementation Orientation—a concern for seeing to it that plans and programs are carried through on a timely basis.

Sense of Identification—willingness and ability to identify with the goals and aspirations of the organization, to be loyal to it.

Leadership—influences and inspires those in the organization.

Other factors or traits that are important are calmness (ability to retain composure under pressure), contentment with himself and the organization, although possessing a healthy dissatisfaction with the status quo, commitment to one's work, caring about one's subordinates and peers, and courage—as expressed partially in a willingness to take a position.

It should also be noted that in evaluating an individual's performance, over time, it may appear that suddenly something has gone amiss, or that over the last few years there has been a slow but steady decline in performance levels. There may be physical reasons for such a decline. The position may have become more difficult with changing times and conditions, valuable subordinates may have left or perhaps it is a superior who has changed. But aside from those possible explanations, the individual may have begun the burnout process. The pressures of many top jobs are such that educational administrators fall prey to becoming burned out executives. It is, therefore, in the best interests of the organization to be concerned about its most valuable resources, highly skilled executives. Some of the steps that can be taken by the individual to avoid falling into the category of the burned out executive include:

1. Don't carry vacation time over several years—take vacations each year —nonworking vacations of different types and frequencies at different times and places;

2. Develop hobbies, outside interests, community and organizational involvements that don't create added or similar tensions or always call for the same kind of effort demanded by normal work activities;

3. Change the pace of work: try to arrange different kinds of special staff and line assignments within the organization of both short and long duration, take advantage of continuing education opportunities;

4. Allow sufficient time to relate to your family, to be involved in their activities and where appropriate, to have them knowledgeable and involved in your activities;

5. Provide time for moments of solitude for questioning and evaluating one's own goals, directions, and needs;

6. Set realistic goals and new challenges; and

7. Provide outlets for talking about the pressures and letting off steam.

Whatever mix of objectives and criteria are used, the individual should be aware of the performance evaluation system, be consulted about, and be informed of the results on a timely basis, with full opportunity for discussion and reaction to the individual doing the evaluation. It is to be hoped that the results contained in the formal annual or semi-annual evaluation will not be a surprise to the individual being evaluated, since throughout the year he should be getting feedback on his performance so that he can attempt to adjust his behavior and performance promptly, rather than awaiting the formal evaluation.

Motivation

Performance evaluation and motivation are very much linked. As indicated previously, motivation is a vital factor in an individual's success, assuming he has the technical and personality skills. And, in many educational institutions, financial compensation is not as strong a motivation as in private industry because of the limits set by Boards of Trustees, state legislatures, the nonprofit status of education, and so on. Thus, the institution must seek to provide a good deal of challenge and stimulation in the job, psychic and job involvement rewards, in addition to reasonable financial compensation.

Some of the things discussed already will serve to motivate individuals, but in addition, specific concern must be given to capitalizing on the individual's natural drive and motivation, as well as utilizing tools and techniques to encourage high motivation and morale. Assuming one has chosen good people for the job in the first place and looked for indications of high drive and motivation to success, there are specific things an organization can do to motivate good people. An organization can:

1. Set high standards of performance, conduct, personal integrity, and concern for the organization and its people. Too often, educational institutions expect too little and rationalize by saying, "well, we don't pay enough," or "we're not as prestigious as other colleges," or "how can we compete against _____.";

2. Achievement of established goals should always be praised, but outstanding performance warrants special recognition. Illustrations of the forms such special recognition can take are: a letter from the President or Vice President, a special awards dinner or luncheon, a press release or special news article in the campus staff and/or student papers or in professional journals or local newspapers, a special meeting with the President or Vice President, an outstanding performance award, plaque, medal, a day off, some new equipment, etc.;

3. Innovation, creativity, a better way of doing things should be encouraged at all levels. To accomplish this, various types of suggestion systems with appropriate rewards might be established. In addition, at higher levels, an individual should be given some time to develop what appears to be a sound innovation. We ought to encourage some daring without a fear of failure;

4. Individuals should be encouraged to utilize their capabilities to the fullest. As educational administration becomes more complex, there is a tendency to lose sight of individual differences and the ability of some to move faster than others. The organization should seek to give the talented more to do, to loosen the rigidities of supervision and clearances (within appropriate standards of delegation, responsibility, and good control procedures), so that the individual, whatever his title or grade level, can begin to feel more of a master of his job, his schedule, his time, more of a contributor, decision-maker, and leader rather than merely one who follows orders; and

5. Poor performance should be noted, and after attempts to help the individual improve and, with appropriate warnings, demotion or termination should result (subject, of course, to the various procedures of union agreements, faculty practices, etc.). The paternalism that characterizes many institutions has its attractive aspects. But a sympathetic and even indulgent attitude toward staff must be tempered by the establishment and enforcement of the standards of performance. Where employees perceive that poor performance is tolerated and perhaps even rewarded, the disincentives and demoralized reactions that result are highly damaging to the institution.

Educational institutions must strive to develop an atmosphere in which individuals feel that they, as individuals, are important to the organization, no matter what their level or title, that the job they perform is important and of value to the organization, and that the organization itself is doing something important for its students and for the community.

It should be noted that public institutions frequently have to deal with a state or municipal civil service system. In general, civil service systems make it considerably more difficult to reward or discipline and, in many instances, administrators expend considerable effort in devising ways, within the structure of the system, to achieve flexibility in giving salary increases, promotions, re-classifications, and so on. A further complication is introduced if there is also a collective bargaining system covering those employees included in the civil service system because there may be some overlap between the two systems, thereby creating more paperwork, concern about violating provisions or regulations, and reducing managerial flexibility.

Some suggestions have been put forth for adapting the objectives of a civil service system to the special characteristics of the educational environment. These are:

1. Rather than written examinations, often scored to two or three decimal places, the principal determinant of promotions should be a performance appraisal and potential assessment system;

2. Written examinations both for selection and for promotion should be employed only where their validity can be demonstrated. Oral examinations should be used more extensively. Scoring of examinations should be rounded off to the nearest whole number so that the appointing or promoting authority has a broad choice. In some categories of employment, exact scores may not be necessary, Pass-Fail or Excellent, or even Pass-Fail may suffice, giving the appointing authority broad leeway;

3. The requirement to select *the* top person on a list should be modified to allow for selection from the top three or five;

4. In choosing new employees, the emphasis should be evaluation of qualifications, experience, assessment by prior employers, and/or an oral or practical examination;

5. Examinations, when used, should be for broad categories of positions, rather than narrow examinations for very narrow specialities within a broad category. "Selective certification" should be used to appoint specialists from within the group of qualified individuals. Examina-

tions should be given frequently so that the recruiter is not faced with lists of people who two or three years later do not wish to change jobs or cannot be located;

6. Salary increases should be based on performance;

7. Positions should be evaluated frequently to ascertain changes and remove barriers posed by overemphasis on credentials which may not be necessary for the position;

8. More upper level positions should be classified as management positions—once individuals reach a certain rank, promotion beyond should be at the discretion of management;

9. The system should not discriminate against "outsiders." There should not be separate lists for those in the system and those outside, with all those on the list within the system being placed before even the highest ranked "outsiders" are placed.

10. A flexible system of probationary periods should be instituted with the duration of the period bearing some logical relationship to the position; and

11. The granting of tenure should come after a careful review and should require a positive action rather than being granted automatically after a set period of service.

Those who would lobby for the application of some of the principles spelled out above, must be prepared to argue persuasively for their importance to effective administration in institutions *and also* to demonstrate that the increased subjectivity to be introduced will incorporate sufficient safeguards. This is, of course, particularly important in the context of affirmative action.

Some other aspects of good human resources management should be briefly mentioned. Although education and training is the "product" of the institution, often the education and training of its staff is overlooked. In-house training, discussion, and problem solving classes or groups should be formed and appropriate attendance at outside training sessions and conferences should be permitted and encouraged. The cost/benefits however, of such participation should be evaluated since there is a tendency in the education world for many conferences.

Many people who come into educational administration have had little formal training in educational administration and for that matter, in management concepts, techniques, and tools. Thus, whether it be in terms of encouraging attendance at job-related courses, or pursuit of an academic degree, the institution should encourage the education and continuing education of its administrators at all levels. The payoff of properly chosen training is not only in job knowledge and performance, but also in motivation.

Communication is important, and it should flow upward as well as downward. It is good for those working in an institution to know the views of the Trustees, President, Vice President, etc. This can be accomplished through annual reports, material in the university community newspapers, newsletter materials, as well as occasional staff meetings. Upward communication can be accomplished through inviting people to talk or write to appropriate individuals, to question and answer columns in the newspaper, to various types of advisory or consultative groups. The goal should be to share appropriate information, both good news and bad, so that individuals feel that they are indeed part of the institution. Communication also involves an announced procedure for dealing with individual or group grievances or concerns so that these concerns are brought to the attention of a responsible official in a timely manner. The resolution of the matter may not always be to the satisfaction of those pressing the grievance, but at the very least, staff should feel that there has been a fair hearing and reasonable consideration.

The education enterprise expends the largest portion of its budget on people. Thus, human resource management should be of vital concern. It is a most important and serious matter, and one that requires the attention and concern of the highest level administrators at the institution.

Chapter Nine

FACULTY ISSUES AND CONCERNS

A president once referred to his college as being crowned with distinction and characterized the faculty as the jewels in that crown. Unquestionably, a distinguished and dedicated faculty (note that both qualities are necessary) is the hallmark of a great institution.

It is possible to discuss specific aspects of college and university administration at length, with relatively brief reference to the faculty, or perhaps no reference at all. But it is not possible to deal comprehensively with issues in higher education management without including a substantive discussion on faculty-related issues.

Administrators and faculty members feel strongly about the way in which they relate to each other. Consequently, any discussion of this relationship will inevitably evoke strong emotional reactions on both sides. It is the purpose of this chapter to discuss, under one heading, some of the principal issues and concerns that relate specifically to faculty. These include the role and obligations of the faculty, collective bargaining, tenure, and retirement.

A. ROLE AND OBLIGATIONS OF FACULTY

The role and responsibility of faculty is a matter which has become of major concern to administrators, trustees, faculty, and students. This concern has come about because of the financial and recruitment pressures facing higher education; demands for increased productivity and accountability; the pressures of collective bargaining; discussion about usurpation of the traditional role of faculty; debate about collegiality and governance; student consumerism; a greater need for flexibility and quick reaction time; and increased emphasis on management techniques. (See Governance, Collective Bargaining, and Student Consumerism.)

A central issue confronting institutions regarding the role and obligations of faculty is the question as to what extent and in what ways faculty should participate in the governance of the institution and what implications this participation or any limitations on participation may have for collective bargaining and for the concept of collegiality.

Faculty members believe that there is an attempt to narrow their role at the institution, to treat them more as if they were employees on a production line than as joint participants in the governance of the institution or indeed, as most of them see themselves, the very core of the institution. Further, as institutions seek to meet financial pressures, faculty members tend to see themselves as the bastions for upholding standards and traditions and for carefully evaluating "unorthodox approaches" that seem to cater to transient fads and tastes.

The faculty also sees an attempt in the name of progress, flexibility, and facing reality, to usurp their traditional role of formulating and approving courses, curriculum, programs, and the role of peer evaluation in selection, promotion, and tenure. (As noted in the section on the role of government, federal regulations in regard to affirmative action also impinge on the peer review process.) In addition, there is controversy over activities that some faculties have engaged in, including playing a decision-making or advisory role concerning selection and retention of administrative officers, budget development, resource allocation discussions, construction and plant improvements, academic facilities and support services, involvement in obtaining research grants, and space utilization.

Administrators seeking to fulfill their own roles more effectively, and in the belief that they more closely represent the institution in its totality, tend to want to restrict faculty involvement to "purely academic matters" such as curriculum and to limit their activities in management or fiscal areas to an advisory or consultative role at the most.

The conflict briefly described above is often resolved within the "real-world" context of governance dynamics—who has the power to do what to whom, when, or who has the power to decide, delay, or dilute. In turn, many of these governance issues become a part of the collective bargaining process.

Another central issue relates to defining the nature and extent of the faculty obligation. As noted in the discussion on monitored workload as a means of supporting salary charges in the chapter on Sponsored Activity, historically few attempts have been made at any clear definition of faculty responsibilities and, not surprisingly, to the extent that they are defined at all, one is more likely to find a detailed definition in the public institutions resulting from state pressures than in the independent institutions. This lack of definition accords with the concept that a distinguished faculty should be accorded substantial latitude and discretion in the carrying out of their activities.

Some erosion of this philosophy has begun to take place in response to a number of pressures. One clear component in the student unrest of the 60s was that students were attracted to particular institutions and programs because of courses purportedly being taught by noted professors only to find that the teaching was, in fact, done by teaching assistants and that the distinguished professors, generally absorbed with research and other professionally enhancing activities, were virtually inaccessible.

Another source of pressure has been the federal government which, through the methodologies employed in support of research at colleges and universities, has contributed significantly to the tension between faculty members and their institutions. As discussed in the section on Federally Sponsored Activity, the use of a cost reimbursement instrument (whether a grant or contract) for funding research and other federally sponsored activities, has compelled an attempt to secure an accounting for faculty time or effort.

In the reasoning of federal officials, if a portion of a faculty member's salary is charged to a grant budget on the assumption that a certain proportion of that faculty member's activities will be devoted to the sponsored project it is reasonable to expect that there will be some realistic means of verifying that the estimated amount of effort was in fact expended. This line of reasoning dismisses an assessment of the results of the project as not germane to the issue of cost reimbursement. What is important, federal officials assert, is that funding support is provided to offset the cost of an effort, translated into a percentage of salary, and what must be verified is that that degree of effort was in fact incurred in carrying out the project.

Implicit to this reasoning is that the faculty member's obligation to the institution is a full-time one, and that in order to verify that a given percentage of the faculty member's time or effort was devoted to a particular activity, in this case the sponsored project, it is necessary to identify the proportion of time or effort devoted to all activities carried out in fulfillment of the faculty member's obligation to the institution. Linked to this has been a growing attention to nonuniversity related activities such as outside consulting and the establishment of limits on these activities on the theory that extensive outside activity impairs the ability to carry out activities directly related to fulfilling university obligations.

Recently, the federal government, in an attempt to ease the problems and abrasions associated with faculty effort reporting, evolved the "monitored workload" concept, discussed earlier in the section on Federally Sponsored Activity. This concept was aimed at eliminating the necessity for after the fact faculty effort reporting and was geared to specific identifiable events such as the awarding of a sabbatical leave, receipt of a grant or failure to receive a grant that was planned for, dropping or adding a course, and so on, as means of determining whether there was any substantive or material change in the apportionment of a faculty member's effort. However, a major ingredient to the acceptance of this concept is that it is predicated on the initial formalization, at the inception of each academic period, of the faculty member's obligation to the institution. Resistance to this kind of formalization remains strong.

The arguments over outside consulting activities of faculty exemplify the frequent dichotomy between faculty and administration and the thorniness of some of the issues. Administrators argue that the faculty are compensated on the basis of a full-time obligation. (As noted, administrators have made this argument less as a consequence of their own convictions and initiative than as a response to the pressures from federal and state officials.)

The problem arises in defining what constitutes a full-time obligation and in determining when that commitment has been met. As discussed under Productivity, faculty obligations have never been truly subject to time quantitative measures, nor would most thoughtful observers contend that they should be. Even the "onerous" federal requirements for documenting salary changes to grants and contracts speak in terms of percentage of effort. Contact hours constitute one tangible time measure of a faculty person's involvement.

But the six to nine hours a week that this frequently represents fails to take into consideration course preparation, counseling, committee work, and other administrative activities. There are wide variations in the amounts of time devoted by individual faculty members to each of these activities governed by the type of course, graduate or undergraduate, basic or advanced, whether or not it requires lab work, how frequently it was taught by the faculty member previously, and other factors relevant to the actual effort required including the dedication and conscientiousness of the faculty member. Faculty spokesmen contend that they work anywhere from 60 to 80 hours a week or more and that, hence, if one thinks in terms of the traditional 40 hour week, there is ample room for outside activity without detracting from the fulfillment of faculty obligations.

A working compromise at many institutions has been to allow one day a week to be devoted to outside consulting activity and this has been accompanied by regulations, in some instances quite elaborate. But the issue has not been fully resolved by this compromise.

As noted earlier, there has traditionally been little or no effort to define faculty obligations and the manner in which they are to be fulfilled, much less to monitor the discharge of faculty commitments. As also noted earlier, it is perhaps ironic that faculty efforts to resist undue impositions have sometimes produced collective bargaining agreements that result in defining faculty obligations with far greater precision.

It can readily be acknowledged that a rigid imposition of measurement standards would be highly detrimental to the academic environment. But as federal and state influences grow, through the vehicle of their funding support, accountability demands will create increasing pressures for a substantially improved means of defining faculty obligations and of assuring that they are fully and properly discharged.

In return for certain improvements in salaries and fringe benefits, administrators have increasingly attempted to list or define what faculty members are expected to do or how they are expected to act. It is not uncommon for a collective bargaining agreement or some other document to spell out certain requirements in regard to faculty responsibilities, in addition to standard workload. Some faculty are opposed to such articulation of responsibilities perceiving this as insulting or denigrating. Other faculty members regard a statement of responsibilities as innocuous, and a statement of the obvious. Where such a statement has been articulated, a problem often arises as to how it can be implemented. Often there is no mention in the statement of implementation or verification, at other times a rather complicated procedure might be set up.

Indicated below are some of the elements of faculty responsibility that have been identified in instances where a formal statement was used; and an example of an enforcement clause for a collective bargaining agreement. (In a noncollective bargaining situation, the statement might be found in the faculty handbook.)

General Faculty Obligations

1. Each full-time faculty member shall hold at least four (4) office hours per week during the academic year when classes are in session. The faculty member shall distribute office hours over at least two days as best to serve the interests of his or her students. Faculty teaching during evening hours should schedule some of their office hours at these times. Regular part-time faculty shall schedule one (1) office hour per course taught. Office hours shall be posted and on file with the Department Chairman;

2. At times of advisement and pre-registration, as established in the academic calendar, faculty members assigned to these duties by the Dean or Chairman shall make additional office hours available by appointment. In addition, faculty members upon adequate notice shall perform programming duties during general registration as assigned by the Chairman. If the Chairman is unable to make the assignments, then the Chairman's designee shall do so;

3. Each full-time faculty member shall maintain a significant presence on the campus for teaching, office hours, sponsored research and training, committee work, planning activities, meetings, research, advisement, et al. Common university practice is four (4) working days or the equivalent when classes are in session. Such time shall include time spent in teaching in off-campus locations as part of one's base load and shall also include normal off-campus academic activities. During the academic year when classes are not in session faculty members shall be available as required by their Chairman or Dean for meetings, committee work, advising, etc., upon adequate notice;

4. Faculty members should refrain from shortening, lengthening, cancelling, adding, or rescheduling of classes. If, however, such changes are necessary or in the interest of academic enrichment, the faculty member shall make every effort to seek agreement in advance from the affected students. If the necessary change will affect more than one class meeting, the faculty member is expected to gain approval of the appropriate Chairman and Dean, and adhere to university policies and procedures concerning such matters as minimum contact hours and the scheduling of classrooms. One class meeting means that no change will take place at any one time that will affect several

class meetings. In the event of illness or unavoidable absence, every attempt should be made to notify appropriate personnel in sufficient time;

5. Each faculty member is expected to meet administrative requirements as to recordkeeping, sending requested information promptly to the Registrar, Bursar, Deans, Chairmen, and other administrative and academic offices and officials;

6. A faculty member should establish and announce early in each term policy on attendance, course requirements, and criteria for grading and should keep students abreast of any changes which may be desirable as the course develops. During the term, the faculty members should present to students, within a reasonable time, information on any evaluation made of their academic performance and progress. At the end of the term, a faculty member is expected to submit final grades to the Registrar in accordance with the university academic calendar, and to counsel academically delinquent students;

7. Each faculty member shall make every effort to attend commencements and faculty meetings;

8. Except in rare circumstances and with the Dean's approval, faculty members shall not provide private counseling, tutoring, lessons, or consultations for members of the student body for a fee; all reasonable assistance by faculty members to the student is to be encouraged as part of the total educational process;

9. Each faculty member shall make every effort to attend convocations;

10. Faculty members should make every effort to provide full and accurate advisement and academic counseling to students. The administration shall make every effort to provide to faculty advisors necessary information and materials;

11. Faculty members shall abide by the general regulations applicable to the university community; and

12. A faculty member, in any opinion or certificate which he may give as to the merits or claims of any business undertaking or of any scientific or practical invention, shall not use the name of the university other than for purposes of affiliation.

The following is an illustration of an "enforcement clause." "Nothing in the procedures set forth below shall restrict any administrative officers of the university in due exercise of their expected role of leadership such as in the promotion of academic excellence, operational efficiency, harmonious relationships, or efforts toward mutual resolution of problems within the university.

"The procedures below are established by the administration to encourage faculty compliance with contract obligations. If students feel that they need assistance in seeking informal resolution, or in utilizing these procedures, it is advised that they discuss the problem with the faculty member concerned and/or their advisor, Chairman or Dean. In the best academic tradition, students are always encouraged to take their concerns to the office of the Dean of Student Affairs, which shall provide assistance in the resolution of problems. However, when a complaint of alleged violation of faculty contract obligations is made, the following means of encouraging compliance shall be followed:

"1. With reference to contract items 8, 10, 11, and 12, it shall be the responsibility of the Dean of the college or school, or the Dean of Academic Affairs, as appropriate, to insure compliance. With reference to contract items 7 and 9, the Dean of the college or school shall insure faculty participation and adequate representation at convocations and commencements;

2. With reference to contract item 2, the Department Chairman, program director, division or sequence Chairman shall be responsible for coordinating the scheduling of student advisement and programming, with due account to faculty preference and adequate notice;

3. With reference to contract items 1–6, the initial responsibility for encouraging compliance shall reside with the designated Chairman or program director. When a violation of any of these items is alleged, the following procedure shall be used:

   a) An alleged violation shall be reported by any concerned party to the Department Chairman, program director, division or sequence Chairman, who shall have an informal discussion with the faculty member involved, in an attempt to effect a mutual resolution of the issue;

   b) The department or school personnel committee shall be consulted by any concerned party in the following instances:

      (1) No resolution has been achieved under step a) above;

      (2) It is alleged that there are repeated violations of the same obligation;

   c) If there is no resolution in step b) above, the chairman of the personnel committee of the department or school or any concerned party shall refer the matter to the appropriate Dean of the college or school, who shall consult with the faculty member;

d) If there is no resolution in step c) above, the Dean of the college or school or any concerned party shall refer the matter to the contract obligations committee, which shall consist of two representatives appointed by the administration, and two faculty members appointed by the steering committee. Two students shall be permitted to observe the presentation of facts in the case. The committee shall meet on a confidential basis with those parties it deems appropriate to a full and complete review, to effect an informal settlement. If no satisfactory resolution is effected, the statement of the majority opinion of the contract obligations committee, if any, together with the minority opinion, if any, shall be shared with the principals to the action. These statments shall be placed in the faculty member's personnel file, along with any statement of rebuttal from the faculty member. All such statements shall be transmitted by the committee to the President of the university and to the President of the union, who shall jointly be responsible for the release of any information to parties other than members of the administration or union officials."

The matter of properly defining the role and responsibility of the faculty will continue to be a concern influenced by external events and pressures, as well as traditions, internal events and personalities. As mentioned elsewhere in this text, tensions between faculty and administration are normal and predictable. Many faculty members are truly dedicated to their institutions, some are highly self-centered and self-aggrandizing although they will always tend to justify their actions as motivated by the interests of the institution. In a system which tends to reward faculty members on the basis of publications and other externally oriented evidences of academic distinction as contrasted with distinguished pedagogy, institutional loyalty tends to be a concept honored more in the breech than the observance. The observation regarding the impact of federal policy is equally applicable to those who govern the university. That is, we have to look to the kinds of incentives that a system and set of policies creates. If for example, trustees are concerned to have faculty members at their institution spend more time with students, they should look to whether the rewards in the system create sufficient motivation for that to occur.

The issue of faculty role and responsibilities coupled as it is with gov-

ernance, can quickly become the flash point in collective bargaining and/
or in administration/faculty relations and can lead to confrontations.
Sensitivity to the traditions and current concerns of both sides, consistent
and thorough attempts at communication, focusing on objectives and
goals and good human relations, can go very far toward avoiding con-
frontation.

B. COLLECTIVE BARGAINING

As of May, 1978, faculty members had chosen collective bargaining agents
at 600 campuses and rejected unionization at 77. This reflects not only a
very substantial number of unionized campuses but also clearly a very
strong trend in the direction of unionization. Of the collective bargaining
agents selected, the American Association of University Professors was
selected at 55 campuses; the American Federation of Teachers at 213; the
National Education Association at 244; AAUP-NEA at 11 (joint agents),
and independents and others at 77 campuses. This also suggests that
faculty members, understandably, seek to be represented by a collective
bargaining agent that is identified with education, but not necessarily
one that specializes in higher education.

Collective bargaining either in actuality or as a potential issue on a
campus, raises matters of great concern to administrators, governing
boards, and faculty. It is often both an economic and an emotional issue.
Some faculty members believe that economic conditions and retrenchment, as they impact on job security, warrant militant union action.
Others show deep concern for the possible destruction or serious impairment of collegiality because of collective bargaining.

The traditional concept of collegiality involves a coming together of
senior scholars to create an environment of mutual enrichment that will
enhance their further scholarly development while also providing learning opportunities for younger scholars such as students. It must be acknowledged that a number of factors have contributed to the erosion of
collegiality, at least in its traditional form.

The complexity of today's institution of higher education and the external forces which impinge upon its operations have created a significant role for "administration" which, under the concept of collegiality
as universities evolved historically, was a minor appendage. The age of
consumerism has seen a change from the very early role of the student as

one who sat rather submissively at the feet of the institution's senior scholars to a more active role in seeking to participate in the governance process and to have a voice in regard to the "product" being provided to him. Government and community influences have helped to steer universities into becoming multiversities with programs becoming more diverse and the environment becoming more "pragmatic" and, if not less scholarly, less purely academic. Other external forces (see discussion on sponsored activity) have influenced a shifting of faculty loyalties away from their institution. External influences, due partly to financial pressures, have become so significant a factor that not even the "independent" institutions can be said to function with any substantial degree of independence or discretion.

Viewed in the context of these and other contributing factors that could be mentioned, faculty unionization may be regarded as a consequence of the erosion of collegiality but also as a force which considerably accelerates that process. Those who are concerned with the management of our institutions of higher education need to have a full appreciation of the philosophic and operational implications of collective bargaining.

The statistics cited at the outset of our discussion indicate clearly that there is a strong trend in the direction of faculty unionization and that this is one of the most significant institutional developments that has occured during the past decade. Those associated with institutions whose faculty are not currently unionized need to develop a perspective and a policy of how they will react to the potential of unionization. They will also need to develop some understanding of role changes that collective bargaining will bring about. This discussion focuses primarily on faculty collective bargaining because the changes brought about by unionization of faculty are the most pervasive, but many other categories of staff will also be engaged in collective bargaining.

The most significant change is that, in contrast to collegiality, faculty unionization produces, by definition, an adversarial relationship. This means that the bargaining process tends to emphasize differences in interest between the bargaining parties rather than mutuality. As an illustration, under the traditional concept of collegiality, a faculty pressing for a compensation increase and confronted by a response from the administration that financial circumstances must limit that proposed increase, will want to evaluate the financial circumstances, and to participate in exploring other alternatives for containing costs. Having done so they may ultimately accept the limitation which the administration initially sought to impose. A unionized faculty, by contrast, is apt to ask for the fullest possible disclosure of financial information, but may then take the posture that the faculty want, need, and deserve an increase and the matter of funding the increase is the administration's problem and not theirs.

At an institution where the relationship between the faculty and the president is a hostile one, the faculty, even though not unionized may, in fact, exhibit more militancy than *some* unionized faculties. Unionization, or the lack thereof, is not the exclusive factor influencing the degree of cooperation at an institution. However, as a generalization, it is safe to say that unionization diminishes cooperation.

Reasons for Unionizing

Why do faculties unionize? The obvious response is that they see unionization as the means by which their interests will be protected or advanced. Many faculty members continue to view unionization, philosophically, as inappropriate to the collegial environment. That they nonetheless unionize in some instances is, therefore, reflective of deep seated concerns and discontent. In some instances, at least, good communication, openness, a climate of respect and trust and, most important, a responsiveness to legitimate concerns, has meant that no attempt was made at unionization.

However, external factors, in regard to which institutional administrators may have little or no control, may induce faculties to unionize despite their general reluctance. A primary motivating factor is job security. Faculty members see such factors as declining enrollments, a plethora of PhDs, a less favorable or supportive attitude toward education by the federal government legislators and the general public, a shifting of educational priorities with some programs becoming obsolete, the closing of an increasing number of independent institutions that are no longer financially viable, the imposition of restrictions, constraints, and requirements by state and federal authorities that may limit their flexibility, increase their workload, and impact unfavorably on their prospects for advancement and, finally, the beginnings of a breach in the hallowed bastion of tenure, brought about principally by severe financial exigency. All of the above can create a climate of insecurity sufficient in strength to compel faculty members to turn to unionization as the only available vehicle for adequate protection of their interests.

A survey was undertaken at two institutions, one a complex partly public university and the other a small private, both primarily liberal arts colleges.* At the former no serious organizing drive was attempted. At the latter, unionization was strongly rejected in an election conducted in 1975. The survey sought to discern why unionization was not successful at these two institutions in contrast to the substantial number of campuses that had adopted unionization.

The degree of trust in the decision-making process of the institution was concluded to be a major factor in influencing the desire for collective bargaining. The survey also reinforced the conclusion that faculty members continue to be highly ambivalent on the subject of collective bargaining.

When asked if they thought it would ever be appropriate for college professors to go on strike approximately 50% responded affirmatively. Similarly, approximately 50% felt that collective bargaining is consistent with the professional standing of college professors and the majority felt that collective bargaining would neither raise nor lower such standing (or could not predict the impact). On the other hand, approximately half of those questioned indicated that they thought collective bargaining would have a negative impact on higher education.

The Ladd-Lipset survey, reported in the February 13, 1978 issue of the Chronicle of Higher Education (this is an ongoing opinion survey on faculty-related issues reported regularly in the Chronicle) indicates that about 73% of faculty (based on a 1977 survey) indicated that they would vote pro-union "if an election for a collective bargaining agent were to be held now at (their) institution."

About three-fourths of the faculty in 1975 and 1977 surveys credited bargaining with bringing increased salaries and better benefits, while about two-thirds of the faculty in both years saw collective bargaining as resulting in an "overemphasis on rules and regulations," and that it "reduces collegiality between administrators and faculty."

The rate of unionization of faculties has slowed, primarily due to the fact that less than half the states have enacted legislation permitting collective bargaining and also because the choice of unionization always involves the issue of who the agent will be if bargaining takes place. Thus, a professor may be sympathetic to the concept of bargaining, but opposed to the views, style, and personality connected with a particular organiza-

*Jones and Driscoll, *Analyzing Attitudes Toward Unions,* "Two Case Studies in Higher Education," May, 1978.

tion. The three largest organizations, leaving aside independent unions or combined groups, involved are the American Federation of Teachers, National Education Association and the American Association of University Professors.

Internal By-Products of Faculty Unionization

Aside from diminishing the atmosphere of cooperation, what are some of the impacts of faculty unionization? The internal governance structure of the faculty may be affected. The traditional leadership of the faculty as represented by such bodies as faculty senates may not be identical to the union leadership. This circumstance not only creates an unhealthy atmosphere of rivalry but poses a substantive problem for institutional administrators. Do they continue to deal with faculty committees such as the committee on curriculum, the committees on tenure and promotion on the same issues and in the same way? How do the joint deliberations with the traditional faculty committees affect the institution's collective bargaining position? Somewhat related questions are raised such as "should part-time faculty and various professional school faculty be in the same collective bargaining unit as arts and sciences faculty? How does the law apply? Is there a community of interest?" Obviously the administration that must bargain with more than one faculty unit finds the process to be enormously complicated.

The administration's governance structure will inevitably be impacted. Traditionally, the Department Chairman has been the administrator's key link to the faculty and a principal guarantor of academic quality within his discipline. More often than not, despite the fact that he may have been elected by his peers, he has been generally regarded as a member of the "management team" and tended to function as one who brought an understanding of institutional imperatives to his department constituency and served as an advocate of his department to the administration. In many instances the Department Chairman has now become a member of the collective bargaining unit. This means that the administration has lost an invaluable member of its "middle management team." Other governance issues are raised such as the role and responsibilities of the Board of Trustees, the President and the Deans.

There is a substantial cost impact. Grievance procedures and preliminary, informal, and formal negotiations will make time demands on administrators and normally will require staff augmentation. Increased costs will be incurred for legal fees, arbitration, transcripts, duplication, and so on. Space and support services are normally furnished to union representatives and faculty members who function as union representatives are normally granted at least partial relief from their academic responsibilities.

A considerable degree of formality is introduced to an environment that had formerly been governed by a high degree of informality. The collective bargaining agreement, in time, becomes increasingly explicit and detailed in spelling out "working conditions and relationships." The administration is impelled to develop more detailed operating procedures to insure consistency. Grievance decisions and arbitrator's findings are circulated and become a guide to day to day operations. Administrators are induced to more fully document actions and conversations and tend to operate with extreme caution to avoid violation of the collective bargaining agreement on the one hand or the inadvertent granting of concessions on the other.

A high degree of rigidity is introduced. Positions, once gained, are not readily relinquished. Consequently, the potential for program innovation may be reduced and this may be particularly critical in today's environment.

Institutional administrators are confronted with heavy and costly demands for data gathering both to respond to union informational requests and in preparing a collective bargaining position. In this latter connection, administrators will generally find in the faculty bargaining unit, an adversary that is at once more intimately knowledgeable of institutional operations and nuances, more thoroughly analytic (it is not unusual for faculty members to spend more time in analyzing data than do administrative staff), more perceptive, and more articulate in its advocacy than any of the entities whom administrators have previously had to face in justifying the annual budget. This requires the administration to develop more detailed data, to perform a more comprehensive analysis of that data, and to engage in a more thoughtful planning and balancing of priorities. In this respect the discipline that collective bargaining imposes is a very healthy one for the institution.

In the case of public institutions, the collective bargaining process may lead to a power flow from the individual campus to the central administration, and often to the state legislature or the governor's office. Because these latter bodies are necessarily involved with balancing institutional needs along with a wide variety of other priorities, the perspective that is introduced is necessarily less favorable to the institution and the faculty than when decision making was confined to the campus and only institutional priorities were being balanced. This is an instance in which faculties may find that unionization has particularly operated to their detriment.

Planning for Negotiations

Planning for negotiations is essential. This involves understanding what are "musts" for the administration as well as what are "musts" for the faculty and the risks one is prepared to run for these "musts." Strategic as well as tactical planning is necessary. The Administration's negotiations committee should be carefully chosen and various responsibilities assigned. The Board of Trustees, generally through a special Labor Relations Committee, must be involved throughout. Top administrators should be consulted in drawing up the Administration's proposals, as well as in preparing responses to the union's proposals. The top administrators should also be thoroughly briefed as to the progress of negotiations. If necessary, contingency plans for a strike must be very carefully drawn up with good communication and involvement with those concerned. Planning also involves a thorough understanding of policies, practices, and costs involving the collective bargaining unit (their salaries, fringe benefits, workload, and personnel plan provisions), other institutions and their collective bargaining units, and the impact of changes on the institution and on other employees, the short and long run implications of changes, and so on.

Although one can hope for, and sometimes obtain, understanding of a university's fiscal and management problems by the faculty union, administrators should anticipate a high degree of intractability and a substantial indifference to the financial constraints confronting the institution. Faculty union representatives cannot allow themselves, any more than can any other union representatives, to be receptive to an administration contention that they cannot afford to meet union demands.

One should expect that negotiations will almost always go down to the wire since it is difficult for union leadership to sell a contract to the membership weeks, days, or even many hours before the deadline (normally the start of classes).

One can hope for and often obtain a high level of discussion and accuracy in union announcements to their members, however, there may be small or large misrepresentation of the administration's position, or selective presentation of the contract negotiations. In fairness, the administration may also be guilty of the same.

Beyond compensation, one should expect increasing concern by the union regarding job security, tenure, sabbaticals, class size, workload, governance, and administrative freedom to modify, eliminate, or introduce programs.

Language becomes critical. Although there are times when it is wise not to dot every "i" and cross every "t," or to define everything precisely, the collective bargaining agreement is a complex legal contract governing a dynamic ongoing relationship which gives rise to many interpretive issues. In many cases, an arbitrator will finally decide, and the risk can be very great for either or both sides. There may be times when it is best not to have an "outsider" rule on fundamental issues, but if the language is ambiguous and agreement cannot be reached, the outsider may get involved. And the process of grievances and arbitration over what was meant or not meant in a phrase, or what the bargaining history shows, can severely damage the relationship between the parties.

Student Involvement

Increasingly, there will be pressure for some type of student involvement in the collective bargaining process ranging from being kept informed, to acting as observers, to serving as members of one or both teams, to functioning as a "third force." Actual student presence in collective bargaining may inhibit frankness of discussion, encourage "playing to the galleries," lead to attempts to capture or use the students. In the view of many professionals the negative results of actual student involvement, both in terms of the collective bargaining process and the after effects, far outweigh any benefits.

A reasonable compromise may be to place the Dean of Students on the collective bargaining team or to arrange briefings for students and solicit their written views. There will certainly be pressure by students on administrators to protect their interest in the contract, such as through faculty responsibilities provisions and enforcement procedures. They may also be concerned to prevent large settlements leading to higher tuition and/or decreased services or funds for student oriented activities. These are manifestations of student consumerism.

There is always the risk that, for whatever reasons, confidentiality of bargaining will be broken. Thus, newspapers, electronic media, well-meaning legislators and governmental executives, may all wish to get involved in resolving an imminent or existing crisis. One must now be prepared to fight battles outside the collective bargaining room while still hoping to preserve an atmosphere that allows civil discussion and problem solving in the room.

At times, the lack of professional experience in negotiations (Union Committees often change from negotiation to negotiation) may lead to emotionalism at the bargaining table, inability to reach accord or to separate vital from nonvital interest, or an unwillingness to recognize and retreat from an untenable position. Further, the union leadership may not be able to withstand pressures from various interest groups in their membership and therefore seek to have something for everyone. Thus, outside mediators can sometimes be helpful.

Although in the overwhelming majority of cases, reasonable compromise will prevail in collective bargaining even after full-blown rhetoric and strike votes, there is of course, the ultimate threat at independent universities, and, despite laws to the contrary, at public universities, of a strike. This may come about because of mistakes, inadequacies, hostile feeling built up over time, and events and threats becoming self-fulfilling. Or it could result from truly unacceptable conditions and practices that are deemed unreasonably favorable to the faculty, or the administration. One side may perceive that it had been disadvantaged or taken advantage of in times when collective bargaining did not exist, or in application of the new contract, or interpretations of previous contracts, or other tensions may be caused by seemingly reasonable faculty requests which, because of financial constraints, cannot be responsibly met, or by power, political, philosophic, or personality motives of union or administration leadership.

Both sides might concede and reason that strikes, slowdowns, or sick-outs would probably lead to a decline of enrollment and income, immediately as well as in future years, increased governmental interference, suits against a university for recovery of tuition, and in effect, the beginning of the end. However, the situation might be such that the antagonists feel they must embark on the dangerous road for any or all of the reasons given above.

In fact, even without an actual strike, sufficiently long, drawn out, hostile negotiations with enough strike threats and possibly the faculty joining with the students in opposing tuition or class size increases, might well result in a sufficient decline of enrollment and income to bring about the same major upheavals as would be caused by strikes. Another path on the way to the same results would be an administration which, faced with sufficient threats, yields to buy "peace" and shortly after the contract is signed recognizes that it is financially unable to live up to the terms of the contract. Or, a settlement reasonably and responsibly arrived at, may turn out in the course of the contract, to be financially impossible to meet because of unanticipated declining enrollment and income, or increasing costs.

Thus, either as a result of strikes, or a contract that for one reason or another turns out to be unacceptable, the following alternative outcomes are possible, in addition, of course, to no change from the status quo:

1. A hardening of attitudes, many grievances once the settlement is finally reached, constant testing of language of the contract and of rights and responsibilities;

2. Change in institutional leadership (including Board of Trustees) and/ or union leadership including the style, freedom and power of the leaders;

3. Cost/Benefit Analysis—Optimal Resource Allocation Studies, and such leading to reallocation and perhaps cutback in faculty, administrative staff, supporting staff, facilities and services, academic programs, courses and facilities—these have to occur within the constraints of tenure rules and financial exigency declarations which may not solve the problem quickly. Further, substantial declines in the areas mentioned may lead to the loss of existing students and good faculty and staff and may create difficulties in recruiting others;

4. Tuition increases—within the constraints of the pool of students willing and able to pay, the increasing tuition may result in declining enrollment leading to, in fact, reduced income. Another problem with tuition increases is that they may set off a continuing cycle of faculty-student antagonism with students believing that tuition increases have come about because of "unreasonable" faculty demands. Of course, faculty might claim that the university could still grant the increases without raising tuition;

5. Merger with other institutions—instead of accomplishing the goal of combining the best of each institution, mergers sometimes enhance and enlarge the worst of both—problems of programs, tenure, administrative staffs, and so on, have to be worked out;

6. Changing the nature of the institution from a university to a college or vice-versa, or from a four-year institution, to a two-year institution, either first two or last two years, or vice-versa. This may be just a delaying tactic in terms of what eventually happens, and the ability to

pay may still not be enhanced;

7. Bankruptcy—going out of business is an unhappy, but possible, alternative as Boards of Trustees begin to assert their views as to responsible action. Of course, this process would probably take a while and several changes of administration. One can delay by selling off endowments, land, and other assets;

8. For independent institutions, an alternative might be to become a public institution or to subject itself to very strong public guidance and control by virtue of special State subsidies—this would obviously change the nature of the institution. Faculty unions don't appear to worry too much about bankruptcy because they believe that state governments will subsidize or take over the institution. However, this may be an overly optimistic view. Few states will be inclined to take over private colleges or universities in the face of economic strains and the general view of legislators about the inefficiencies of college administrations and the "easy" life of professors. This disinclination may be reinforced by a judgment that the institution is not a high quality or distinguished institution.

Academic collective bargaining can be different from private or public sector bargaining models, even though, thus far, it has followed the other models without any significant differences.

We can hope for greater cooperation between both sides in reaching understanding of mutual problems and then forging new types of agreements based upon the realities of the particular institution's condition.

Whether it is through a partnership arrangement with the union or on its own because of the need to fulfill its contract obligation or forestall unionization, collective bargaining will compel university management to realistically assess and formulate specific philosophy, goals, programs, and activities.

The approach, strategy and tactics in regard to faculty collective bargaining will be a vital factor in determining the nature, as well as the future, of the institution. Legal developments will also have to be carefully monitored.

Future of Collective Bargaining

A case now being heard by the U.S. Supreme Court* may have a very significant impact on faculty collective bargaining.

* SOURCE: National Labor Relations Board and Yeshiva University Faculty Association.

The United States Court of Appeals for the Second Circuit ruled that Yeshiva University does not have to bargain collectively with a faculty union because the faculty members can be considered managerial personnel. Judge William M. Mulligan, writing the unanimous opinion, stated that faculty members play such an important role in determining Yeshiva's personnel and policy decisions that "they are, in effect, substantially and pervasively operating the enterprise." Judge Mulligan said that the record in the case "strongly supports the contention of Yeshiva that its full-time faculty, acting at times through committees or department chairmen and at other times as a body, exercises supervisory and managerial functions" as described by the National Labor Relations Act.

"The record here discloses that in many instances the full time faculty of the schools of Yeshiva, without question, effectively recommend the hiring, promotion, salary and tenure of the faculty of the university in a manner which can hardly be described as routine or clerical. They further perform managerial functions not only by their personnel decisions, but by adopting the standards of admission, the curriculum, the grading system and the graduation requirements of their school. Moreover, in particular cases, the hiring of deans, the physical location of a school, teaching loads, and even the tuition to be charged were controlled by the full-time faculty."

The case is likely to be decided by the Supreme Court on its particular facts. But the pervasiveness of faculty influence on the governance of Yeshiva University is sufficiently typical of the circumstances at most independent institutions that if the lower court decision is upheld, there are potentially profound implications for the future of faculty collective bargaining. (The case has since been decided and the Supreme Court affirmed the lower court decision that Yeshiva University faculty were "management" rather than "employees" because of the pervasiveness of their influence on the governance of the institution.)

C. TENURE—RETIREMENT

The subject of faculty tenure is a complex and highly sensitive one in the college and university environment. In basic terms the issues related to faculty tenure are not unlike those related to job security in general, such as civil service security. A primary argument in favor of a security provision is to minimize the impact of political influences which have no relevance to capability or performance.

This takes on a special connotation in education because educational institutions are or should be a marketplace for the free exchange of ideas. This connotation gains force from the recollection of the McCarthy era when loss of employment was one of the methods of intimidation used to suppress unpopular ideas.

Arguments against the tenure concept refer to the fact that security can also be synonymous with complacency and can contribute to intellectual stultification or to an attitude of indifference to the institution. An inevitable consequence of a security system, in a nonexpanding situation, is that promising young scholars will find their access both to promotion opportunities and to initial employment restricted, and institutions will have, at best, an impaired ability to selectively improve the quality of their faculty and to deal flexibly with financial stringencies which may call for retrenchment.

As the once firmly entrenched concept of tenure comes under increasingly critical scrutiny, the most forceful argument made by those who propose re-examination of the concept is that there are now available sufficient legal protections outside the tenure system to avoid the kinds of abuses that characterized the McCarthy era.

It is natural that faculty will strongly resist attempted incursions on tenure and an increased movement toward unionization is a predictable response to such incursions. But higher education is not only a labor intensive enterprise; the preponderance of its resources are concentrated on the academic side—and properly so. This means that any significant retrenchment effort will have to focus on academic programs and, increasingly, in light of the current difficulties in reducing or eliminating programs, on tenure.

Termination of tenured faculty has generally been deemed legally permissible under circumstances of "financial exigency." The determination of what constitutes financial exigency can be subject to interpretation. In late 1977 the Nebraska Supreme Court ruled in *Schriver vs. Creighton University,* Neb. Sup. Ct., 1977 that a tenured faculty member may be terminated because of financial exigency within his or her school or department, even though the institution as a whole is financially sound.

"To rule otherwise," said the court, "would mean subjecting the University to a financial drain which might jeopardize the entire institution." In this case, the School of Pharmacy at Creighton had operated at a deficit for five years. Schriver was terminated due to budget cutbacks. The University's faculty handbook lists financial exigency as a cause for terminating tenured faculty members.

Since another professor was available to teach Schriver's subject, the process used for selecting Mr. Schriver for termination was considered by the court to be fair and reasonable, enabling the University to maintain the most viable program for the School of Pharmacy.

The percentage of tenured faculty at many institutions is increasing dramatically, particularly among white males. As has been cogently observed, it is not possible to have an affirmative action program when there are no jobs. In some instances tenure rates institution-wide are approaching the 60–70% range and may be at or close to 100% in given departments. This circumstance is further compounded by restrictions on the ability of institutions to impose mandatory retirement. In lieu thereof, some institutions have offered early retirement incentive arrangements to senior faculty members.

Various approaches have also been tried dealing specifically with the subject of tenure, short of an attempt at outright abolition. These have included:

1. Contractual periods of employment—three to five years, with various types of renewal procedures, or with no renewal procedures;

2. Contractual period of employment when tenure is not granted for reasons other than merit—the individual would be guaranteed employment for some period and if conditions changed in his department or school, he might achieve tenure;

3. A quota system for tenure (i.e., percentage restrictions) in a particular department, school or university-wide with contractual periods of employment for those denied tenure for reasons (generally financial) other than merit;

4. Early retirement systems;

5. Multi-disciplinary approaches, refresher courses, and the retraining of faculty so that tenured faculty can teach in other, more needed, areas and fields; and

6. More stringent requirements and the establishment of more demanding standards of qualification for granting tenure, including longer probationary periods and more careful evaluations in the years prior to reaching the tenure decision.

The approaches cited above have sometimes been formalized within the framework of the collective bargaining agreement and in a non-bargaining situation have either been imposed by authority of the trustees or worked out within the context of a collegiality system. It is by no means evident at this stage that there is a significant trend toward utilizing the approaches cited. But a reassessment and potential departure from the tenure principle can become a central issue for an institution, depending on the combination of circumstances which it confronts as financial pressures increase.

Retirement

As noted in the preceding discussion, institutions have a dual incentive to attempt to stimulate early retirement. The first is to provide for or facilitate the continuing flow of young intellects into the faculty ranks that is essential for the continued vitality of the institution. The second is to alleviate the financial situation of the institution, not only by replacing a senior higher salaried faculty member with a junior lower salaried person, but also by replacing a tenured position with a nontenured one.

Early retirement has also been traditionally more attractive to faculty than to those in other callings. This is largely because the diversity of faculty activity and those activities related to professional development tend to insure that the retired faculty member will find ample opportunities for using his newly available time for activities that are at a minimum, personally fulfilling and may also be materially rewarding. But early retirement has become less attractive with the increasing inflationary impact on retirement income.

The most recent legislation, aimed at preventing discrimination against the aging, exempts faculties from its provisions until 1982, but subsequent to that date, prohibits the mandating of retirement before the age of 70. A less recent enactment, ERISA, also impacts on retirement considerations. This act, also popularly known as the pension reform act, was intended generally to regularize pension practices to insure that pension plans are properly funded and specifically to avoid abuses such as the discharging of long-term employees, just short of the time when they acquired vested pension benefits.

The college and university environment has not generally been subject to the abuses that gave rise to ERISA, and the excellent TIAA-CREF plan that embraces most faculty and administrators is probably the most successful approach to accommodating mobility with no impairment of pension benefits. Nonetheless, the specific compliance requirements of

ERISA, particularly as they relate to funding, have introduced another level of complexity in the general considerations related to early retirement policy.

It was indicated earlier that institutions have, either on an ad hoc basis or as part of a formalized program, sought to induce early retirement by offering a retirement benefit somewhat greater than a calculation using the normal formula would produce. A variation on this approach is to arrange for a phased retirement during the course of which workload and compensation are reduced over time.

Social Security benefits have become an important factor in these considerations. Increasingly, institutional administrators are linking the retirement income intended to be generated by the pension plan with projected Social Security benefits. Since many institutions contribute both to Social Security and the pension plan (these contributions are the major components of a fringe benefit rate which ranges from 15 to 25% of salaries), it is appropriate that they consider the Social Security benefit in determining the amount of pension to be funded. This also introduces a consideration in connection with early retirement plans. For example, a professor may be induced to elect early retirement prior to the age at which he becomes eligible for Social Security benefits. Under those circumstances, some institutions have, in "negotiating" early retirement provided for an interim payment of increased pension benefits approaching or equivalent to the level of Social Security benefits until such time as the professor becomes eligible to receive his Social Security benefits.

The salient point is that institutional management and planning must take into consideration its faculty mix. It must examine, over time, what is happening to rank distribution, proportionality of tenured and non-tenured faculty, diversity (including ethnic and racial mix), and to access and promotion opportunities for young faculty. Such examination was always essential and is now more critical because of heightened financial pressures. The issues related to tenure, retirement, and the related costs are among the factors to be considered in the trade-off decisions associated with formulating a policy that is aimed at insuring the academic and financial viability of the institution.

Chapter Ten

SOME SIGNIFICANT MANAGEMENT ISSUES

A. PRODUCTIVITY

To some, the term productivity evokes an image of a factory assembly line; and the advocates of status quo in higher education do not hesitate to conjure up this vision while contending that that term has no place in higher education. However, there is a growing body of thought that attaches a much broader connotation to productivity. Economists, among others, would assert that any enterprise that consumes resources should be subject to measures of the effectiveness and efficiency with which those resources are used or applied. The important and fundamental question is: what are the measures that are appropriate to a particular enterprise?

It is difficult for many to accept that the higher education enterprise may not be as readily susceptible to the measures of productivity and efficiency that economists seek to apply to other enterprises in the profit sector. But it is also true that without the ability to apply such analyses to education, it is difficult at the macro level to make informed value judgments on the level of funding for education. An example would be that a judgment to the effect that the proportion of state tax dollars expended for education is low should necessarily be tempered by productivity considerations.

Productivity measures as they might apply to higher education are, at best, very crude and it is contended by those who oppose any attempted application of the concept of productivity to higher education that the production process is constrained by the limitations of student-teacher ratios which have tolerance limits beyond which quality of instruction is impaired. It is further contended that unlike the industrial world, there are no viable options in higher education to substitute one type of capital or labor for another.

However, as discussed in a number of other sections (e.g., in the discussion on the role and responsibilities of faculty and in the discussion on faculty effort reporting), we are accustomed to a style, particularly within our universities as contrasted with four year colleges or junior colleges, in which faculty obligations are loosely defined and they are accorded substantial latitude in the fulfillment of those obligations.

Consequently, we have had relatively little success in determining, with any degree of reliability, the manner in which faculty members apportion their time among the various activities that may be embraced within their academic responsibilities. Much less has there been any successful attempt to analyze how the faculty go about these various activities. In regard to the latter, the tendency has been to accept, as given, the various methods of instruction, research, counseling, and committee activity.

Clearly, no one would suggest the application of traditional work measurement techniques that might currently be applied to non-professional activities. But there would appear to be some potential value in learning more about how faculty time is consumed and in learning more about how the faculty interact with students. Given the nature of the learning process at the higher education level, as contrasted with elementary and secondary teaching techniques, it would appear that student-faculty ratios should be viewed in a somewhat different context. New approaches to instruction (e.g., university without walls and technological advances, and the use of TV and computer assisted instruction) would also seem to have some implications for student-faculty ratios.

Few would question that at many institutions, there is significant potential for reduction in non-academic expenditures. Mechanical operations such as copying and printing, repetitive operations such as typing and other clerical activities, maintenance and custodial work, and the use of telecommunications and data communications equipment all constitute areas where the application of analytic and systematic techniques can produce dramatic savings. Energy, purchasing operations, handling of supplies, and the management of auxiliary enterprises are other areas in which a savings potential exists. By thinking through what is done, how it is done, whether it needs to be done at all, or whether the methodology needs to be changed and by applying managerial, mechanical, and computer advances, many institutions have the potential to reduce non-faculty staff by ten to twenty percent, without reducing the level of service and, possibly, accompanied by an improved level of service.

But efforts to achieve economy of operations cannot continue to be confined to non-academic activities. Despite our legitimate reservations regarding the ease and validity with which we can apportion faculty efforts, measure and compare costs among institutions, educational administrators are going to have to engage in such analyses or they will be performed by others. We have already noted that the United States Office of Education is requiring institutions to report annual expenditure data in accordance with the NCHEMS PCS (program classification structure), and that state legislatures are increasingly using a formula approach to fund the education budgets. These budgets are generally related to full-time equivalent (FTE) students.

However crude, the cost per credit hour is a measure of resource and output relationships; it has utility at least in the sense that the rate of variation over time can signal the necessity for further analysis. Given the changes in the needs and desires of students, an examination of course enrollments in elective subjects over time in relation to cost—or even so gross a measure as department size—will inevitably impel a reduction in numbers of sections, elimination of some courses, and even of departments, in some instances. Even the core curriculum cannot remain immune from critical reassessment, particularly as the institution views its prospects for effectively recruiting students in an increasingly competitive marketplace. This reassessment could, in fact, take the form of reaffirmation. But it is not inappropriate to recognize that what constitutes "core" can be a changing concept.

Given both the need to consider productivity concepts and considering also the limitations of such concepts as applied to the higher education enterprise, at least one thoughtful observer has suggested that, for education, input-output analysis has utility as a planning tool rather than as an after-the-fact measurement.

William Toombs has stated "In the industrial production process, outputs are well established and can often be converted into comparable monetary terms by pricing mechanisms. Priorities can be ordered around the dominant principle of profitability. Historical review of input-output ratios offers guidance for adjustments to improve productivity. These decisions can be made on the basis of limited information with assurance that their consequence, if significant, will appear in those ratios. . . . the production process can usually be managed directly with both the settings and the behaviors of production subject to adjustment."*

In regard to education he comments ". . . the absence of a single organizing principle for output that is stable over time, all but nullifies historical data. They are little more than incomplete descriptions, interesting but not reliable enough to permit generalized principles. Productivity analysis in the usual framework of comparing inputs with outputs after the fact is replaced by the process of planning. If outputs must be established, de novo for each analysis, the exercise shifts completely from one of productivity adjustment based on past experience to a comprehensive operation of planning. The utility of the usual productivity question, Has it improved?, disappears and the central issue becomes, How can improvement be designed? The schematic for describing the issue now becomes: Outputs Defined—Inputs—Environment—Process—Outputs Achieved. What productivity is to the business community, planning is to education."†

There is one particular facet of college and university activity that falls broadly under the rubric of productivity, in the sense that one can draw a relationship between outputs and resource requirements and that relates to attracting and retaining students. Anecdotal evidence suggests that if, in general, too little attention is paid to both, disproportionately little attention is paid to the latter.

Much time, attention, money, and concern is spent on assessing performance in regard to recruitment of new students this year as contrasted with the previous years in particular programs, departments and schools. Significantly less attention is paid, in general, to the question of retention of students or what is the rate of attrition, drop-outs, stop-outs, and transfers. It should be noted that decidedly more emphasis on retention is in evidence of late. Aggressive admissions offices barrage potential students with mailings and attention, and do a great deal of follow-up as to why an application has not been sent in, or deposit sent, a registration completed, and so on. By comparison, relatively little has been done in regard to potential drop-outs, stop-outs, transfers, or to those who have in fact left the institution. When one considers the cost of recruiting, selecting, and processing new students, it is worth considering the comparative in-

---

*Toombs, W., "Productivity—Burden of Success," *ERIC/Higher Education Research Report* No. 2, 1973.
†Ibid.

cremental cost of concentrating more effort on retention in relation to the comparative impact on maintenance of enrollment levels.

Many institutions find that 25% to 50% of all enrolled freshmen do not graduate from the institution. This has implications for the selection process. But institutional administrators need to determine whether the rate could be modified if more attention and effective resources were devoted to early warning of potential drop-outs, sound counseling and follow-up, outreach to *all* students not just those identified as "problems," and the provision of adequate and timely services. Important in all this is a sense of concern about the student and what's happening to him. This concern has to be shared by individuals other than the counselors or the staff in the Dean of Students Office. The professor, chairperson, dean, administrator, clerk, and security officer all have a role to play in preventing attrition.

Personnel-related costs constitute the largest cost area in an institution; but, through improved management, considerable savings or increased effectiveness and efficiency can be achieved in other areas of university expenditures such as maintenance, supplies, equipment, energy and utility costs, construction, advertising, publications, vehicles, telephones, insurance, travel and entertainment, purchasing procedures. (To cite a small example, many institutions expend thousands of dollars annually by paying sales and other taxes on supplies, travel and entertainment expenses, general purchases, and gas. This expenditure could be avoided by filing the appropriate tax exempt certificate with the vendor or supplier.) A careful view of scholarship funding can yield important results by determining whether no-need scholarships are achieving their intended purpose or are merely costly, whether too much or too little of the institution's funds are being spent, whether full use is being made of work-study and other governmental grant and loan programs, thereby permitting greater funding for student needs at less cost in the institution's own funds. Accounts receivable may not be receiving sufficient attention (although the federal government has certainly focused attention on them in relation to student loans). Educational institutions have not been aggressive enough in collecting money owed by students. By using sound and sensitive collection practices including letters, calls, collection agencies, and attorneys considerable sums can be recovered.

In general, all of us who are concerned with higher education must recognize that we will have to learn to do a better job of managing higher education in an economy of scarcity. It is not so much the projected decline in traditional enrollments that will produce this scarcity. The term traditional is an important qualifier in projecting enrollment trends. It is the economic conditions that prevail in today's society.

Even if we succeed in containing inflation more effectively than we give evidence of being able to do at this writing, higher education will still confront an economy of scarcity. This is, in large part, due to the fact that in the last half century we have evolved a concept of the quality of life as a society that has created an enormous increase in the demand for tax supported services.

Much of this is related to the social philosophy that has evolved (and, in general, transcended political party affiliation) reflecting a greatly heightened concern for the disadvantaged—those disadvantaged by virtue of race or social or economic status, the physically handicapped, the convicted felon, among others—accompanied by an attempt to deal with their problems constructively and to create a better life for them. There also seems to be a growing sense that with the increasingly prohibitive costs associated with health care services, we need to adopt measures that will insure a minimum level of quality health care to all.

We are reaching the point, assuming we have not already reached it, where the resource demands associated with the services we seek to provide cannot be supported by our tax structure without making that structure confiscatory. The taxpayer's revolt, or the Proposition 13 psychology, suggests that many of our citizens believe that our structure is already confiscatory. Or if they have not yet reached that conclusion, they believe that the quality and quantity of services being received is non-commensurate with the level of taxes.

What this means for higher education is, that, as the value oriented resource allocation decisions take place at both the federal and the local level, higher education is going to have a more difficult time in competing for the resources believed by educators to be needed. The same impact is in evidence in private giving as well, as potential benefactors are confronted by increasing pressure from competing worthy causes. (Estimated voluntary support for higher education, including foundations, increased from $1,270,000,000 in 1967 to $1,891,000,000 in 1976. While in absolute terms the increase is impressive, it failed to keep pace with the rate of increase in current fund expenditures.)

Consequently, just as has been the case with health care, increasing attention will necessarily be concentrated on more cost efficient techniques for delivering higher educational services. We may reject the *term* productivity as it applies to education. But the *concept* of productivity, as it connotes an improved relationship between outputs and the resources required to attain these outputs, must inevitably be applied to higher education.

B. MANAGING IN A COMPUTERIZED ENVIRONMENT

The availability of the computer as a tool for facilitating the administration of institutions of higher education has created the potential for significantly improving the effectiveness of that administration.

The computer is used for information storage and retrieval and creates the capability for arraying, integrating, and displaying data in a variety of combinations and formats to assist in interpreting and analyzing. It is used to record and calculate financial data for such purposes as accounting and budgeting. It is used to process transactions, which involve repetitive functions. Some examples are processing an application for admission, registering a student, storing a test, reporting and recording a semester grade, preparing a bill for student fees, preparing a paycheck, and preparing alumni mailings. It is also used as a control mechanism, such as precluding the processing of expenditures against a budget line item that is fully expended.

With the advent of simulation modeling, the computer is also used as a tool to aid in the budgeting and planning process. It can reduce the volume of information through exception reporting, by reflecting only matters that need attention, by clear graphic displays or projections, and by sophisticated treatment which reduces multiveriate data to univeriate form whenever possible. It provides for trial runs and simulation of decisions by automatic projections of the probable effects of present trends and experimental studies of the effects of policies prior to commitment.

Small wonder that, with the multitude of sophisticated applications, institutions spend millions annually to install computer equipment, operate, program, and maintain the hardware. In the face of such a major expenditure those concerned with college and university governance should be alert to at least three areas that warrant consideration:

1. The need for requirements reviews as an essential preliminary to buying or developing a software application system;
2. The importance and utility of hardware and software measurement

systems as a means of insuring that existing systems meet institutional needs in a cost effective way; and

3. The role of chargeback systems and like methodologies in managing computer resources effectively.

In many instances, data processing resources are not utilized to optimum effectiveness and substantial amounts of computer dollars are wasted because the users of data processing services and those charged with providing those services have been unable to communicate well with each other. One consequence of this communication problem is reflected in the development of the software programs necessary to utilize the computer effectively for a given application.

When a new system is to be installed, the development of the system should properly begin with a requirements study which seeks to identify in what ways the various users of the system will be drawing upon the system for such things as information reports, addressing such matters as particular data elements required, frequency of information requirements, and report formats. User requirements need to be assembled, evaluated, prioritized, and costed out.

Institutions should seek to avoid a circumstance in which an elaborate system is installed which ignores the special needs of a significant user. Similarly, to be avoided is the incorporation of systems enhancements which have little value relative to their cost. All too frequently systems design and programming efforts are performed by data processing personnel, based on their best judgments as to user needs because an effective dialogue with users has not taken place. On the other hand, it is very often the case that users will state their requirements in the context of the manual system they have last used (i.e., they are perhaps unconsciously constrained in identifying requirements by what they believe to be limitations in capability). A meaningful dialogue between users and systems designers is important to convey to users the technical potential of a new system as a means of identifying new or unmet needs.

On many occasions, institutions have felt that they could dispense with the necessity of a requirements review by purchasing a software application package. While the acquisition of a software package may indeed avoid a costly systems development and programming effort, such acquisition should always be preceded by the performance of a requirements review which will inevitably result in identifying necessary modifications to the system. Failure to take this vital step can be anticipated to result in subsequent problems which will ultimately entail an expenditure for modification far in excess of the original cost to acquire the software.

The effectiveness and efficiency of data processing operations need to be evaluated with considerable thought to assist in answering the following kinds of questions.

What are the hardware needs? Is the institution most effectively served by using one highly sophisticated main frame computer to serve both academic and administrative needs, or should each area have its own dedicated computer resource? To what extent do users have a need to access the computer for information retrieval or for data entry? How instant must that access be? (As in many other aspects of modern technology, we adjust upward very quickly in the use of computer resources and tend to prefer instant access, particularly when we are not fully aware of the cost of an "interactive system" as contrasted with one that has a somewhat slower reaction time.) What are the applications that truly require computerization?

There are tools available which enable an institution to analyze the manner in which it is utilizing its computer hardware and supporting resources. An effective approach would utilize both hardware monitors and software monitoring programs. Essentially, hardware monitors are small, special-purpose electronic counting devices that attach electrically to the computer. Software monitor programs are loaded into the computer's core memory to examine, periodically, the contents of various registers, accumulating information on the status of each computer resource.

In establishing the extent to which each piece of equipment is being used and the distribution of idle time among the various pieces of equipment, monitoring serves as a basis for optimizing both equipment configuration and its usage. This has significance, not only as a cost reduction device, but also as a means of cost avoidance. The apparent lack of capacity will frequently prompt an institution to acquire the latest generation of computer. In part this is also a manifestation of the new toy syndrome. But capacity is the function of an interaction among all hardware units, all of which have operating speeds that vary radically. Hence, it is important to determine whether a significant increase in capacity can be achieved by replacing one or more peripheral units in lieu of investing in a new computer.

Another major consideration relates to demand. Differing information needs and differing program priorities, as well as differing ways in which a program aimed at accomplishing a particular purpose is written, will all bear on the capacity demands. It is, consequently, important to periodically employ performance measurement techniques as a means of optimizing utilization and minimizing cost. It is also important to utilize an arrangement such as a user's committee, which meets regularly to order priorities, evaluate usage and plan for future needs. If provided with sufficient cost data, such a committee can, among other things, serve as a vehicle for evaluating needs and patterns of usage as a means of avoiding excessively costly demands.

Chargeback systems are employed with increasing frequency in connection with computer utilization, as well as with other types of services. The concept of a chargeback system is that all users of computer services pay for such services on the basis of a formula that is intended to insure equitable charges to all users and that the data processing operation is self-supporting. Since in major institutions, federally sponsored activity will normally be a heavy user of computer services, the necessity for a chargeback formula that is demonstrably equitable is evident. However, equity does not preclude the use of differential pricing rates related to peak or off-peak usage, provided that the priority system for allocating machine time is an equitable and rational one.

Many, but not all, chargeback systems are integrated with the budget process. This means that each user department receives an allocation of funds for computer utilization in the annual budgeting process based on a projection of needs. This process can be self-defeating and indeed doubly dangerous to the institution if the allocation for data processing is not subject to line item control as "hard money" rather than "soft money." That is, some institutions have made the mistake of allowing user departments to transfer funds budgeted for computer utilization to other uses. The dual consequence of this is that the costs of the computer operation will not be recovered, while budgetary transfers to other areas of expenditure will result in over expenditures because there are no true budgetary resources to support such expenditures.

When functioning properly a chargeback system can serve to constrain users from arbitrary, unreasonable, or excessive costly demands because users are required to pay for their use of computer resources. Users who pay are also likely to demand more efficiency, effectiveness, and responsiveness from the data processing organization. However, an effective system requires that the budgetary allocation be meaningful to the user department and also that that department be in position to exercise some meaningful control over the computer budget. Consequently the system cannot simply be a technique for the allocation of costs and it may also have to provide that the user department is permitted to place the internal computer resource in competition with outside services, whether for systems development or processing.

C. THE USE OF CONSULTANTS

It is well recognized that one of the most valuable attributes of the outstanding manager is the ability to select and effectively utilize good subordinates. Identifying occasions when it is appropriate to use outside resources and knowing how those resources can be utilized effectively, can also be extremely important.

The heightened necessity for improved management and for effective husbanding of resources, lends added importance to the selective and prudent use of consulting assistance to augment internal resources. As with other types of entities, there are three principal reasons for the use of consultants by educational institutions:

1. To secure independent, objective, professional advice and judgments on issues of high sensitivity and significant political ramifications;
2. To enable execution of special projects which internal staff are capable of performing but cannot be freed from day-to-day responsibilities to achieve in timely fashion; and
3. To secure highly specialized skills which may not be available except at the largest institutions and sometimes not even there.

There is still another important reason for utilizing consultants less widely perceived and understood than those cited above. The successful management of a significant project (e.g., the installation of a major software system) requires unique talents. An institution may possess an abundance of technical expertise and management skills that are highly suited to administering day-to-day operations but not nearly as effective in the management of major projects. Consultants possess superior project management skills, if not by reason of natural aptitude then because this is an activity in which they engage constantly as contrasted with the college or university administrator.

In determining when and how to utilize outside consulting assistance, the first critical step is to clearly define the work to be performed, the results to be achieved, and to delineate the respective responsibilities of consultants and internal staff. Concurrent with this step is the thoughtful identification of the likely ramifications, political and other, of the work to be performed. When consulting assignments fail, it is often because of lack of adequate definition and equally often because management has not thought through the consequences of the projected undertaking, with the result that the institution is not ready or has not prepared itself for the change.

There are a variety of sources for consulting assistance, depending on the kind of skills required, ranging from staff members or faculty at other institutions to specialty firms to public accounting firms. The latter have developed a wide range of consulting skills intended originally to serve audit clients, but now widely used to serve non-audit clients as well.

In recent years, the question as to whether it is appropriate for accounting firms to provide consulting services to clients whom they also serve as auditors has become the subject of controversy. (See the section on Auditing.) Those who would preclude accounting firms from rendering consulting services to audit clients, or would limit the range or types of services provided, argue that the independence of the accounting firm as auditor cannot be effectively preserved when that firm also functions as consultant.

The concern regarding a potential compromise of independence is understandable, but there are some cogent responses. Many would contend that the most compelling assurance of independence stems from the professional integrity of the firm. Those who are inclined to utilize the consulting services of their public accounting firms do so because they believe those firms have already developed an invaluable knowledge and understanding of the institution, its organization, internal dynamics, and staff. They also believe that the ongoing relationship with the accounting firm insures the integrity and reliability of the consulting services.

Another issue in regard to selection of a consultant is that of competition. It is well recognized that competitive bidding procedures are not as fully suited to the procuring of professional services as they are to procuring products or nonprofessional services. Moreover, a price competition that induces the successful bidder to accept a project at a price that does not offer an adequate return, encourages the cutting of corners in ways that may not be readily apparent to the buyer.

Nonetheless, the sharp focus on propriety and stewardship, particularly in the public sector, has caused many institutions to regularly use competitive bidding procedures. When they do, it is particularly important that specifications be carefully drawn so as to maximize the likelihood of receiving truly comparable bids. In many instances, the difference between the highest and lowest bid can reflect differences in both scope and quality of performance. It is consequently important to give thought to the characteristics that are most important for effective performance of the particular project and to develop weighted selection criteria based on those characteristics. When this is done, even when heavy weighting is accorded to price, the institution will more readily be able to recognize circumstances in which the low bidder is seriously deficient in several respects and to justify rejection of the low bid under those circumstances.

A major consideration in selection should always be whether the proposed consultant demonstrates a sufficient understanding of the problem to be solved or situation to be improved and displays a sound, thorough, and orderly approach to performing the project. The consultant selected should be able to present credentials which reflect understanding of the education environment and experience in performing similar projects. Reference checks should be routinely made, and those performing the checks should attempt to insure that they are securing the reactions directly or indirectly of those who have been most closely associated with the consultants. On the other hand, subordinate staff have, at times, displayed defensive reactions to consulting services and the inquirer must consequently be sensitive and alert to biased reports.

The nature of consulting is such that it is not realistic to expect that a firm will be able to fully predict two, three, or more months in advance of the inception of a project the staff that will be assigned. This can be a particular problem with educational institutions where the decision-making process is frequently a protracted one. Nonetheless, for any significant consulting assignment, it is both reasonable and essential that the key personnel to be associated with the project be identified in advance. The client needs to assess the qualifications of the key personnel to be assigned and also to determine that the "chemistry is right."

Some firms utilize their senior and most impressive personnel in a marketing role with no prospect that these individuals will ever be involved in the project. This can be avoided by utilizing a formal contractual arrangement containing a key personnel clause. Such a clause specifies the names of key personnel to be associated with the project and provides that approval of the client must be secured before any substitutions can be made for the key personnel.

The requirements to carry out particular projects may vary widely, but it is normally important that the institution plan on assigning some staff to a consulting project on at least a part-time basis. It is highly desirable to have a key staff member function as liaison with the consulting staff. It is appropriate for the institution to monitor the consulting effort to insure effective and timely performance but care must be taken to avoid the kind of monitoring that is counterproductive.

Institutions engaging consultants should be cognizant of their own responsibility to facilitate the consulting effort and to help create an environment in which the consultants can perform effectively. It is important not only to clearly delineate consultant and client responsibilities, but also to accord sufficient latitude and flexibility to consultants to carry out their responsibilities.

Many a consulting assignment has floundered because client staff impeded the consultants from performing their work through misguided attempts at helpfulness or overzealous monitoring. Often this occurs without the knowledge of the key university official who approved the consulting assignment.

The *good* consultant brings to the consulting assignment analytic and diagnostic skills, an understanding of and sensitivity to the dynamics of the college and university environment, a broad base of experience in dealing with similar circumstances in environments that are both similar and different, and specific project management and project execution skills. The institutional management that has developed the ability to properly identify circumstances that call for consulting assistance, articulate the situation to be addressed or work to be performed with clarity and specificity, prudently select the appropriate consultant, and judiciously utilize the consulting talents in the most appropriate way, will have developed a highly useful and cost effective means of augmenting internal resources.

Chapter Eleven

EDUCATIONAL LAW, TRUSTEE LIABILITIES, AND RISK MANAGEMENT

Increasingly, those associated with college and university administration need to concern themselves with the legal implications of their activities. One of the more striking evidences of this fact is the growth in the number of full-time attorneys employed on the staff of colleges and universities. Those institutions that do not have counsel on their own staff generally employ outside counsel on a retainer basis. In the past ten years, there has been a very dramatic increase in litigation involving institutions of higher education with legal claims asserted individually or jointly against institutions and against their directors, trustees, officers, faculty, and staff.

What are the liabilities of institutions and what are the liabilities of the trustees in particular? There has traditionally been a legal distinction between corporate directors and university trustees, but one which seems to diminish with the expanding role of university trustees. Both may be said to have a trust or a fiduciary relationship. In the case of the corporate director, this relationship is with the stockholders.

The entire management of corporate affairs is committed to the corporate directors and they are required to act in the utmost of good faith and best judgment and for the common benefit of all stockholders. Stockholders of corporations can bring suit for a breach of these fiduciary duties. Educational corporations do not have stockholders, nor do they have specific identifiable beneficiaries. Their beneficiaries are a number of groups such as students, alumni, faculty, donors, and the public. They have, consequently, been classified along with nonprofit charitable organizations as charitable trusts. However, public educational corporations are agents of state government and trustees are consequently responsible to state government for the performance of their duties. The trustee is required to subordinate his personal interest to the diverse group of beneficiaries indicated above. The care taken must be that which a "normally prudent man" would take under similar circumstances, while giving his best judgment.

Following the Cambodian crisis in 1970 and the tragic events at Kent State University, a suit was brought against the Chancellor of Washington University for $7.7 million. The student plaintiffs claimed that the relaxation of normal academic rules and the failure to call police quickly enough during an anti-ROTC demonstration caused them to lose valuable classroom and extra-curricular experience. The trustees and administration of Indiana State University at Terre Haute were sued for $50,000 for failing to take prompt police action against student demonstrators who damaged campus property in the early spring of 1970. Such cases reflect that, although colleges and universities historically have enjoyed a far-reaching legal immunity from many claims, this immunity has virtually disappeared.

Trustees are finding that the heightened emphasis on accountability extends to them as well and they will become increasingly active in their governance role (assuming that the spectre of legal liability does not discourage them from Board participation) because of the extent to which they are pressured to be knowledgeable of and, hence, accountable for the full range of college and university activities. They are faced with the prospect of suits based on alleged neglect of their proper functions of reviewing management, evaluating policies, and providing reasonable answers to deficits and other financial crises.

In recent years, the much publicized circumstances involving speculative investment and pyramiding of endowment funds at one major institution and the virtual collapse of financial administration at another, leading to the resignation of the President, raised questions as to trustee liability. The serious regard for potential trustee liability is evidenced by one university board that provided liability insurance protection for trustees in the amount of $1,000,000.

As another aspect of the increasing number of legal issues confronting colleges and universities, there are at least thirteen major pieces of federal legislation that now govern various aspects of college and university behavior and hence raise compliance issues with legal ramifications. These are:

- The Equal Pay Act of 1963
- The Age Discrimination in Employment Act of 1967
- The Minimum Wage Laws
- The Unemployment Insurance Requirements in the Employment Security Amendments of 1970
- The Social Security Act
- The Health Maintenance Organization Act of 1973
- The Employment Retirement Income Security Act of 1974
- Wage and Salary Controls under the Economic Stabilization Act of 1970
- The Occupational Safety & Health Act of 1970
- Regulations Implemented under Civil Laws by the Environmental Protection Agency
- Title VII of the Civil Rights Act of 1964 dealing with Equal Employment Opportunity
- Executive Order 11246, as amended requiring Affirmative Action to Correct Past Discriminations in Employment
- Sex Discrimination Regulations under Title IX of the Education Amendment of 1972.

The distinction between public and private institutions respecting their status before the courts continues to have significance, although the distinction has become less clear, particularly in relation to the federal courts. In the 1960s a group of students at Alfred University were suspended following an anti-ROTC demonstration. Alfred is a private liberal arts college but is also the host campus for one of the State University of New York contract colleges dealing in ceramics. The court of appeals ruled in this case that the ceramics students (presumed to be students of a public institution) would be entitled to due process and all the substantive guarantees of the Bill of Rights. Liberal arts students would not.

Whether or not private institutions are susceptible to suit before the federal courts and to the guarantees of the Constitution is deemed to depend, at least in part, on the degree of government involvement. Government involvement can be broadly interpreted to include not only fiscal interdependence but also regulation and control. However, even fiscal interdependence is subject to broad interpretation. In one instance, a state court ruled that a private institution was subject to the federal

Constitution because of the extensive use of *state* funds to build residence halls, because of the number of students receiving state and federal financial aid, and because of various state and local tax exemptions. The latter two circumstances are clearly widespread. Moreover, private institutions receive nearly twice as many federal dollars as the public campuses. Hence, in legal terms, as well as in other respects (see discussion on public and private institutions in Financing Higher Education) it is not unrealistic to predict that the distinction between public and private institutions is rapidly disappearing.

An inventory of institutional activities can provide an indication to those concerned with college and university administration as to the range of vulnerability or exposure. The categories within such an inventory would vary with the compiler. However, a reasonably representative list would include:

1. Recruitment, promotion, discipline, and termination of personnel;
2. Curricular and research activities (such as, research investigations involving human subjects);
3. Consulting and public services programs;
4. Support services activities and auxiliary enterprises;
5. Student services (housing, food, health, etc.);
6. Student activities;
7. General and financial administration; and
8. Public relations.

The Insurance and Risk Management Committee of the National Association of College and University Business Officers established the following more comprehensive classification of higher education liability perils (Committee Minutes 1974)

1. Criminal Acts;
   Embezzlement—employee dishonesty;
   Environmental—pollution;
   Malfeasance—employee and/or directors; and
   Manslaughter—campus security.

2. Tort (Civil) and Equity Acts;
   Advertisers, authors, and publishers liability;

Athletic events (players, spectators, coaches), recreational facilities, programs, instructional, intercollegiate contests (events);

Automobile (including mobile equipment) fleet, drivers, and non-ownership operation;

Aviation liability;

Bailee liability (care, custody, and control);

Boiler and machinery liability;

Campus security—normal operations, false arrest, and all related internal tasks;

Construction liability (contractor, students, public, donor, board);

Dental malpractice—products and services;

Directors and officers (errors and omissions);

Discrimination;

Easement and other property liability—access appurtenances, etc.;

Ownership liability, rights of others, e.g. eminent domain, etc.;

Elevators, escalators, including collision liability;

Employers, including safety and health hazards;

Workmen's Compensation, Federal Employment Liability Act, Longshoremen and Harbor Workers, Jones Act, Unemployment Compensation;

Discrimination (civil damages);

Fire—legal liability;

Fringe benefits and employee benefits;

Hold harmless or waiver agreements; consent travel forms, etc.;

Institutional agency—employees, invitees, licensees, trespassers, volunteers, etc.;

Libel—slander, defamation of character, invasion of privacy, etc.;

Liquor law liability;

Malpractice—errors and omissions, negligence;

Medical doctors, dentists, nurses, specialists, pharmacists, paramedics, hospital personnel;

Veterinary medical personnel (institutional personnel);

Clinical practicum, psychological conditioning, counseling;

Audio—speech centers, personnel, etc.;

Nuclear liability—products and general;

Oceanography—maritime liabilities;

Pharmaceutical liability;

Pollution—environmental hazards;

Premises and operations;

Professional liability, errors, omissions, negligence (ordinary and gross) (administration and professional discipline personnel);

Product liability—food services, medical products (blood, prosthetic, etc.);

Program liability—travel, research (foreign and domestic);

Protective liability (contractual in large measure);

Residence liability;

Riot, civil commotion;

Watercraft;

Worldwide premises and program liability.

3. Contractual Acts;

Artifacts, art objects (bailee, exhibitor, etc.);

Authority operations;

Equipment;

Franchise operations;

Implied contracts, e.g. catalogs;

Joint—e.g. affiliation agreements;

Products and services;

Real estate—leasehold operations;

Staff—fringe benefits, tenure, etc.

All of the above constitute areas of activity in which legal advice may be required and which constitute areas of concern for trustees regarding the potential liability of their institutions and their own liabilities.

Without being prescriptive, it is nonetheless possible to set forth several very fundamental principles and caveats in respect to the legal aspects of higher education administration. These are included in the following list:

1. It is important that all those associated with the management of the institution are made fully aware of their potential liabilities. In this connection an SEC investigation report set forth four principal stan-

dards for directorial performance that are equally pertinent to college and university trustees:

- Outside directors violate their duty if their presence has no impact whatever on the company's operations or affairs;
- Outside directors cannot blindly rely on the fact that the company employs accountants, lawyers, investment bankers, and other professionals;
- Directors should familiarize themselves with the company's business and question management in more than a perfunctory manner;
- Management must make available to outside directors sufficient information concerning corporate affairs to enable them to adequately discharge their responsibilities. (See section on Reporting.)

2. Institutional affairs should be conducted in a manner that is fully sensitive to areas of exposure and to potential legal liabilities resulting from institutional activities.

3. Thoughtful consideration should be given to the most effective means of providing adequate legal support to the institution within its resource limitations. Where full time legal counsel is employed by the institution such counsel should be involved in all significant administrative activities and deliberations and not merely consulted on such obvious matters as contractual relationships. While smaller institutions frequently cannot afford to engage full time specialists in many disciplines that are commonly found on the staff of large universities, full time counsel may well be the one area of specialization that an institution can ill afford to forego. The institution that relies on occasional or ad hoc legal assistance is apt to be dealing with potential liabilities in a reactive, rather than preventive manner.

4. Institutions should explicitly establish and effectively implement a thoughtfully conceived and carefully developed program of risk management.

RISK MANAGEMENT

The average lay person practices risk management in his or her every day affairs, frequently on an instinctive basis, without being explicitly aware that risk management is being practiced. The head of household determines the amount of life insurance that is appropriate for family protection, based on a variety of trade-off decisions. The amount of premium cost constitutes an ultimate limitation on the amount and type of life insurance procured.

But there is a wide range of premium cost that will be deemed tolerable, predicated on considerations such as number and ages of children, age and predicted earning power of surviving spouse, and general financial condition of the family, including but not limited to, amount of debt, value of other assets, status of mortgage, and existence or non-existence of mortgage insurance.

A decision on the deductibles when procuring auto insurance will be predicated on considerations such as the age and condition of the car, the potential magnitude of cost in the event of accident and the premium cost. Efforts will be made to minimize risk or to limit premium cost. For example, a woman may elect to keep her expensive jewelry in a vault and to take out day insurance when the jewelry is to be worn for a special occasion. The owner of an automobile involved in an accident may, if there is no personal injury involved, elect not to report the accident to his insurance company and to bear the cost of repair.

Clearly, these same principles have even greater applicability to an institution when considering an insurance program. Some years ago, the curator of a fine arts museum at a prestigious institution was involved in a dispute with the chief financial officer—the kind of argument that business managers all too frequently lose. The overall financial condition of the institution had deteriorated to the point where the financial officer was compelled to examine every potential avenue for reducing costs. It was within this context that premium costs for fine arts insurance came under scrutiny and a proposal was advanced to increase the deductible.

The curator appealed to the President in outraged indignation, contending that the fine arts objects ought to be fully insured because they were priceless and irreplaceable. "Precisely the point," responded the chief financial officer. "If the objects cannot be replaced, all that the insurance premiums can do is to provide funds that will enable us to procure some roughly equivalent substitute. Under those circumstances, since the risk of loss is minimal and the premium cost high, we ought to limit the premium by increasing the deductible." This was one instance in which the chief financial officer prevailed.

Broadly speaking, an institutional risk management program involves:

—a comprehensive identification of exposures and potential liabilities;

—a thorough and continuing evaluation and selection of indemnification coverage which balances premium costs against the level of risk assumed with self-insurance; and

—an institutional style which integrates risk management concepts into the day-to-day administration of the institution so that exposures are reasonably and realistically contained.

Stated differently, the two major components of risk management, when undertaken either by individuals or by an entity such as a college or university, are loss financing and loss prevention. The matter of loss financing is a highly important one for institutions because the sums involved can be quite substantial and the cash flow implications, significant.

There are a wide variety of plans that can be utilized as an alternative to the payment of premiums and passing on the risk or some significant portion of the risk to the carrier. The adoption of these plans is motivated either by financial considerations, such as the substantial premium cost of malpractice insurance or by the fact that carriers may be reluctant to insure certain types of risk.

The essential features of these plans are that they provide an increased cash flow to the institution and involve a greater assumption of risk by the institution. This latter characteristic causes the trustees to be reluctant to depart from the more traditional approach. But institutions have available to them both experience history and analytic tools with which to evaluate that experience, determining the frequency and severity of losses in probability terms, along with the pertinent considerations to determine retention requirements and make other necessary decisions in connection with a self-insurance program. These are essentially the same analytic tools that would be used by an insurance carrier. But this is a complex and specialized area where consulting assistance may be required.

An approach to self-insurance that has been used predominantly in the profit sector because of its tax avoidance features, but is beginning to be adopted by some institutions, is the use of a captive insurance company, either domestic or off-shore (e.g., domiciled in such locations as Bermuda, the Cayman Islands and the Channel Islands). This is a separate corporate entity formed to provide insurance coverage for its "parent," and third parties. Professionals in the field deem it inadvisable to use a captive unless there is also the intent to insure third parties. In the university sector, this raises issues of unrelated business income. Basically, the captive is a loss-retention vehicle. Identified advantages of the use of a captive are reduction of cost through elimination of unnecessary services or performance of services at less expense, funding of uninsurable or unreasonably priced coverages, and greater control and flexibility in respect to the insurance program. Disadvantages are principally the initial capitalization requirement and the incurrence of limiting company expenses (i.e., expenses associated with normal state requirements that filings must be through admitted carriers).

A prime advantage of a captive insurance company, vis-á-vis a strict self-insurance program, is improved access to reinsurance markets. Offshore captives have also been used to lessen or avoid the impact of cumbersome or restrictive state regulatory activity.

A self-insurance program, whether or not associated with the use of a captive insurance company, is likely to stimulate a greater awareness of the necessity for concentrated and systematic attention to the second major element in a risk management program which is loss prevention. As indicated in the discussion on Educational Law, it is possible to comprehensively identify areas of potential exposure associated with the range of college and university activities and to systematically analyze the potential frequency, severity, and likelihood of occurrence.

This analysis is very much a part of the analysis required to determine the most appropriate form of loss financing. The additional ingredient introduced here is the cost of preventive measures that may either reduce the potential of a loss occurrence or minimize its consequences. An important element in any loss prevention program is to induce academic and non-academic administrators to incorporate loss prevention concepts into the administration of their day-to-day activities. For example, does the Dean of Students or other appropriate university official, who is involved in preparations for a rock concert to be held in the campus stadium, give full consideration to all of the potential risk and liability implications and to what preventive measures might be necessary?

In the chapters on computers and on budgeting, the concept of a "chargeback" system is discussed in the context of a budgetary device for properly apportioning the costs of some types of support services. In appropriate instances, it is also an effective device for stimulating effective management. Risk management may be one such area. The apportionment of the costs of an insurance program as part of the operating costs of institutional department and activity centers may serve to make administrators more risk conscious. But whereas in the example of data processing support services it is important that the funds budgeted to a department for this purpose not be susceptible to transfer, it is precisely the potential for transfer to another budget line, or the reverse, that provides the incentive in the case of risk management.

Chapter Twelve

FINANCIAL REPORTING AND ACCOUNTING

Considerations such as increasing competition among institutions in the face of declining enrollments, heightened attention to financial conditions due to increased fiscal pressures and greater awareness of trustee responsibilities and liabilities in their stewardship of the institution, have resulted in a new focus on institutional accounting practices and on financial reporting as a management tool.

College and university accounting and financial reporting has been traditionally governed by accounting concepts reflecting not only the nonprofit character of these institutions, but also the special ways in which they obtain and must render an accounting for their funding support. Those not previously exposed to financial affairs of colleges and universities are frequently perplexed by the forms of accounting and reporting. A profit-making enterprise would normally be expected to utilize some form of cost accounting which permits such determinations as the overall cost of a product line or service in contrast to the income it generates, as well as the cost to provide additional increments of that product. College and university accounting does not normally utilize cost accounting concepts.

An exception to this should immediately be noted. There are instances, increasing in number, in which colleges and universities do engage in cost accounting. For example, the attempt to recover costs associated with federally sponsored activity (see discussion on Sponsored Activity) leads to the use of cost accounting techniques, albeit imprecise, to establish the cost, both direct and indirect, of that activity. But, for the present, at least, cost accounting is used only for special purposes.

FUND ACCOUNTING

The prescribed method used to account for and report on the financial condition of colleges and universities is fund accounting. This is a means of accounting for the disposition of funds by funding source with no specific focus on the effectiveness with which funds are put to use. Institutions receive support from a variety of donors and external funding sources which may place restrictions on when the funds may be used (e.g., a donor may stipulate that only the income from a gift may be expended), or for what purpose funds may be used (e.g., a gift may be earmarked for scholarships).

This poses something of a dilemma for institutions in regard to fund raising strategy. On the one hand, the institution is in the most favorable circumstance when it is free to use funds flexibly and without restriction. On the other hand, prospective donors are frequently most receptive to appeals that are aimed at their special interests (see discussion on Development).

The purpose of fund accounting is to evidence the manner in which the institution has discharged its stewardship responsibilities for the funds provided to it and to provide assurance that the funds have been preserved and expended in accordance with the special conditions imposed when they were provided. There are two principal reference sources on college and university fund accounting. They are *College and University Business Administration* (CUBA) published by the National Association of College and University Business Officers, and the *Audit Guide* published by the American Institute for Certified Public Accountants (AICPA).

The official description of fund accounting principles is contained in *College and University Business Administration*. It establishes the means by which the variety of restrictions pertaining to funds, whether externally imposed or imposed by the trustees, are systematically accounted for. Two guiding fund accounting principles are established. These are:

1. Accounts must be classified in balanced fund groups in the books of account and in the financial reports. Recommended fund groups include six categories: current funds, annuity and life income funds, loan funds, plant funds, endowment and similar funds, and agency funds. Other funds and subsections of these funds may be established when needed; and

2. All financial transactions must be recorded and reported by fund group.

The emphasis is, in both instances, on the treatment of each fund as a separate entity with no intermingling.

Current Funds are funds which are available for current operations, whether unrestricted or for special purposes, restricted by the donor or another provider of funds. The three major categories of current funds are:

- Funds available for general and educational purposes including: administrative staff; instructional staff; library system; maintenance and operations; student services; organized activities related to instructional departments; and sponsored and non-sponsored research;
- Funds for student aid;
- Funds for operation of auxiliary enterprises such as dining halls, bookstores, and so on.

Loan Funds are, as the term implies, available as loans to students, faculty, and staff. These funds may be provided from several different sources such as government appropriations, income from designated endowment funds and must be grouped by type. Additions to this fund group are not treated as revenue to the institution and are instead entered directly into the loan funds.

Endowment and Similar Funds are funds whose principal is non-expendable but is invested to generate income. Typically, endowments arise from gifts in which the donor specifies that the principal may not be expended until a certain date or until the occurrence of a specified event (term endowments) or in which expenditure of principal is indefinitely proscribed (perpetual endowment).

Trustees or governing boards may choose to voluntarily set aside otherwise unrestricted funds and limit the expenditures of principal. These are quasi-endowment funds, at one time called "funds functioning as endowment" and one of the objectives achieved in maintaining the separate identity of the three classes of funds is not only to insure that the restrictions are observed, but also to insure that the trustees are aware that the opportunity exists to modify the treatment of Board designated funds, where necessary by appropriate Board action. It is, in fact, the case that Boards have often failed to take advantage of this opportunity. Because endowment funds are a major fund source to many institutions (including many public institutions!) a number of significant subprinciples have been developed in connection with endowment fund accounting and management.

Annuity and Life Income Funds are those funds acquired by an institution subject to annuity contracts, living trust agreements, or gifts and bequests reserving life income to one or more beneficiaries. As emphasis is placed on deferred giving in institutional fund raising programs (see section on Development), it becomes increasingly important to adequately account for these funds and to make certain that the income is appropriately distributed and that donor stipulations are otherwise observed until the time when the fund becomes fully available to the institution. CUBA also requires that an actuarial determination be made to ascertain the split between the liability of the institution and the remaining fund balance available to the institution with the liability to be stated in present value terms predicated on life expectancy tables.

Plant Funds fall into four distinct categories:

1. Funds to be used in obtaining additional plant property;
2. Transfers from current funds for replacements or renewals;
3. Funds for debt service; and
4. Investments already made in plant properties.

These funds are generally derived from gifts and bequests, government appropriations, borrowings, special student fees, and transfers from other institutional funds. Plant properties are valued at cost (acquisition not replacement) and the depreciation concept is still rarely applied.

Agency Funds are funds in respect to which the institution functions exclusively in a custodial capacity, in other words, it merely serves to retain, dispense, and account for the funds. The most typical illustration of this custodial relationship would be student activity fees. But trustees and others concerned with the financial stewardship of the institution should be alert to the fact that both policy and liability considerations have led to changes in the handling of agency funds as a consequence of which institutions are not necessarily neutral, and at times, do exercise limited control over these funds.

The accounting system is to be maintained on an accrual basis, rather than a cash basis. As an example, in the case of a major purchase, an encumbrance system would decrease the funds available at the time of the issuance of the purchase order; an accrual system considers a legal obligation to have been incurred when the goods are received. A cash system decreases the fund balance only when the invoice is paid. From a budget management or expenditure control perspective, an encumbrance system might well be regarded as superior.

But it is important to constantly bear in mind that the efficacy of an accounting system can only be fairly evaluated in the context of its intended purposes. CUBA very explicitly declares that the determination of net profits and net worth is not only inappropriate for a non-profit institution of higher education, it is not even possible. The purpose of university accounting is, consequently, to provide a clear disclosure that stewardship obligations have been properly fulfilled.

Stated differently, college and university fund accounting and reporting, as it is presently structured, focuses primarily on whether funds are expended for the purposes for which they were provided and whether restrictions that may have been associated with the provision of the funds are properly observed. The focus is not, or has not been, on the relationship between income and expenditure, nor on the cost effectiveness of operations.

FINANCIAL REPORTING

In terms of financial reporting, three statements are deemed minimal for adequate reporting. These are:

1. A Balance Sheet;
2. Statements of Changes in Fund Balances for each fund and pertinent subgroup; and
3. A Statement of Current Funds Revenues, Expenditures and Transfers.

- *The Balance Sheet*—the recommended format for the balance sheet follows the account form with assets presented on the left and liabilities and fund balances on the right. Each fund (or subgroup within a fund) is balanced and totaled separately. No grand totals are accumulated. At least two funds must be divided into separately balanced subgroups. The current fund must disclose restricted data separately from unrestricted, and the unrestricted presentation may show the auxiliary enterprise accounts separately. The plant fund must be separated into an unexpended balances subgroup and an invested-in plant section. Unexpended balances may be further segregated into subgroups of funds for acquiring properties for renewal of and replacement of plant facilities and for debt services. Fund balance accounts within each fund or subgroup are often subdivided to reflect the distinct nature or source of the funds.

- *Statement of Changes in Fund Balances*—this statement explains the changes from the beginning fund balance by showing the additions and deductions during the year. Separate statements are prepared for each fund or subgroup within a fund. An alternative multicolumnar form, showing each fund or subgroup in a separate column may be prepared. When separate statements for each fund or subgroup are used, they are presented in multicolumnar form to disclose the significant elements of each fund balance separately. For example, unrestricted current funds have separate columns for allocated and unallocated portions of the balance.

- *Statement of Current Fund Revenues/Expenditures and Transfers*—this statement is roughly equivalent to the income statement in a commercial enterprise. However, it does not purport to show the results of operations. In fact, *College and University Business Administration* takes the position that since service, rather than profit, is the primary objective of an educational institution, no useful purpose would be served by an attempt to present the results of operations. What this statement does reflect are the changes in the current fund account. Since temporary borrowings among funds is permissible, a careful analysis of revenue and expenditures before transfers and a review of transfers themselves will help to make this statement more meaningful.

The nonaccounting professional, Trustee, President, Dean, etc. might look for the following information from these three standard documents in order to gain an overall perspective on the financial status of the institution:

1. Trends—one year to the next and over several years;

2. Percentage of total income derived from tuition and fees; governmental contracts, gifts, endowment income, auxiliary enterprises. How these percentages change over time and why;

3. Categories of expense and their percentage changes over time and why;

4. Amount of financial aid assistance, particularly in comparison to tuition and fee income; and

5. Income versus expenditures.

Exhibits 1–5, extracted from *College and University Business Administration,** illustrate the three types of statements. In examining the balance sheet one revealing area of comparison is the unrestricted cash balance in the current fund in contrast to the previous year. A diminishing balance may raise danger signals even if the overall financial condition of the institution appears to be healthy. An increase in accounts receivable raises another area of concern. How good are the University's collection procedures? To what extent may such receivables have to be written off eventually? What is happening to unrestricted current funds in contrast to current fund liabilities and to the restricted fund balance in contrast to unrestricted. The restricted fund balance is a direct result of development or fund raising activities, and if it is growing at too rapid a rate relative to the unrestricted, this suggests that not enough effort is being made to secure funds that can be freely used for general operations.

Endowment fund trends are significant because it is important that endowment fund income continue to contribute at least the same proportionate share of revenue. Quasi-endowment is also significant because it represents a potential source of flexible funds. Because of the importance of unrestricted fund balances, there is a need for institutional management to constantly focus on the restricted endowment and on quasi-endowment funds to insure that unneeded restricted funds are effectively used to meet the central purpose of the institution to avoid draining limited unrestricted fund balances. At the extreme cy-pres proceedings are available. This is a legal proceeding which provides relief from restrictions when circumstances have occurred which make fulfillment of the original intent of a bequest no longer tenable or practicable.

As noted earlier, the financial statements are particularly informative

---

* *College and University Business Administration,* Third Edition, NACUBO, 1974.

when read in conjunction with each other. An analysis of "due to's" and "due from's" is more apt than the balance sheet to provide a true indication of how the institution is using its funds and of potential areas of vulnerability. The Statement of Changes in Funds Balances adds another dimension of analysis and provides one perspective to constituents on relationships between activities and funding sources such as the relationship between tuition and fees and current educational and general expenditures.

Institutions, public as well as independent, are increasingly utilizing external audits, stimulated at least in part by external funding sources such as the federal government. The independent auditor examines and states an opinion on the financial statements, and also provides assistance, expert advice, and an independent point of view on accounting and fiscal problems.

The *AICPA Audit Guide* is the key reference document that governs the performance of independent audits and the rendering of auditors' opinions. The AICPA Statement on Auditing Standards No. 1* outlines four standards for the auditor's report.

1. The report shall state whether the financial statements are presented in accordance with generally accepted accounting principles;
2. The report shall state whether such principles have been consistently observed in the current period in relation to the preceding period;
3. Informative disclosures in the financial statements are to be regarded as reasonably adequate unless otherwise stated in the report; and
4. The report shall contain either an expression of opinion regarding the financial statements, taken as a whole, *or an assertion to the effect that an opinion cannot be expressed*. (Italics added by the authors.)

The inability to express an opinion is commonly referred to as a "disclaimer." Opinions may also be "qualified." Either circumstance should be a source of concern to readers of financial statements, since they may suggest the possibility that the financial statements do not fully and fairly reflect the disposition of institutional funds or even perhaps that some questionable accounting treatment raises an issue as to whether fiduciary responsibilities are being properly discharged. Since generally accepted accounting principles offer some latitude to the auditor in the resolution of doubtful questions, the inability to issue an unqualified opinion is not to be taken lightly.

Exhibit 1. Balance Sheet

June 30, 19___

With Comparative Figures at June 30, 19___

Assets

Current Funds

	Current Year	Prior Year
Unrestricted		
Cash	$ 210,000	$ 110,000
Investments	450,000	360,000
Accounts receivable, less allowance of $18,000 both years	228,000	175,000
Inventories, at lower of cost (first-in, first-out basis) or market	90,000	80,000
Prepaid expenses and deferred charges	28,000	20,000
Total unrestricted	1,006,000	745,000
Restricted		
Cash	145,000	101,000
Investments	175,000	165,000
Accounts receivable, less allowance of $8,000 both years	68,000	160,000
Unbilled charges	72,000	——
Total restricted	460,000	426,000
Total current funds	1,446,000	1,171,000

Loan Funds

	Current Year	Prior Year
Cash	30,000	20,000
Investments	100,000	100,000
Loans to students, faculty, and staff, less allowance of $10,000 current year and $9,000 prior year	550,000	382,000
Due from unrestricted funds	3,000	——
Total loan funds	683,000	502,000

Endowment and Similar Funds

	Current Year	Prior Year
Cash	100,000	101,000
Investments	13,900,000	11,800,000
Total endowment and similar funds	14,000,000	11,901,000

Annuity and Life Income Funds

	Current Year	Prior Year
Annuity funds		
Cash	$ 55,000	$ 45,000
Investments	3,260,000	3,010,000
Total annuity funds	3,315,000	3,055,000
Life income funds		
Cash	15,000	15,000
Investments	2,045,000	1,740,000
Total life income funds	2,060,000	1,755,000
Total annuity and life income funds	5,375,000	4,810,000

Plant Funds

	Current Year	Prior Year
Unexpended		
Cash	275,000	410,000
Investments	1,285,000	1,590,000
Due from unrestricted current funds	150,000	120,000
Total unexpended	1,710,000	2,120,000
Renewals and replacements		
Cash	5,000	4,000
Investments	150,000	286,000
Deposits with trustees	100,000	90,000
Due from unrestricted current funds	5,000	——
Total renewals and replacements	260,000	380,000
Retirement of indebtedness		
Cash	50,000	40,000
Deposits with trustees	250,000	253,000
Total retirement of indebtedness	300,000	293,000
Investment in plant		
Land	500,000	500,000
Land improvements	1,000,000	1,110,000
Buildings	25,000,000	24,060,000
Equipment	15,000,000	14,200,000
Library books	100,000	80,000
Total investment in plant	41,600,000	39,950,000
Total plant funds	43,870,000	42,743,000

Agency Funds

	Current Year	Prior Year
Cash	50,000	70,000
Investments	60,000	20,000
Total agency funds	110,000	90,000

Exhibit 2. Statement of Changes in Fund Balances Year Ended June

	Current Funds	
	Unrestricted	Restrict
Balances, July 1, 19___	$837,800	$ 355,1
Excess of revenues over expenditures and transfers	45,600	
Governmental appropriations		380,0
Endowment income		47,1
Gifts and grants		198,9
Sponsored research		1,351,5
Other sponsored programs		52,0
Other sources		3,1
Interest and investment income		
Income added to principal		
Accrued interest on sale of bonds		
Transfers from (to) other funds		(30,0
Additions to physical properties from—		
Current funds		
Unexpended plant funds		
Gains (or losses) on sales of securities		
Expenditures		(1,749,2
Refunds to grantors		(23,5
Expiration of term endowment	21,000	
Uncollectible notes charged off		
Death and teachers' cancellations		
Payments to beneficiaries and annuitants		
Bonds retired		
Note payments		
Interest paid		
Disposals of physical properties		
Balances, June 30, 19___	$904,400ª	$ 585,1

ª The Governing Board has allowed $125,000 of this balance for specifi

Note. If the multi-columnar fund balance statement is used, details o

balance sheet.

186

Loan Funds	Endowment and Similar Funds	Annuity and Life Income Funds	Plant Funds		Agency Funds
			Unexpended	Net Investment in Plant	
$383,180	$1,313,700	$223,300	$ 969,200	$25,178,900	$119,500
			600,000		
140					
36,400	33,000	10,000	75,000	20,000	
			10,000		36,700
4,200		11,700	27,000		
	3,000				
			3,000		
4,000	103,000	(3,000)	416,800		
				80,000	
			(651,400)	651,400	
	14,700	(1,000)	500		
			(187,200)		
	(21,000)				
(1,160)					
(460)					
		(13,000)			
			(112,500)	112,500	
			(15,000)	15,000	
			(70,000)		
				(73,400)	
$426,300	$1,446,400	$228,000	$1,065,400	$25,984,400	$156,200

rating purposes.

year end fund balances (as illustrated in Forms 4 through 13) should be shown in the

Exhibit 3. Statement of Current Fund Revenues, Expenditures, and Other Changes
Year Ended June 30, 19___

| | Current Year | | | Prior |
	Unrestricted	Restricted	Total	Year Total
Revenues				
Tuition and fees	$2,600,000		$2,600,000	$2,300,000
Federal appropriations	500,000		500,000	500,000
State appropriations	700,000		700,000	700,000
Local appropriations	100,000		100,000	100,000
Federal grants and contracts	20,000	$ 375,000	395,000	350,000
State grants and contracts	10,000	25,000	35,000	200,000
Local grants and contracts	5,000	25,000	30,000	45,000
Private gifts, grants, and contracts ...	850,000	380,000	1,230,000	1,190,000
Endowment income	325,000	209,000	534,000	500,000
Sales and services of educational activities	190,000		190,000	195,000
Sales and services of auxiliary enterprises	2,200,000		2,200,000	2,100,000
Expired term endowment	40,000		40,000	
Other sources (if any)				
Total current revenues	7,540,000	1,014,000	8,554,000	8,180,000
Expenditures and Mandatory Transfers				
Educational and general				
Instruction	2,960,000	489,000	3,449,000	3,300,000
Research	100,000	400,000	500,000	650,000

	Unrestricted	Restricted	Total	Total
Public service	130,000	25,000	155,000	175,000
Academic support	250,000		250,000	225,000
Student services	200,000		200,000	195,000
Institutional support	450,000		450,000	445,000
Operation and maintenance of plant	220,000		220,000	200,000
Scholarships and fellowships	90,000	100,000	190,000	180,000
Educational and general expenditures	4,400,000	1,014,000	5,414,000	5,370,000
Mandatory transfers for:				
Principal and interest	90,000		90,000	50,000
Renewals and replacements	100,000		100,000	80,000
Loan fund matching grant	2,000		2,000	
Total educational and general	4,592,000	1,014,000	5,606,000	5,500,000
Auxiliary enterprises				
Expenditures	1,830,000		1,830,000	1,730,000
Mandatory transfers for:				
Principal and interest	250,000		250,000	250,000
Renewals and replacements	70,000		70,000	70,000
Total auxiliary	2,150,000		2,150,000	2,050,000
Total expenditures and mandatory transfers	6,742,000	1,014,000	7,756,000	7,550,000

Other Transfers and Additions/(Deductions)

	Unrestricted	Restricted	Total	Total
Excess of restricted receipts over transfers to revenues		45,000	45,000	40,000
Refunded to grantors		(20,000)	(20,000)	
Unrestricted gifts allocated to other funds	(650,000)		(650,000)	(510,000)
Portion of quasi-endowment gains appropriated	40,000		40,000	
Net increase in fund balances	188,000	25,000	213,000	160,000

Exhibit 4. Liabilities and Fund Balances

Current Funds

	Current Year	Prior Year
Unrestricted		
Accounts payable	$ 125,000	$ 100,000
Accrued liabilities	20,000	15,000
Students' deposits	30,000	35,000
Due to other funds	158,000	120,000
Deferred credits	30,000	20,000
Fund balance	643,000	455,000
Total unrestricted	1,006,000	745,000
Restricted		
Accounts payable	14,000	5,000
Fund balances	446,000	421,000
Total restricted	460,000	426,000
Total current funds	1,466,000	1,171,000

Loan Funds

	Current Year	Prior Year
Fund balances		
U.S. government grants refundable	50,000	33,000
University funds		
Restricted	483,000	369,000
Unrestricted	150,000	100,000
Total loan funds	683,000	502,000

Endowment and Similar Funds

	Current Year	Prior Year
Fund balances		
Endowment	7,800,000	6,740,000
Term endowment	3,840,000	3,420,000
Quasi-endowment—unrestricted	1,000,000	800,000
Quasi-endowment—restricted	1,360,000	941,000
Total endowment and similar funds	14,000,000	11,901,000

Annuity and Life Income Funds

	Current Year	Prior Year
Annuity funds		
Annuities payable	$ 2,150,000	$ 2,300,000
Fund balances	1,165,000	755,000
Total annuity funds	3,315,000	3,055,000

	Current Year	Prior Year
Life income funds		
Income payable	5,000	5,000
Fund balances	2,055,000	1,750,000
Total life income funds	2,060,000	1,755,000
Total annuity and life income funds	5,375,000	4,810,000

Plant Funds

	Current Year	Prior Year
Unexpended		
Accounts payable	10,000	——
Notes payable	100,000	——
Bonds payable	400,000	——
Fund balances		
Restricted	1,000,000	1,860,000
Unrestricted	200,000	260,000
Total unexpended	1,710,000	2,120,000
Renewals and replacements		
Fund balances		
Restricted	25,000	180,000
Unrestricted	235,000	200,000
Total renewals and replacements	260,000	380,000
Retirement of indebtedness		
Fund balances		
Restricted	185,000	125,000
Unrestricted	115,000	168,000
Total retirement of indebtedness	300,000	293,000
Investment in plant		
Notes payable	790,000	810,000
Bonds payable	2,200,000	2,400,000
Mortgages payable	400,000	200,000
Net investment in plant	38,210,000	36,540,000
Total investment in plant	41,600,000	39,950,000
Total plant funds	43,870,000	42,743,000

Agency Funds

	Current Year	Prior Year
Deposits held in custody for others	110,000	90,000
Total agency funds	110,000	90,000

Exhibit 5. Schedule of Current Funds Revenues

Year Ended June 30, 19___

	Total	Unrestricted	Restricted
Educational and General			
Student Tuition and Fees			
Tuition	$ 893,600	$ 893,600	
Laboratory	29,600	29,600	
Incidental	15,400	15,400	
Extension division	25,500	25,500	
	$ 964,100	$ 964,100	
Government Appropriations—			
State government	$2,426,100	$2,126,000	$ 300,100
Federal government	261,900	200,400	61,500
	$2,668,000	$2,326,400	$ 361,600
Endowment Income	$ 39,000	$ 12,000	$ 27,000
Gifts—			
Alumni	$ 341,500	$ 332,200	$ 9,300
Churches	31,600	21,600	10,000
Foundations	65,400	60,800	4,600
Industrial	7,400		7,400
Other	26,800	26,800	
	$ 472,700	$ 441,400	$ 31,300
Sponsored Research—			
Federal government agencies	$ 631,000		$ 631,000
State agencies	377,000		377,000
Private sponsors	200,000		200,000
	$1,208,000		$1,208,000
Other Separately Budgeted			
Research	$ 61,000	$ 61,000	

Exhibit 5. continued

	Total	Unrestricted	Restricted
Other Sponsored Programs—			
State agencies	$ 15,000		$ 15,000
Federal agencies	12,000		12,000
Private sponsors	10,000		10,000
	$ 37,000		$ 37,000
Recovery of Indirect Costs—			
Sponsored Programs—			
Federal agencies	$ 25,000	$ 25,000	
State agencies	5,000	5,000	
	$ 30,000	$ 30,000	
Sales and Services of			
Educational Departments—			
College of Education	$ 24,400	$ 24,400	
Engineering testing materials	18,800	18,800	
	$ 43,200	$ 43,200	

As an illustration, a teaching hospital may have elected to self-insure for malpractice liability and may have set up a reserve for that purpose. Such a reserve should be supported by an analytic study. The absence of an appropriate analytic basis would be the occasion for a qualified opinion in which the auditor would be indicating that in the absence of appropriate analytic support there is no reasonable way to determine whether the reserve is adequate, inadequate, or excessive.

As the concern about the financial condition of colleges and universities mounts, so too is there a growing concern about the adequacy of fund accounting and the associated financial reports.

In a study on university financial reporting* Fritzemeyer and Snyder concluded the following:

- Forty-one percent of the published university financial reports are unaudited and such reports have a greater incidence of noncompliance with recommended practices, for example 22 percent of the unaudited reports are on the cash basis;
- Less than half of the financial reports contain supplemental statistical and financial highlight information, with a higher proportion of audited reports containing this type of information than unaudited reports;
- A significant proportion of audited reports, eight percent, use an unacceptable accounting principle of such consequence as to require a qualified opinion;
- Less than half the reports, both audited and unaudited are in compliance with the recommended classification of current funds revenues and expenditures;
- A significant portion of reports, both audited and unaudited, do not show an equalization of restricted current operating funds revenues and expenditures.

One can reasonably conclude from the foregoing that there is a clear potential for improved financial reporting by colleges and universities. Trustees and other constituents, as their interest in the affairs of the institution becomes more intense, are concerned as to whether the financial reports presented to them by the institution are sufficiently comprehen-

*Fritzemeyer, J. R. and Snyder, G. E., "The Present Status of University Financial Reporting" published in portfolio, *NACUBO Business Officer*, September, 1978.

sive and presented with sufficient clarity to permit them to truly understand the current circumstances of the institution and to evaluate trends in terms of their potential impact on the institution.

Some business officers, on the other hand, are concerned about information demands, not only because of the burdens they impose which many institutions are ill equipped to meet, but also because of the concern that more information will encourage trustees and others to attempt to involve themselves in the details of day-to-day operations. There is, at present, no clear agreement as to the areas or level of operating detail which should be immune from "outside interference." For example, there is a wide variation in the degree of involvement in collective bargaining negotiations by trustees, state agencies, and others. At one extreme, the administration will have full authority to negotiate and will have the latitude to make the necessary adjustments within budget to accommodate the results of the negotiation. At the other extreme, the administration will have no active role in the negotiation. (See discussion on Collective Bargaining.)

One of the accounting treatment issues that is the subject of increasing discussion is depreciation accounting. Federal cost principles governing reimbursement under grants and contracts currently permit the application of a use allowance to assets in lieu of depreciation.

Since such allowance can be collected in perpetuity, it obviously bears no relationship to the useful life of the asset or even to its cost or value (although it is calculated against acquisition cost). The use allowance is not a popular concept with those responsible for federal costing policy and there is reason to believe that, as in the case with the Medicare Cost Principles, depreciation will ultimately be mandated in connection with federally sponsored activity.

As a general practice, colleges and universities have not historically utilized depreciation accounting. A few institutions do not even reflect their investment in plant assets on their books. Increased discussion on depreciation has been stimulated in part by the revelation of a very substantial degree of deferred maintenance among institutions. (In 1977 a study highlighted that over $22 billion in new funds was needed to provide for the major renovation and repair needs occasioned by the cumulative effects of deferred maintenance.)

This has prompted some observers to suggest that institutions adopt depreciation accounting, as a means of reflecting the diminished value of the assets. A separate but related issue pertains to the possible funding of depreciation as one means of accumulating funds for needed renewal, replacement or expansion of physical plant.

In the *AICPA Audit Guide* and in the 1974 edition of *College and University Business Administration* provision is made for the recording of depreciation in plant funds, but not for any charge which would result in an addition to the cost of operations in current funds.

It is questionable whether the original cost of buildings, some of which may be over 100 years old, has any relevance to the cost of current operations, and consideration must be given to the fact that the cost was funded from special sources, such as federal, earmarked capital fund drive donations, and state appropriations. Additionally, if it is the desire to fund major renovation, repair, or replacement from current funds, the impact on current revenues and expenditures must also be recognized and it is likely that a tuition increase will be required.

But, on the other hand, some institutions believe that the advantages of charging current funds with depreciation outweigh the disadvantages. At one institution a use charge is levied against current fund operations for costs associated with plant fund use. The use charge consists of current year interest on long-term debt, plus an amount equal to current year depreciation of plant assets. The annual charge is assigned to operating activities on the basis of space occupied, and is paid to the plant fund in cash. In turn, the plant fund meets requirements for debt service renewals, as replacements, and supports the cost of internally-financed construction projects. However, it is also important to note that this practice not only reflects the way in which this particular institution perceives its future needs, but also its current financial circumstances.

What this type of discussion reflects is more than a concern over some technical aspect of accounting. It is more broadly a concern about the relationships among financial accounting and reporting and the patterns of financing post secondary education in the context of today's economic environment. In respect to physical plant, it has been the tradition that major expenditures for physical plant have been financed predominantly by private philanthrophy, federal grant, or state appropriation.

It seems evident that these sources of funding will, at a minimum, not be abundantly available. But the need for major plant expenditures will continue, not so much for expansion, as for modernization, adaptation to new purposes, and modification such as reducing energy costs. A related, but separate problem is that which is associated with deferred maintenance.

The broader question raised in discussions such as those related to depreciation accounting is as to whether present financial accounting and reporting tends to bring costing and financing issues into sharp enough focus to facilitate informed financial management decision-making.

In this context what is being called for is a broader range of internal reports and information, both financial and non-financial, for management purposes, than is now routinely disseminated to administrators and trustees. Among the elements that would appear to be necessary, the following can be cited as illustrative:

1. Historical trend data. Aside from what has occurred during the year, what has happened to the financial condition of the institution over time?

2. Narratives that describe and explain the reasons for and significance of particular data; e.g., is a shortfall in endowment fund income, as originally budgeted, a reflection of a change in investment policy, unpredicted market conditions, or some other circumstance? What are its consequences for the overall income projections and for the budget?

3. Non-financial statistics and data. Increasingly trustees are being furnished this data, sometimes in response to their demands, but frequently at the initiative of administrators in order to provide a context for financial information and a basis for making meaningful decisions regarding the future of the institution. For example, consider what is happening to enrollments, in absolute numbers, in diversity of students, in academic levels of students (S.A.T. scores, etc.) in retention rates; what are faculty trends, such as in regard to tenure and rank distribtuion, salary levels, retention rates, research and other accomplishments? What is happening to tuition measured in terms of frequency of increases, as a proportion of income, and in relationship to scholarship funds?

4. Comparative data from other institutions. Business officers and others involved in university administration are appropriately concerned about the potential use of comparative data for invidious comparisons. The complexities and variations among institutions are such that one must indeed be wary of comparing a statistic (e.g., tuition rates, the cost of the food service operation, faculty compensation levels) at institution A and institution B without having a full appreciation of

the myriad conditions that may give rise to the difference. Nonetheless, it is only natural that those concerned with the condition of the institution will seek some benchmarks for assessing the trends at their institution by looking at what is happening to other peer institutions. Faced with that natural tendency, college and university administrators may find it desirable to gather and selectively distribute such information at their own initiative, accompanying it with appropriate cautions as to how it can be used and, indeed, as to which other institutions may appropriately be regarded as peers.

An adequate internal reporting system is necessary for effective management and control. Control over any given item is a function of the lowest level in the organizational structure with authority and responsibility for the incurrence of that cost, and to assure the best control each level must be kept advised of its operational status.

In substance, the internal reporting format should resemble a responsibility accounting system which identifies the levels where a cost is controllable and permits evaluation of performances at each level. Reports would disclose on a regular basis how effectively resources are being controlled and utilized to carry out the actions for which budgeted resources were made available. Progress reports would show specific kinds of information, useful in administration and decision-making, such as the operations of restricted current funds, sponsored research projects, or construction projects. Special project reports would be prepared as needed. In addition to the detailed reports for each budget unit, summary reports should be prepared for the appropriate administrative officers for review and any necessary action.

Possible Reporting System

The following report formats *illustrate* a four-level responsibility reporting system that has proved effective.

Fourth Level—This report, which is illustrated in Figure 1 is to be prepared for the lowest identifiable budget unit; an academic department within one of the schools, for example, or an administrative office within the general administration, or the bookstore within the auxiliary enterprises. A separate report showing each expense item within a unit, together with its annual budget appropriation, budget prorated to date, actual expense to date, and the variance, is prepared for each budget unit. Although it does not account for encumbrances or unencumbered balances, as *College and University Business Administration* recommends, it could be adapted to include such recommended procedures. The totals from these reports are carried over to the level three reports, and become line items there.

A University Responsibility Expense Report

Department_____

Item	Current Month	Annual Budget	Budget Expired	Actual Year to Date	Variance
Salaries and Wages:					
Academic					
Technical					
Clerical					
Etc.					
Total Salaries and Wages					
Travel and Subsistence:					
Employee Travel					
Entertainment					
Total Travel and Subsistence					
Equipment Purchases					
Supplies and Other:					
Office and General					
Postage					
Honorarium					
Staff Benefits					
Etc.					
Total Supplies and Other					
Charges to Other Departments (Cr.)					
Total Department Expense					

*Also referred to as Department Report and Cost Center Report.
Frequency—Monthly.
Distribution—Department heads and their immediate supervisors.

Figure 1. Fourth Level Report.*

Third Level—An illustration of this report appears in Figure 2. A report is prepared for each minor organizational group, such as a school or a college, totals for each of the budget units in the group are brought forward from the fourth level reports, and the total budget-expenditure picture for the group is shown. It is prepared monthly, as are the other three reports.

A University Summary of Responsibility Expense Report

Organization	Current Month	Annual Budget	Budget Expired	Actual Year to Date	Variance
College of Arts and Sciences: Office of the Dean Classics Etc. (14 departments in total)					
Total					
School of Business Administration Office of the Dean Etc. (55 departments in total)					
Total					
Etc. (14 additional groupings)					

*This report is a summary of responsibility expense report totals within each organizational grouping. It should summarize the totals from each group of responsibility report, so that subtotals can be directly related to the second and first level reports. Frequency—Monthly.
Distribution—Deans and key administrative personnel.

Figure 2. Third Level Report.*

Second Level—Two basic differences are reflected in the format of the report. The report itself shows totals of revenue and expense for the major organization group, and is supported by individual supplementary schedules, showing the revenue and expense of each minor group within the major one. Since this report incorporates revenue into both the pri-

A University Statement of Revenue and Expense
Undergraduate and Graduate

Direct Revenue:	Annual Budget	Budget Expired	Actual	Variance
Tuition and Fees				
Grant and Contract				
Overhead Recovery				
Endowment Income				
Gifts				
Student Aid				
Sales and Service				
Other				
Total Direct Revenue Line #1				
Direct Expense Line #2				
Funds Available for Indirect Expense Line #3				
General Revenue:				
Endowment Income				
Gifts				
Other				
Total General Income Line #4				
Total Funds Available Line #5				
General Expense Line #6				
Net Funds Available for University Line #7				

School of Business Administration

	Annual Budget	Budget Expired	Actual	Variance

*Statement of Revenue and Expense for each income-producing segment within the organization.
Frequency—Monthly.
Distribution—President and Vice Presidents. Parts of level 2 may be distributed to Deans.
Note: This side of the report will be made up of individual sheets on a ring binder, so that each sheet can be reviewed against the totals to which it applies.

Figure 3. Second Level Reports.*

A University Statement of Revenue and Expense

Total University

Direct Revenue:	Annual Budget	Budget Expired	Actual	Variance
Tuition and Fees				
Grant and Contract Overhead Recovery				
Endowment Income				
Gifts				
Student Aid				
Sales and Services				
Other	_____	_____	_____	_____
Total Direct Revenue	Line #1	_____	_____	_____
Direct Expense	Line #2	_____	_____	_____
Net Funds Available for University	Line #3	(Line #1–	Line #2)	_____
General University Expense:				
Physical Plant				
Administration				
Student Development				
Inter-Dept. Charges (Cr.)	_____	_____	_____	_____
Total General University Expense	Line #4	_____	_____	_____
Net Result of Operations	Line #5	(Line #3–	Line #4)	_____

MEDICAL AND DENTAL SCHOOLS

	Annual Budget	Budget Expired	Actual	Variance

*Statement of Revenue and Expense for the University in total and for each income-producing segment within the organization.
Frequency—Monthly.
Distribution—President and Vice Presidents.
Note: This side of report will be made up of individual sheets on a ring binder so that each sheet can be reviewed against the totals to which it applies.

Figure 4.   First Level Reports.*

mary report and its supporting schedules, this means that the data brought forward from the level three reports must be supplemented with revenue information. Also, both revenue and expense are classified into direct and indirect categories on the primary report to provide a two-step contribution reporting format. One indicates the margin available after direct revenue minus expense, and the other shows the margin for general purposes after indirect items of the major group. Figure 3 illustrates this form.

Information for preparing the second and first level reports is given following Figure 4. It will be noted that level two reports include only income-producing organizational groups or segments.

First Level—This report is prepared for the entire university in basically the same format as level two reports, with schedules for each major organizational group supporting the primary report. The contribution margin each major group gives to the university is applied against university indirect expenses, and the difference reflects the net results of operation. First level reports are illustrated in Figure 4. *This reporting system is designed for current funds only.*

EXPLANATION OF DATA IN FIGURES 3 AND 4

Income-producing segments are defined as:

- Undergraduate and graduate schools
- Medical and dental schools
- Law school
- Hospital
- Auxiliary enterprises

The explanation will be related to the undergraduate and graduate schools, but it applies to each of the income-producing segments.

The report is designed to show revenue and expense information for the undergraduate and graduate schools in total and to explode this total into the individual schools within the undergraduate and graduate schools. These schools might include the following:

- College of arts and sciences
- School of business administration

- School of foreign service
- School of language and linguistics
- Graduate schools
- School of nursing
- Summer school

With regard to the descriptive information in the left column:

- Direct revenue is all revenue that can specifically be identified with an individual school and any auxiliary enterprise (such as bookstore or dormitory.)
- Direct expense is the total expenses of the responsibility centers organizationally assigned to an individual school within the undergraduate and graduate schools.
- Funds available for indirect expense represent the difference between direct revenue and direct expense. It is a key line in the evaluation process. It identifies those income-producing areas where financial problems may exist. It is the key to deciding which areas should be analyzed in detail to determine the specific activities that require immediate management attention.
- General revenue is the revenue that can specifically be identified with the undergraduate and graduate schools, but cannot be specifically identified with the individual schools within the undergraduate and graduate schools.
- Total funds available is self-explanatory.
- General expense. Same description as for general revenue.
- Net funds available for university identifies the funds that each income-producing segment is providing to cover the "general university expense."

The areas to be explicated within the remaining income-producing segments are as follows:

- Medical and dental schools
    Medical
    Dental
- Law school

- Hospital
- Auxiliary enterprises
    - —Printing
    - —Bookstores
    - —Dormitories
    - —Food service
    - —Pay parking

Early in this chapter two principal reference documents were identified: *College and University Business Administration* and the *AICPA Audit Guide*. There is a third very important document that should be referred to before concluding this discussion. Late in 1978 a monograph was published culminating over 18 months of joint effort by the National Association of Business Officers and the Association of Governing Boards. This was an effort of major significance dealing with the financial responsibilities of Governing Boards and in the process focusing on background information that allows Board members to see the context in which decisions are made, describing financial policy issues of concern to Governing Boards and providing illustrations of financial data useful to Governing Boards. This monograph is likely to be significantly influential in setting a pattern for reporting to Trustees.

It is axiomatic that decisions are only as good as the information on which they are based. As those associated with the management of our educational enterprise are confronted with increasingly critical decisions regarding the future health and viability of their institutions, we may expect an increasing emphasis on information systems and on the rendering of meaningful financial management reports.

Chapter Thirteen

COST ANALYSIS, BUDGETING AND PLANNING

Accounting conventions and techniques must be oriented to the objectives intended to be served. It is, therefore, important to understand what given techniques can and cannot accomplish and to periodically assess whether what is capable of accomplishment is sufficient to meet current objectives.

In the earlier discussion on fund accounting it was pointed out that fund accounting is intended to enable institutions to evidence that the funds provided to them have been expended for the purposes for which they were provided and, more broadly, that all conditions and restrictions associated with the provision of these funds have been observed.

Since the above statement reflects what has been the traditional objective of accounting for colleges and universities, it is no criticism of fund accounting to say that it does not serve other objectives. More pointedly, fund accounting was never intended to reflect whether funds were spent wisely or efficiently nor was the intent to provide a means to clearly identify the cost of specific programs or operations, although, as was noted, in the earlier discussion, colleges and universities have had to utilize cost accounting techniques in certain specialized areas. For example, federal support for research is preponderantly on a cost reimbursement basis.

Few knowledgeable observers will be inclined to dispute that the characteristics and capabilities of fund accounting are no longer fully adequate to meet the accounting needs that confront colleges and universities today.

Among the things that fund accounting does not and was not intended to do are:

- It does not highlight the relationship of resources to programs;
- It does not deal with the relationship between direct and indirect activities;
- It does not evaluate the impact of capital investments or expenditures on current programs; and
- It does not fully reflect organizational expenditure authority.

An economic climate in which even the most prestigious and amply endowed institutions have been struggling to overcome or avoid annual operating deficits, has created the need for additional techniques to assist institutions in husbanding and allocating resources so as to enable them to fulfill their missions within the limitations of their financial means or to determine that financial limitations compel a reassessment of mission.

COST ANALYSIS

It is in response to this changed and still changing economic climate and the demands imposed by it that techniques such as cost accounting or cost analysis have been the focus of increased attention. This has been a source of profound concern to many college and university business officers. Their concern stems not from a failure to recognize the imperatives in today's environment that call for these techniques. Their concern is rather that these imperatives are so strong that they will encourage development and utilization of costing techniques in a manner that is injudicious and insufficiently sensitive to the complexities of the university environment. They are concerned that a focus on costs by constituents will inevitably invoke invidious comparisons that are invalid unless they fully consider all of the factors that account for differences.

Colleges and universities are labor intensive environments in which faculty compensation is a major element of current operating costs. Colleges and universities are also joint product environments such as the classic illustration, cited in the section on sponsored research, of the physician in a teaching hospital with a university faculty appointment who is treating a research patient while being observed by a group of medical students and hence is engaged in teaching, research, and patient care simultaneously. Hence, there can be a certain element of arbitrariness in the allocation of a substantial portion of operating costs. There can also be a wide variation in the cost of instruction among purportedly similar institutions based on such facts as the manner in which the institution is organized, the financial circumstances and sources of funding that may give rise to certain requirements for cost allocation, and the quality of instruction.

The enlightened business officer does not eschew the use of costing techniques which are probably essential to survival in today's environment. Rather, he voices his concerns to avoid incautious and indiscriminate use of these techniques. It is against the background of such concerns that current techniques should be viewed.

The most comprehensive and definitive examination of cost analysis in higher education can be found in the four volume "A Study of Cost Analysis in Higher Education"* by Carl R. Adams, Russell L. Harkins, and Roger A. Schrader. The study was funded by the Ford Foundation and sponsored by the American Council on Education. Its major segments include: The Literature of Cost and Cost Analysis in Higher Education; The Production and Use of Cost Analysis in Institutions of Higher Education; Site Visit Descriptions of Costing Systems and Their Use in Higher Education; and The Future Use of Cost Analysis in Higher Education.

Some of the observations and conclusions from this study bear citation:

- Over the years there has been almost a fixation with average costs. Issues of management costing, responsibility accounting, and managerial cost accounting have been virtually ignored;
- The literature contains very little discussion of the use and utility of cost analysis. The role of costing information in decision-making has not been addressed;
- There has been very little reporting of empirical studies or of application successes and failures; and
- The literature has not provided a basis for classifying the differences in internal institutional information needs as opposed to the information needs of persons or agencies outside the institution.

It is perhaps appropriate to pause at this juncture and to ask the questions: What is cost analysis and what utility does it have? There are a

---

*"A Study of Cost Analysis in Higher Education," Carl R. Adams, Russell L. Harkins, and Roger A. Schrader, The American Council of Education, 1978.

variety of definitions of cost analysis in use. One generalized definition would be that cost analysis seeks to deal with the relationships between a specific objective (i.e. a product or service or output) and the resources required to attain that objective.

The broadness of that definition encompasses a number of concepts related to cost analysis. It embraces the concept that an examination of historical costs can or should be useful to predict future costs. It embraces the concept that a structured examination of costs in conjunction with a value analysis can assist in cost-benefit trade off decisions. It embraces the concept that the manner in which resources are marshalled and directed toward achieving the desired objective bears on whether the objective is being achieved in a *cost effective* manner.

It could also embrace other cost analysis concepts such as inputed cost, which is the cost of resources that are foregone because one alternative was selected rather than another. Economists also use the term opportunity cost to express this concept. Finally, but not all inclusively, it embraces the concept that costs need to be examined in terms of differences in cost behavior. That is, the amounts and kinds of resources necessary to achieve a particular objective can vary at different times, in different settings, and in different circumstances. An example of the latter, that might be termed downside rigidity, is that generally the incremental addition to the cost associated with a workload addition will be somewhat greater than the incremental reduction in cost when that same amount of work is eliminated.

The difficulties in measuring outcomes, and in ascribing resources to particular objectives in a joint product environment and the complexities of cost behavior in higher education render cost analysis an imperfect tool which must be used with considerable sensitivity, discretion, and judgment in connection with internal decision-making and which has limited utility for comparison among institutions.

Among the variety of cost analysis techniques that can be identified, one form of categorization would identify full costing, variable costing, and standard costing. Standard costing has little utility for or application to the educational environment. It relies on the establishment of predetermined costs and places strong emphasis on variance analysis to focus on the reasons for significant departures from the originally planned allocation of resources. The use of the budget as a control mechanism in some universities has certain analogies to standard costing.

The closely linked concepts of the variability of costs and marginal or incremental costs are useful and even important. But their potential for providing a basis for decision-making or action in the short run is nonetheless quite limited. The former concept says that, at a given point in time, costs have differing degrees of flexibility that can be identified on a rank from fixed to variable. A fixed cost will presumably be unaffected by a change in activity in the short run whereas a variable cost will fluctuate or has the *potential* to fluctuate in direct relationship to the pattern of activity.

It is particularly to be noted that the concept of cost variability is significantly time oriented. For example, the tenured faculty member who retires converts his compensation cost from fixed to variable thus providing the institution with the option as to whether to replace him. It is immediately apparent that the time line introduces another important characteristic to the concept of variability and that is convertibility. Different fixed costs become convertible to variable costs at different points in time.

This is perhaps a more significant analytic tool for institutional administrators than simple or unqualified variability analysis. While undoubtedly, institutions will have to respond to exigent short run circumstances and should have an analytic basis for such response, the capacity to respond adequately is limited and the longer run analysis of cost relationships is of much more importance to the viability of the institution.

Marginal cost, it should be noted, is more circumstance than time oriented. To illustrate, the scheduling of an additional class could involve, under circumstances where sufficient classroom space is available, virtually no operations and maintenance costs because all that is involved is the use of a vacant classroom for possibly three hours a week. By contrast, if classroom space is fully and optimally used, the scheduling of another class would require the creation of additional classroom space (e.g. by conversion of existing space, rental, and so on).

Clearly institutional administrators need to engage in both short term and long term analysis and can be assisted in doing so by employing, selectively, thoughtfully, and discriminatingly, a number of different cost analysis techniques. A shortfall in enrollment can produce an income shortfall that calls for an immediate response. Variability and marginal cost analysis can assist in identifying the potential for reducing costs and hence the quantification of the amount that must be sought from other income sources to make up the shortfall.

The full costing approach is one that requires that all costs both direct and indirect associated with an activity be identified. This approach to cost analysis is probably the most widely used technique in higher education and is regarded as the most fruitful.

The most ambitious and most widely accepted attempt at full cost analysis in higher education is being made by the National Center for Higher Education Management Systems (NCHEMS). Its initial effort was to develop a set of standard definitions and procedures for collecting information about disciplines and student degree programs, outcomes of instructional programs, and general institutional characteristics. The orientation of this approach termed Information Exchange Procedures (IEP) was, as the title suggests, to facilitate comparisons among institutions. It was, for this reason, appealing to state officials who were seeking to "get a handle" on the costs of their public institutions and to the federal government because of the cost of education allowance associated with fellowship grants and other reasons.

The costing component of IEP was tested during 1972–73 by a group of about 60 institutions and evaluated by the Costing Standards Committee of the National Association of College and University Business Officers (NACUBO). The evaluative comments were quite critical and resulted in a joint project by NCHEMS and NACUBO funded by the United States Office of Education to develop revised procedures for determining historical full costs. A report was published in September, 1977 but a further revision is now in process. This document in contrast to the IEP stresses cost information for internal management, rather than for information exchange.

The procedures associated with this full costing approach call for:

- Developing an activity structure;
- Developing an instructional workload matrix;
- Crossing over current fund expenditures to the activity structure;
- Calculating direct instructional discipline unit costs;
- Calculating direct student program unit costs;
- Allocating indirect costs;
- Calculating full unit costs; and
- Analyzing components of cost information.

Significant deficiencies, both in respect to the efficacy of the costing information as data for internal management, and for use on a comparative basis, are readily acknowledged by those associated with development of the procedures. They cite as a caveat, in regard to comparability, the illustration of two institutions reporting data for their graduate-level chemistry disciplines. Differences in purpose will inevitably result in non-comparable data, although the data has the prima facie appearance of comparibility; one may be training high school chemistry teachers and the other training students to be research chemists.

The NCHEMS procedures do not purport to deal with the issue of quality, clearly a major measurement consideration. In 1975, NACUBO published a paper entitled *Fundamental Considerations for Determining Cost Information in Higher Education* subsequently incorporated in Chapter 4:5 of NACUBO's *Administrative Service* in which they made the following cogent statement on quality:

"In commercial organizations, cost generally can be assigned to well-defined and measurable products or services. In higher education, however, the services of instruction, research and public service, may not be measurable or separable in terms of units of output. For example, the instructional process produces an output sometimes referred to as an acquired body of knowledge; however there is no consensus on how to measure the acquired knowledge as an output. (It should be noted that there is a growing emphasis on seeking ways to adequately measure acquired knowledge as a means of evaluating institutions) Full-time equivalent students, student credit-hours, student contact hours, student headcount, student major by level, and degrees awarded are examples of costing units of service used to measure the instructional process in lieu of output measures. These units are not measures of quality or efficiency."

NACUBO has also set forth in this chapter 12 costing standards. These are:

- The purposes for which cost information is to be used should determine work within which cost information is developed
- Cost information should be based on the accrual method of accounting
- Cost data should be reconcilable to official accounting data
- Non-financial data should be reconcilable to official institutional records
- Definitions used in cost determinations should be applied uniformly
- Cost information and related costing units should cover the same period
- Cost information should be consistently determined

- Cost should be attributed to a cost objective based on a crucial or beneficial relationship
- Indirect cost should be allocated based on quantitative measures that can be applied in a practical manner
- Common cost incurred to provide two or more services should be allocated in an equitable manner
- Capital cost of a cost objective should reflect the applicable expired capital cost of the period
- Cost information should be accompanied by a disclosure statement

Underlying *any costing system* in higher education is the recognition that faculty costs constitute the single largest cost component and also constitute a primary base for the allocation of other costs. Attendant to this recognition is the necessity for faculty activity analysis. As noted in the discussion on federally sponsored activity, research institutions have been singularly unsuccessful in accomplishing meaningful faculty activity analysis, for reasons which include faculty attitudes and the fact that as noted on several occasions, their efforts produce joint products. Faculty activity analysis has been the most abrasive issue in the administration of federally sponsored research. The difficulties in apportioning faculty costs in non-research institutions are perhaps different in degree, but not in substance.

This is not to say that cost analysis techniques are without value. The point is rather that the costing imprecisions that are endemic to the academic institution and its activities should lead us to: avoid engaging in overly elaborate analyses in the vain hope of attaining precision; be sensitive to the manner in which we use cost data being ever mindful of its limitations; and finally, and perhaps most importantly, be certain that the purpose to be served is always uppermost in our thoughts, when we engage in cost analysis—and that the technique used is appropriate to that purpose.

Subject to these caveats it is clearly desirable that cost oriented decisions with significant cost implications, such as setting room and board rates, setting tuition rates, changing course requirements, and accommodating an enrollment decline, be made utilizing such cost analysis tools as are available in preference to ignoring the cost implications or treating them superficially. There are gross analyses, which can be made with available cost analysis techniques that can be quite useful. For example, a state university used unit cost data and faculty activity analysis to gain a better understanding of the appropriate support level for its social science programs. Cost data comparisons with several institutions served to confirm the perception that, relative to other disciplines, undergraduate social sciences are consistently low cost disciplines and, hence, should not be compared to dissimilar disciplines on a single campus. This tends to illustrate that even in the dangerous area of comparison, certain gross comparisons among institutions can have high utility.

BUDGETING

The budget process is a critically important element of higher education management. In discussing the budget it is necessary to begin with some general observations and then deal with specific procedures.

As used generally, the budget is a means by which resources are allocated to permit the accomplishment of one or more objectives. But with rare exceptions, the budget development process in higher education is essentially incremental and, hence, does not normally contemplate a reallocation or redistribution of resources, either in the short term or in the long term when the budget becomes the long-range plan.

Instead, there tends to be an annual examination in which the impact of projected salary and wage increases (clearly the most significant cost element in this labor intensive environment), and other increases reflected in the budgets of the various cost centers, is considered in relation to income projections. In instances where expenses are anticipated to exceed income, several alternatives are considered.

In the past, a frequently encountered alternative was to incur a deficit. Other possible alternatives are to seek a means of increasing income (such as through a tuition increase) or to seek a means of reducing costs. Such cost reductions have frequently been sought in the areas that have the least political sensitivity. For example, as noted earlier, colleges and universities have engaged in a dangerous degree of deferred maintenance.

The process may be more elaborate, but what has been described is the essence of what, in many instances, takes place. In a profit making environment, the budget is necessarily more dynamic because of its relationship to sales and to varying levels of production. In the college and university environment, the conditions during the course of a budget year are considerably more static. Consequently, the budget is or should be a control mechanism which is used to monitor the manner in which resources are utilized and the rate at which they are being expended. A potential increase in expenditures or shortfall in projected income should be signalled at a sufficiently early point in time to allow for administrators to react.

The budget process that does not effectuate a periodic reassessment of resource allocation decisions and that also fails to deal with variations from the projected budget until year end is a virtually meaningless process. But, in many instances, the budgetary process at an institution is deficient in both respects, despite the fact that the process may be a fairly elaborate one. It might be well at this point to describe a real life example of a process utilized at one major institution.

The process is projected to begin in October, culminating with a final budget plan to be submitted to the Trustees in March. But the process also contemplates tentative budget decisions for a four-year period. The steps in the process include the following:

1. Establishment of general planning variables and constraints. Based on alternative recommendations, the President, in conjunction with the Vice Presidents, will be expected to have made policy decisions on:
   a) A projection of FTE enrollments;
   b) Tuition increases—i.e., establishment of a tentative maximum level;
   c) Salary increases;
   d) Staff benefits;
   e) Projection of utility and fuel inflation; and
   f) Projected gift income.
2. Departmental base budget analysis—in this step departments are asked to submit a base budget analysis and an adjusted base budget request analyzed in terms of two major issues:
   a) What is the specific impact of the projected enrollment trends on each department? The intent is to correlate the general planning assumption regarding enrollment levels with the analysis by individual departments of future base resource needs;
   b) What is the potential for savings from increased efficiency or productivity in the department?
3. Requests for new or expanded programs and quality improvement and reactions to possible unanticipated improvements in the budgetary situation. This is intended to provide a basis for an ordering of priorities in the event that it becomes possible to exceed the base budget.

4. Identification of present programs or activities of the department which can be reduced or deferred in the event that there are:
   a) Budgetary shortfalls in determining the base budget;
   b) Unanticipated serious financial problems at the university after the budget is approved.
5. The budget review process is the final step before presentation of the budget plan for trustee approval. It involves a consolidation of departmental budget requests by the Office of Budget and Planning during the course of which those requests will be reviewed, questions raised and responded to, and unresolved questions brought to resolution through a meeting among the Vice President for Finance, the Vice President who has jurisdiction over the department in question and their supporting staff. The result of the review process is a working budget plan document which presents a refined set of budget options to the President and the Vice Presidents.

The procedure outlined briefly above presents a reasonably representative illustration of a thoughtful approach which attempts to introduce some structure to the budget process, attempts to focus responsibility on the various cost centers to consider some overall budgetary constraints in their planning on a basis consistent with that of all other departments, and attempts to identify alternative courses of action under varying circumstances of a tight or liberal budget.

It is possible to go beyond the kind of procedures described above to achieve a greater degree of systemization and structure in the budget process and to bring together the concepts of cost analysis and budget development. One such approach that has gained prominence in recent years is zero base budgeting.

Zero Base Budgeting

Zero base budgeting is, when used with care and thoughtfulness, a very useful analytic technique. There is too ready a tendency in some quarters to dismiss this and other highly structured techniques, as they apply to higher education management, as mere gimmickry, particularly when they are introduced in a manner which suggests that they will solve all of the institution's problems.

There is rarely an indisputably "right decision" in the college and university environment. More often, decisions of consequence involve choices from among apparently viable alternatives. Consequently, no technique has the intrinsic capability to automatically produce the "right answer." The political process within an institution—using the term in its broadest sense—will continue to be the most influential force in the making of priority trade-off decisions. That is, the power relationships among those within and external to the institution who influence decisions and the dynamics of the decision-making process have more to do with outcomes than the analytic or evaluative techniques employed.

Nonetheless, the structure and the discipline introduced by a technique such as zero base budgeting can make an invaluable contribution to the decision-making process. It forces a systematic and orderly focus on the questions that have to be answered. It compels an explicit ordering of priorities and it requires that advocacy of a specific program or objective be supported by a clearly articulated rationale.

The distinguishing feature of zero base budgeting in contrast to traditional budgeting techniques is that the latter tend to assume historically incurred cost levels as a given and involve the incremental addition of costs due to such factors as inflation and expansion in the scope of activities. Zero base budgeting, which is both a planning and budgeting technique, is premised on the concept that if resource allocation decisions are approached de novo (as if the institution were starting afresh, with no commitments), it is likely that the self-perpetuating tendencies of existing programs and activities will at least be partially overcome by the necessity to justify all costs, not merely those to be added above the previous year's level.

The two key elements in the zero base budgeting concept are the development of decision packages and their prioritization. Both are critical. The decision package must state the purpose of an activity *and also* must identify the appropriate measure of performance for the activity, cost and benefits, consequences of not performing the activity, and alternative courses of action for accomplishing the same purpose.

The requirement to rank activities in order of priority, to evaluate those activities in cost-benefit terms, and to specifically identify the consequences of abandoning those activities suggests, referring to the discussion on cost analysis, that this is one of the most potentially fruitful techniques for overcoming the vested interest resistance to changes and reductions. While such changes and reductions may ultimately be centrally mandated, their imposition is facilitated by the fact that the analytic basis for the onerous decision has been developed by those directly impacted by it. At a minimum, the requirement to consider alternate means of accomplishing the desired objective will provide a strong incentive to responsibility centers or cost centers to develop more cost efficient approaches as an alternative to being compelled to reduce or abandon programs or activities.

Highly compatible with, but separate from, the zero base budgeting approach is another budgetary approach that has come to be known as "every tub on its own bottom." The concept calls for responsibility or cost centers to be assigned a budget which would normally include both direct and indirect costs and asks them to consider the income which they generate in support of their activities in the budget planning process.

This approach to budgeting provides an incentive to responsibility centers to contain costs and to generate income since a normal component of the system is that responsibility centers can accumulate reserves to be used to improve quality and to initiate new programs. Some responsibility centers will inevitably require subsidization from the central administration because their potential to generate income through tuition, gifts, and other sources is more limited. Despite the necessity for subsidization, such responsibility centers may be responsible for programs which are of vital importance to the mission of the institution. But it is clearly important that institutional administrators be fully aware of the extent of the subsidization if intelligent planning and informed trade-off decision-making is to take place.

PLANNING

Planning can be one of the most critical aspects of higher education management and at the same time has generally been one of the most neglected. Few institutions have attempted to project and analyze external and internal trends and their interrelationship with a sufficient degree of sophistication and discrimination. For example, it has been widely recognized that the traditional college-age group (18 to 24 year olds) will decrease nationally between 1980 and 1985 by about 4.1%. But while it is important for institutions to be aware of this general trend in their planning, they must also be conscious that this will be an uneven process and must consequently make a more discriminating determination of the impact on their specific circumstances.

During this period six states will maintain or slightly increase this college age population. On the other hand, in some states the cumulative decline from 1976 to 1985 will exceed 25%, and clearly the impact within states and upon specific institutions within states will also be uneven. Similarly, although approximately ten percent of today's college students is over age 35 and the potential market of older students has been estimated as anywhere between 32 and 19 million people, institutions need to evaluate the implications and ramifications of these statistics in the fullest context and with particular reference to their own circumstances.

In order to suggest some of the implications of the planning process as an aspect of higher education management, there will be some brief introductory discussion, including a reference to simulation; a focus on mission assessment and reassessment, including the necessity for considering innovative techniques and, finally, a discussion on retrenchment planning.

When budgeting is considered within a time line extending beyond one year, frequently five and rarely more than ten, the budget process becomes the planning process. The planning process that takes place over an extended time period inevitably involves variations and uncertainties substantially greater than those encountered in developing a budget for a single year. Because it also contemplates the possibility of phased changes, the planning process, if it is differentiated from the budget process, introduces an added dimension of complexity.

For this reason, sophisticated attempts at planning have involved the development of computerized simulation models. Simulation makes it possible to operate the institution, or part of it, on a computer for a period of time and thereby to test alternative courses of action. The basic idea in simulation is to abstract from a real-life situation certain characteristics that, when assembled in a model, reproduce the actual conditions. The test of the model is how closely it approximates the results that would be obtained in real life. Alternative values can be introduced into the model in successive runs and comparative results obtained without having to rely on real-life experimentation.

Colleges which have developed and successfully utilized such models include Westminster and Morris Brown among others. Because of its far greater complexity the university presents a much greater challenge in simulation. Stanford University appears to have successfully met that challenge with a model, which they call TRADES. This model is driven by several forecasting submodels, each of which is dependent upon the values of a set of primary planning variables controlled by the model user. In its most detailed version TRADES can display 50 income, expense, and asset categories projected for up to 25 years.

MISSION ASSESSMENT AND REASSESSMENT

The planning process that fails to embrace a mission assessment and reassessment, in the context of changed and changing circumstances, is as limited in utility as the budget process that is purely incremental.

In a society that is increasingly consumer oriented, those who are concerned with college and university administration need to recognize that the service of higher education is being evaluated by parents and prospective students, legislators, and the general public in the context of the question "How do educational needs get served at the lowest cost?"

This is not only a question of cost effectiveness. It is more fundamentally a question of the mission of the institution and the educational product that it has to offer. Enrollments are declining because of such factors as diminished population growth, rising tuition costs, and the disenchantment or disillusionment of a college age generation that can no longer view higher education as an automatic path to financial success and "the good life." Institutions that have an acknowledged reputation as high quality institutions are experiencing a "show rate" or "conversion rate" (the ratio of enrollments to acceptances) of as low as 40%. Attrition rates among institutions of higher education are alarmingly high.

Under these circumstances it is incumbent upon institutions of higher education to engage in what for many is a painful self-evaluation. Prideful academics will be inclined to say "this is what we are and have stood for as an institution for many years and those who share the same values will continue to flock to our doors." Pragmatically, a concern for the survival of the institution suggests that all but a handful of highly prestigious, very amply endowed institutions, cannot afford the indulgence of this attitude. They must instead ask themselves "What is our marketplace, meaning what segment of the population do we expect to draw from for our student population? What are the educational needs of our prospective students as they perceive them? Which institutions are competing in our marketplace? What is the special product that we have to offer our prospective students? What is it that makes us unique or special?"

The self-evaluation process should normally be an integral element of long-range planning. The introduction of a marketing perspective means that those charged with governance of the institution will ask not only "how can our educational goals be achieved most effectively?" But also, "to what extent are these goals still relevant? What are the things we do well as an institution and what are the things that we do less well?" It would be difficult to overemphasize the need to sharply focus on such questions as "what is it that makes us special, and what is it that we do particularly well?" Institutions becoming acutely conscious of competitive pressures may make the serious error of attempting to emulate the competition rather than emphasizing and strengthening the particular attributes that make the institution attractive to its segment of the market and which are in fact intrinsic to its identity.

The decisions that can result from this kind of analysis, given the nature of the environment, can be more profound and traumatic than for the corporation that considers the prospect of abandoning an unprofitable product line.

There are indeed some critical philosophical issues to be resolved. At the extreme, few thoughtful observers would argue that the fundamental components of a classic liberal education should be abandoned in favor of courses in driver education. But the growing emphasis on nontraditional education and continuing education needs to be considered by any institution engaged in a meaningful evaluation of its role, and the question must be raised as to whether vocational preparation is not a component of the mission of an institution that seeks to prepare its students to function effectively in today's society.

Illustration—A small liberal arts college with a long and distinguished tradition, loyal alumni, dedicated faculty, a very attractive faculty-student ratio and an idyllic campus setting found itself to be in severe financial straits. A variety of solutions were called for and undertaken, the most major of which was to introduce a number of career oriented programs. This, in turn, involved an evaluation of faculty secondary skills in order to utilize existing faculty in connection with the new programs. The enrollment increase attributable to these measures was prompt and dramatic.

Unfortunately, the self-evaluation process cannot consist merely of adding new programs, it involves a pruning process as well. Spiraling educational costs and the attendant burdens of high tuition are compelling institutions to focus on how to become more cost effective. There are meaningful opportunities to reduce and contain costs in the support areas, but clearly 70% or more of the cost lies in the area of academic program. Despite strong resistance, there is an increasing tendency to examine relationships between the cost of programs and the income they generate. Establishing programs or schools as self-sustaining cost centers, i.e., "every tub on its own bottom" has become an increasingly popular trend. This is not to say that a cost-benefit analysis that is strictly dollar oriented is being engaged in.

It is generally recognized that the "money makers" such as the law school and the school of business will continue to subsidize the "non-money makers," both in terms of tuition income and contribution to endowment. But historically, administrators have not known, cared or dared to examine the extent of this subsidization. When it is determined through analysis that a given program is being heavily subsidized and statistics reflect that there is a minimal student demand for the program, it is time to ask whether that program is indeed endemic to the mission of the institution. While the judgment on the latter question will be affirmative in some instances, leading to the justifiable retention of "unprofitable programs," other programs will inevitably be discontinued when the financial consequences of retention are perceived as sufficiently critical to offset the political problems associated with abandonment.

Innovative Approaches

Coupled with the necessity for mission assessment and reassessment is the necessity for considering innovative approaches that will assist in offsetting some of the negative trends and emphasize fuller and more effective use of institutional resources. The term innovative, when used in this context, is intended merely to connote a departure from current practices at a particular institution. Approaches that will be listed have all been "tried and tested"—some of them extensively. Indeed, it would require considerable temerity for an institution to adopt an untried innovation, despite the obvious fact that each of the practices now current had to be tried some place for the first time. What should be emphasized in considering innovative approaches, is that they must be subjected to thoughtful and critical evaluation to determine which have relevance and value to the particular circumstances of the institution. Subject to that general caveat, a representative compendium of innovative approaches would include, but not necessarily be limited to:

Appealing to students other than the usual 18–21 year old group—"non-traditional" students would include: mature adults, senior citizens, women returning to college and the work force, public servants, military, police and fire personnel who retire early from one career and are ready to begin a second career, the very bright high school junior or senior, the handicapped, prison inmates, individuals hospitalized for long periods, individuals interested in or forced to change careers, and public servants.

Changing the traditional time and place of teaching—early morning, evenings, weekends, better use of summer school, teaching away from the campus in libraries and other public buildings, on trains and commuter buses, on planes, at vacation resorts and camps, in convalescent and nursing homes, in places of employment, shopping centers, prisons, military bases, hospitals, and in individual homes through television.

Emphasizing different teaching methods, technology, and programs—more emphasis on: "university without walls"; independent study; linkages to television programs, cassettes, records, microfilms and microfiche, filmstrips—all of which can be utilized at home, at locations other than the main campus, and on the campus; cooperative education; internships; three year or five year programs; junior year abroad or at another university, academic credit for accomplishments of an intellectual and academic nature outside of the college classroom; credit for qualifying examinations and noncollege courses or training. There might be more and better combinations of undergraduate and graduate programs emphasizing interdisciplinary approaches and shortening the length of study. There could be greater emphasis on general education, quantitative skills, "hands on" experience with computers, continuing education, professional refresher and certificate type programs, special training programs for college graduates such as legal assistants, and cooperative education programs.

Sharing of resources—two or more institutions could share space, equipment, laboratories, staff, special facilities such as computers or theaters. They could join together in regard to joint buying or insurance to reduce costs and in joint research projects, joint lobbying, cultural efforts, and so on. These joint efforts could, but need not, take place within a broader consortium agreement.

Community service programs—can include: academic and training courses for public employees or those employed in local industry at their workplace; providing training in occupational safety and health; offering cultural, recreational, athletic, language laboratory, public affairs, library facilities for general community use; offering various types of seminars, classes, programs and speakers on campus or at community locations; providing various types of clinics for the public; offering expert advice to government, business, labor and industrial organizations; participating as an institution and as individuals identified with the institution in various community activities and organizations.

Improved student recruitment—attracting more students through scholarship programs based on achievement, as well as need, (recognizing that outstanding students such as National Merit Scholars attract other students to the institution) and through loan programs extending well beyond graduation; attracting students through more creative marketing approaches including campus visits and weekend stays, meeting with administrators and professors and attending classes and college activities, using current students actively in attracting new students. More emphasis could be placed on utilizing alumni in recruiting potential students. Reduced tuition could be offered if two or more individuals of the same family are attending the institution (two children, a child and a parent).

Services to students—concern for dormitory living arrangements; apartments rather than the usual dorm room; more options in regard to the food service; better psychological and career counseling service and job placement services; better orientation programs and study skills programs with emphasis on peer counselors as well as professional counselors; indicating a sense that professors and administrators are accessible, supportive, and interested; concern for a wide range of activities available to all students—whether intramural sports, recreational, cultural, or entertainment activities; contact with alumni to build a sense of continuity and tradition; programs to prevent dropouts such as early warning signals and intensive counseling, following up on those who don't re-register, academic "amnesty" permitting a student not doing well in one major to switch to another; follow up on those who have dropped out to urge them to return.

Retrenchment Planning

Separate from, but related to, mission assessment and reassessment is retrenchment planning. For the sake of emphasis, it might be well to suggest that the terms retrenchment plan should be viewed as synonymous with disaster plan. What is connoted is that the institution has reached, or is reaching, a state of financial exigency such that survival of the institution is at issue. Presumably aggressive and comprehensive efforts have already taken place to increase revenues and reduce and contain costs without sufficiently alleviating the deteriorating financial position. At this stage, what is necessary is a very painful and demanding process that goes beyond mission reassessment and focuses on the issue of how and in what ways can an institution scale down and cut back while still remaining vital.

The focus of this discussion is intended to be that retrenchment planning means that the development of a long-range plan should encompass retrenchment considerations and planning, as contrasted with awaiting the necessity for retrenchment action. This would mean that the institution would need to identify a series of "early warning signals" that would indicate the potential necessity for retrenchment actions if projected trends continue. This would also mean that the institution will need to have considered and determined in advance the kinds and extent of retrenchment actions that could potentially be required and that would not be overwhelmingly traumatic or represent so drastic a change as to be tantamount to closing the institution.

Explicit in these considerations is the further evaluation as to whether the projected condition of the institution after retrenchment actions, as related to projections of the external and internal conditions which gave rise to the necessity for retrenchment, will be such that the institution can reasonably be expected to survive. It is a sad, but increasingly frequent reality (see chart on private college openings, closings, and mergers and accompanying discussion) that closing of an institution is one of the alternatives that must also be incorporated into the planning process.

Accordingly, when it can be projected that the institution's financial situation will continue to deteriorate, despite retrenchment actions, retrenchment might nonetheless be called for. But it will be recognized to be a holding or delaying process during which time an orderly transition in closing the institution will be planned for and effectuated. It is evident that the projections and considerations relative to the issue of retrenchment planning are sufficiently complex and demanding that simulation modeling can be a highly effective tool, even for the small institution and, because of their complexity and political sensitivity, retrenchment actions can often be facilitated through the use of outside assistance.

Among the "early warning signals" that need to be considered as possible indicators of the need for retrenchment are the following:

1. Continuing enrollment declines overall, in certain programs, and increasing percentage of enrollment in high cost areas;

2. Decline in applications, in those admitted, and in conversion rate of those who applied and in those who meet present academic standards;

3. Continuing cash flow problems;

4. Continuing depletion of reserves including negative balances in reserve funds;

5. State and/or private aid insufficient to meet changes in cost;

6. Decline in dormitory occupancy;

7. Increasing difficulty in meeting debt service and interest charges;

8. Decreasing amount of unrestricted current and quasi-endowment funds;

9. Decreasing value of endowment funds per FTE (full-time equivalent) student and in percentage contribution of endowment income in regard to the institution's budget;

10. Increased percentage of receivables in relation to total charges and increasing amount of total receivables;

11. Increasing amount of payables;

12. Greater reliance on and use of interfund borrowing from current funds for plant expenditures and to meet working capital requirements for unrestricted current funds;

13. Increasing amount and percentage of student aid funded from the institution's own general operating resources rather than from other sources, rising percentage of student aid expenditures to total revenues from student tuition and fees;

14. Decline in teaching loads, in average number of students per section, in student-faculty ratio; rising number of course sections in relation to the number of full-time equivalent students;

15. Insufficient funds to deal with normal operations including energy costs and maintenance, and growth in deferred maintenance;

16. Increases in tuition and fees approaching or having passed the point where the "competitive" position of the institution is endangered;

17. Inability to compete, because of lack of funds, in scholarships and promotional efforts for new students;

18. Inability to significantly reduce size of staff or costs of operation;

19. Aging of facilities and equipment and many substandard facilities—with no reserves to upgrade or replace these facilities;

20. A high percentage of tenured faculty;

21. Increased rate of turnover of staff, particularly those considered outstanding, and increased difficulty in recruiting quality faculty and staff;

22. Declining growth in contributions from alumni, corporations, and other sources of gifts;

23. Declining growth in funded research;

24. Increasing dependence on tuition and fees income or on state subsidy;

25. Auxiliary enterprises failing to break even in current operations or failing to provide reserves for plant improvements, refurbishments, etc.;

26. Unfavorable change in the ratio of current unrestricted to current restricted funds, with the former decreasing as a percentage of the total and perhaps in absolute terms.

Various studies have been performed in regard to identifying institutions in distress, encompassing a consideration and a weighting of various combinations of the aforementioned factors. But for effective corrective action to take place on a timely basis, distress should be predicted well in advance of occurrence.

Given the nature of the academic environment, it can be predicted that the identification of an imminent distress situation will be disputed and retrenchment actions staunchly resisted. Latent and explicit rivalries and hostilities will surface or become more severe as various elements seek to forestall retrenchment action as it will impact on them, either by hoping or searching for a deus ex machina or aggressively advocating more drastic action in some other sector of institutional activity. For example, those resisting retrenchment may hold forth the prospect of securing increased state aid—whether the institution be public or private. Faculty may resist faculty reductions (within the context of "financial exigency") by referring to extravagance in entertainment, the President's home, athletics, and support staff.

It is in large part because of the anticipation of strong resistance that details regarding retrenchment planning and implementation must be incorporated into the planning process to enable timely and decisive action to take place. The alternative is to deal with financial distress in an untimely, frantic, emotional, and generally ineffectual manner, which is apt to exacerbate rather than ameliorate the financial crisis.

The formidable challenges confronting higher education clearly impose management demands that could not have been imagined twenty years ago. In the face of those demands, sophisticated techniques in cost analysis, budgeting, and planning need to be examined, with full sensitivity to their limitations, but with a view toward assessing their potential utility for improving management effectiveness.

Chapter Fourteen
THE ROLE OF AUDIT

There is a growing tendency among colleges and universities, public as well as private, to utilize both internal auditors and public accounting firms. In the case of the public institution, the state auditor normally serves the function that would otherwise be performed by a public accounting firm. But in an increasing number of cases the state auditor is contracting with a public accounting firm or authorizing the university to do so.

Internal auditing is a staff function that serves management by reviewing the accounting, financial, and other operations of the institution. Organizationally, this function has traditionally been the responsibility of the chief financial officer. But some institutions have assigned reporting responsibility for this function to the office of the Executive Vice President, the President, or the trustees in order to enhance independence.

College and University Business Administration, the fundamental guide to business administrative procedures governing higher education, published by the National Association of College and University Business Officers, explains that the activities of the internal auditor should be directed toward:

1. Determining that the system of internal control is adequate and functioning;
2. Ensuring that institutional policies and procedures are being followed;
3. Verifying the existence of assets shown on the books of account, and ensuring the maintenance of proper safeguards for their protection;
4. Preventing or discovering dishonesty; and
5. Determining the reliability and adequacy of the accounting and reporting system and procedures.

To accomplish the internal audit functions in a fully effective manner, a formal written program for the internal auditing operations should be prepared to define the extent and frequency of the review of the financial and business operations of the institution. The program should include, but not necessarily be limited to, provisions for examination of cash receipts, cash disbursements, payrolls, construction accounts, maintenance activities, inventories, and investments.

On the issue of independence, *College and University Business Administration* does not call for a reporting relationship outside the financial management organizational structure. In fact, it recommends that this function should be the responsibility of the chief business officer. But it further states that the internal auditor should not be assigned line responsibilities and should not engage in any activities that he normally would be expected to review and appraise. *College and University Business Administration* also states that the governing board should "require" an audit by independent certified public accountants who are qualified by training and experience to audit the accounts of educational institutions. The function of the independent auditor is defined to include an examination of the financial statements, as well as bringing to the business office assistance, expert advice, and an independent point of view on accounting and fiscal problems.

The American Institute of Certified Public Accountants has outlined four standards of reporting, all of which are applicable to colleges and universities. These are:

1. The report shall state whether the financial statements are presented in accordance with generally accepted accounting principles;
2. The report shall state whether such principles have been consistently observed in the current period in relation to the preceding period;
3. Informative disclosures in the financial statements are to be regarded as reasonably adequate unless otherwise stated in the report; and
4. The report shall contain either an expression of opinion regarding the financial statements, taken as a whole, or an assertion to the effect that an opinion cannot be expressed.

In essence, the "attest" function, which is still fundamental to the role of the auditor, involves a certification that the manner in which financial transactions are processed and recorded accords with generally accepted accounting principles, and that the financial statements fairly present the financial condition of the institution. There are growing pressures to make such statements more meaningful and informative, and the trustees should particularly focus on whether the financial statements and supplementary reports provided to them yield a sufficiently clear picture as to the condition of the institution. With growth in automation, auditors must have the skills to audit computerized records. Public accounting firms are continuing to expand their skills in this area.

Beyond the "attest" function, an extremely important ingredient has been added to the role of the auditors. The growing concerns about the stewardship of the institution and whether its resources are being properly managed, has given special impetus to expansion of the normal scope of audit to include an operational audit. The operational audit is directed toward the broad objective of assisting in the improvement of financial management. This is accomplished by alerting institutional administrators to the breakdown of operational controls, by pinpointing areas for cost reduction, suggesting potential operating improvements, and by pointing out where deficiencies or lapses in the implementation of functional responsibilities in various areas have significantly affected these areas.

A product of this expanded audit is the management letter. This letter should address the effectiveness of internal systems for the budgeting, allocation, and management of resources and make recommendations for the correction of perceived weaknesses or deficiencies.

The broad experience that public accounting firms possess in performing audits of such diverse entities as banks, insurance companies, hospitals, and industrial concerns, as well as a variety of educational institutions, creates a frame of reference in respect to varying financial and operating conditions that permits the firms to bring a highly useful perspective to the audit and to their management recommendations. The quality of the management letter is one key measure of the audit services the institution is receiving.

Issues of disclosure and confidentiality, as they relate to audit reports and management letters, are highly sensitive and complex and need to receive the thoughtful consideration of trustees. These issues have been brought into even sharper focus in the so-called "sunshine" states which have mandated that the affairs of public entities be conducted with full disclosure to the public.

It is fair to say that even in the non-public sector there is a heightened awareness of the necessity for adequately informing all constituents and the public in general. (See Chapter 2 on Consumerism.)

The responsibility that this imposes in regard to audit reports and management letters in particular is to adopt thoughtfully conceived procedures that permit institutional management to be fully informed by auditors on all matters that should properly come to the attention of management, while also adhering to the spirit of full disclosure in respect to the public.

This may well mean that some matters formerly treated with confidentiality because of their sensitivity and complexity may now be subject to broader disclosure. The wider and more diverse audience will require that these matters be treated much more expansively in order to reduce the likelihood that they will be taken out of context, misinterpreted, or misunderstood.

Concurrent with the trend toward and increasing improvement of operational audits has been the growth in management consulting divisions among the major public accounting firms. This is not mere coincidence. The major public accounting firms have found that they serve their audit clients most effectively when they function as full service organizations. As colleges and universities have become more complex and diverse and as the tools and techniques utilized to manage their operations have become more sophisticated, the range of functional specializations and the role of the functional specialist have expanded. In this context the consultant facilitates the audit in two ways.

First, the consultant can provide specialized expertise that will assist in providing analytic and meaningful management letter comments and recommendations. Second, the consultant provides a resource to which the institution can turn for specialized assistance in implementing recommended improvements.

As noted in the chapter on the Use of Consultants, there has been considerable discussion on the issue as to whether public accounting firms can provide consulting services without impairing their independence. Without question, both the accounting profession itself and these institutions and organizations which it services must be alert and highly sensitive to any circumstances, creating a potential conflict of interest or otherwise threatening to diminish the integrity of the audit. But the profession believes, as do other professions such as the medical and legal profession, that the primary means of insuring integrity is through the self-policing mechanisms employed by the profession.

There are some very demonstrable values associated with the provision of consulting services to institutional audit clients by public accounting firms. The specialized knowledge and pragmatic experience of consultants, coupled with the awareness that they may be called upon to assist in implementing management letter recommendations, makes it more likely that these recommendations will be meaningful and realistic. Too often in the past auditors have been criticized by their clients for making recommendations that were "text book" in nature and not realistic or readily implementable.

The consultant who serves an audit client is also likely to be far more effective and cost efficient because he can draw upon the auditor's knowledge of the institution, its operations, *and* its personnel. Additionally, and perhaps most significantly, the continuity of the ongoing audit relationship tends to lend an element of responsibility and responsiveness to the consulting relationship. The consultant who serves an audit client is not apt to "write and run."

As in most aspects of college and university administration, the procedures utilized in selection of public accounting firms for the performance of audits vary widely among institutions.

Among the factors that should normally be considered in the selection of an auditor, is whether the firm being considered has experience in auditing institutions of similar size, nature, and complexity. If such expertise is not available in the local office, the institution should assure itself as to whether it will be provided by transfer of a partner or senior staff member from another office, who has the requisite experience, or through other means. The availability of specialized skills that can provide a convenient and reliable source of support should be another consideration. The institution will want to have the principal staff members who will participate in the audit identified in advance, since the element of personal chemistry is always an ingredient where professional services are involved.

There is an observable distinction in the practices of public and independent institutions although, as in all other areas, a generality as to a practice that is characteristic of a particular category of institutions suggests that the practice is widespread, but not universal. Subject to that qualification, independent institutions tend, more generally, to feel that they have the latitude to select the firm best suited to their needs, even if that firm has not submitted the lowest fee quotation. Their selection procedures will reflect this emphasis through the attention they pay to other factors.

By contrast, fee will probably be a predominant criterion in the public sector. The emphasis on fee in the public sector is not confined to audit services, but is more broadly reflective of a general approach to contracting for personal services. It is a manifestation, not so much of the absence of latitude to make a selection on grounds other than fee, as it is the perceived inability to make a meaningful distinction among bidders on other grounds.

Accounting firms, in common with other professionals, do not believe that all firms are alike, and indeed it is clear that they are not. Self-policing mechanisms such as the recently introduced peer review procedures, which involve reviews of one public accounting firm by another, unquestionably tend to insure a certain consistency in quality and professionalism. But individual firms nonetheless have unique characteristics and special qualifications that are particularly suited to the specific needs of particular institutions.

Perhaps accounting firms have no alternative but to respond to a market, or one segment of a market, that seeks to treat them as all alike. But they must bear some responsibility as a profession for submitting to a competition on such terms.

Many institutions that engage public accounting firms as auditors have a trustees audit committee. In other instances, selection of an audit firm and interaction with it is a function of the Finance Committee and sometimes of the full Board. The method of handling this is not necessarily based on the size of the institution, but is more likely to be influenced by the size of the Board and whether the trustees are generally organized to conduct their affairs through the committee mechanism.

There is a growing appreciation of the value of an audit committee as an instrument of control as well as a means of enhancing the quality and acceptability of financial reporting practices. While audit committee practices will necessarily continue to vary significantly from institution to institution, certain issues of policy and procedures are universal:

- What relationship should the committee establish with the independent auditors?
- What kind of information should the committee seek from independent auditors?
- What information should the committee seek from the internal auditors?
- How intensive should the committee's investigations be?
- What staff and facilities can audit committees use to accomplish their purposes and how should operations be organized?

- What functions can audit committees perform aside from reviewing the annual independent audit? For example, should they be involved in the budgeting process?

Among the functions of audit committees, the following appear to be gaining the most widespread acceptance:

1. Review of outside auditor's management letter;
2. Meeting with independent auditor:
   a) to discuss the scope of the audit;
   b) to review financial statements;
3. Meeting with the chief financial officer:
   a) to discuss implementing the independent auditor's recommendations;
   b) to discuss internal controls, procedures, etc.;
   c) to review alternative accounting policies;
4. Meeting with the internal auditor:
   a) to discuss adequacy of the internal audit program;
   b) to review findings of internal audit investigations;
   c) to discuss adequacy of staff;
5. Discussion of recent American Institute of Certified Public Accountants (AICPA) and other regulatory agency pronouncements and their impact on institutional accounting practices;
6. Discussion of performance and staffing of accounting and financial departments;
7. Appointment or nomination of the independent auditor; and
8. Participation in the establishment of fees.

Periodic rotation of auditors has been viewed by some as a means of ensuring independence—by avoiding the development of overly close auditor-management relationships—and also of preserving a fresh auditor viewpoint. Countering these advantages are certain significant drawbacks. A newly appointed audit firm must necessarily incur extra audit expenses to accumulate the historical information needed to become familiar with operations, organization, personnel, and special institutional characteristics.

Furthermore, rotation can sometimes lead to a loss of continuity and a lack of familiarity with accounting principles used in prior periods. There is also a cost borne by the institution as a result of the rotation—

related to the time of key administrators and expense involved in familiarizing the new auditors with the institution and its procedures.

Those who advocate rotation of auditors believe that the change:

- Reinforces the objectivity of the audit; and
- Reduces the likelihood that the auditors will fail to detect crucial items because they have not recognized a change in conditions.

But it may be possible for a client to preserve the advantages of rotation without forfeiting the advantages of continuity if the auditing firm's internal policies permit this. Thus an audit committee can explore the recurring auditors' attitude toward:

- Rotation of all personnel involved in audit activities; and
- Revision of audit programs to keep auditing relevant to current conditions.

Rotation of auditors can often be the result not of a philosophic conviction as to its desirability, but rather a dissatisfaction with the quality and responsiveness of the existing audit firm's performance. When a change of auditors occurs, it is important that the audit committee meet with both the administration and the existing auditors to obtain their views on the change. In that way, the committee can determine that there are no unstated differences that could have an impact on future relationships and gain insights that may be useful in avoiding future difficulties.

Since institutions receive their support from a number of funding sources, they have traditionally been required to account separately to these various funding sources and have, consequently, been subject to multiple audits. This is particularly true of institutions that receive federal support, whether in connection with campus based student financial aid programs or federally sponsored activity such as research.

The Federal Office of Management and Budget in its *Circular A-110* establishes uniform administrative requirements for grants and other agreements with institutions of higher education, hospitals, and other nonprofit organizations. These include the requirement that institutional recipients maintain financial management systems which, among other things, provide for examinations in the form of external audits or internal audits. Where internal audits are performed, they must meet the independence criteria established by the United States General Accounting Office publication, *Standards for Audit of Governmental Organizations, Programs, Activities and Functions.*

It is further specified that these examinations should be conducted on an organization wide basis to test the fiscal integrity of financial transactions, as well as compliance with the terms and conditions of the federal grants and other agreements. They should be conducted at scheduled intervals no less frequently than every two years. Finally, it is stated that these examinations do not relieve federal agencies of their audit responsibilities, but may affect the frequency and scope of such audits.

It is within the context of this last provision, and in recognition of the limited availability of their own audit resources, that some federal agencies are encouraging the use of public accounting firms to audit federally sponsored activities as an extension of their regular audits.

This applies particularly to the area of student financial aid which has been a source of major concern. Federal agencies can view their own audit responsibilities as being fulfilled by relying on these audits, provided that they can satisfy themselves as to be completeness and effectiveness of the audit program and test the quality of the audit through review of the workpapers.

In one particular respect, public accounting firms can utilize their unique position to provide an effective service both to their clients and to federal sponsoring agencies. Resolution of audit disallowances and "set asides" has been an especially thorny source of conflict between institutions and federal granting agencies. When federal auditors encounter a circumstance in which costs are inadequately documented or supported, their normal practice has been to set the entire amount of such costs aside.

What these set aside costs connote is not that the auditors consider such costs to be improper charges to federal grants and contracts, but rather that the inadequacy of documentation precludes the auditors from determining with any reliability the extent to which such costs may or may not be valid charges to federally sponsored projects. The set asides may be quite substantial in amount, amounting to millions of dollars in the area of faculty compensation, as an illustration. (See discussion on Sponsored Activity.) This will be further exacerbated when, because of limited resources, federal auditors are unable to perform audits annually or even biannually and, hence, are frequently applying their findings retroactively over several years.

As a consequence of the "set aside" there is left to the mechanism of "audit resolution" the establishment of the extent to which the inadequacy of documentation reflects improper charges which should result in refunds from institutional grantees to the federal government. Although this process has often involved extended fact finding beyond that engaged in by auditors, it has generally fallen short of validating or invalidating charges with any degree of conclusiveness. The resolution thus ultimately results in a negotiation which has produced refunds of hundreds of thousands of dollars by individual institutions. These refunds were frequently not acknowledged by the institutions as appropriate, but utilized as a means of terminating the process. Thus the process has been a source of considerable tension, with federal officials upset at the failure of institutions to provide them with satisfactory information on a timely basis and believing the institutions to be recalcitrant and institutions believing that they are being harassed with excessive and unreasonable demands. (HEW's Office of the Inspector General has issued an internal directive requiring federal auditors to extend their audits when confronted with documentation deficiencies. They are expected to make reasonable efforts to avoid set asides. Since it is likely that resources will continue to be limited, it does not seem likely that this directive will do much to solve the problem referred to.)

Interestingly, the General Accounting Office (GAO) has been as critical of the audit resolution process as have institutions. It has been the contention of the GAO that the refunds negotiated were arbitrary and inadequate in relation to the size of the set aside.

Because the accounting firm that serves as auditor for the institution enjoys a position of trust and confidence with the institution and also with the federal government, and because of its professional independence, it is possible for it to serve both parties and to effectively deal with the problem of audit resolution by extending its audit to encompass federally sponsored activity. It accomplishes this by establishing with the institution an acceptable method for validating charges when adequate documentation is not available. The methodology deemed acceptable will be one that the federal authorities will be equally willing to accept. Institutional staff can then perform the validation techniques with test checks performed by the accounting firm to insure the integrity and proper application of the validation process. This involves many complex issues. But as in many other situations, the intrusion of a third party perceived by both parties to be fair and objective, can make a constructive contribution to the process.

Chapter Fifteen

EDUCATIONAL ADMINISTRATION IN THE FUTURE

Given the dynamics of change in higher education it is perhaps more difficult to predict future trends than for many other segments of our society. Nonetheless, it seems reasonable to assume that in the 1980s the continued viability of many of our higher education institutions will require a searching re-examination of organization and governance relationships, an increased focus on cost effectiveness and on revenue generating activities, a critical assessment of the effectiveness of fund raising and student recruitment and perhaps a reassessment of mission. Further, we can expect that the factors discussed in "Trends Affecting Higher Education" will continue to exert an important influence and call for an appropriate response.

Thus, it seems that in the 1980s, higher education will continue to grapple with the loss of public confidence in the value and utility of higher education, changing enrollment patterns, and a smaller pool of traditional college age students, increased competition among and between institutions and between the public and private sectors, rising costs of higher education to the consumer and taxpayers, increasing concern about effective management in educational institutions, perhaps leading to stricter controls by various state agencies and Boards of Trustees, and erosion of collegiality. Universities and the public will continue to be concerned about falling SAT scores (although the professionals will continue to debate the validity of those scores) and through informed opinion, will discuss social change, school standards, and television viewing as among the causes. There will be concern with collegiate preparation at the secondary school level, and about the extent to which post secondary education remedies or should be expected to remedy basic skill deficiencies. This may in fact bring us full circle back to the question of the value and utility of college. The financial woes of a number of private institutions will continue to worsen and the trend of college closings should continue. Between the spring of 1970 and the fall of 1976, 113 private colleges closed and 15 shifted to public control. During the same period 46 new private colleges were founded and 39 private colleges merged with other private institutions. There are also likely to be mergers among various institutions and the adoption of state laws permitting absorption of some private institutions into the public systems. In any event, as more and more public money is spent for public institutions or in one way or another, as a subsidy to independent institutions, state controls are bound to increase with corresponding concern about the independence of the private sector and academic freedom at all institutions.

The trends seem also to indicate that there will continue to be concern among faculty about protecting their economic security which may manifest itself through unionization. This will be true unless the Yeshiva decision referred to in the section on Collective Bargaining remains the law and serves to inhibit unionization at private institutions.

Other aspects of educational management in the 1980s seem to indicate that the following will pose significant challenges:

1. The need to control library expansion by substituting microforms, computer techniques, various forms of information sharing, various forms of information dissemination—in order to slow down or stop expensive physical expansion;

2. Increased concern for equality of opportunity and facilities in women's sports and abuses in intercollegiate sports in regard to recruiting, academic standards, and academic progression;

3. Continued concern for admission of minority and handicapped students and for selection and promotion of faculty and staff;

4. A new education structure for the federal government which proponents hope will provide for the needs of education while reducing the red tape and multitudes of forms and requirements. The new Department of Education is likely to bring about some change, but further organizational change is necessary to bring about more rational approaches in dealing with major universities; particularly in the area of sponsored research;

5. The need for increased cooperation, communication, and coordination among and between Washington, the states, and the individual institutions;

6. Concern about the future of graduate education as graduate schools find that the traditional market for their students, college and university teaching, is diminishing;

7. Continued interest by the Internal Revenue Service in tuition remission and other employee fringe benefits;

8. The need to be concerned about the proliferation of accrediting agencies in the allied health professions field;

9. A review of the Doctor of Arts concept and its utility;

10. The spectre of deferred maintenance—it is estimated that because of the budgeting crunch institutions have a backlog of over $22 billion in deferred maintenance. Replacing aging buildings and adapting buildings for the handicapped is potentially a major cost item;

11. The continuing concern about upgrading academic requirements and the need for a core curriculum. (The recent response by Harvard is of interest in this connection.);

12. Increasing focus on regionalism as an approach to higher education;

13. Concern about student payment of tuition and re-payment of loans;

14. Continued grappling with state subsidy formulas to recognize that enrollment driven formulas are not appropriate to a time of decline and that consequently there must be more attention to the fixed, mixed, or variable nature of costs;

15. An increasing thrust toward central control over funding and expenditures by state boards of regents and legislators as a means of "conserving" state funds. This will reduce the autonomy and flexibility of public institutions and independent institutions to the degree that they rely on state funding;

16. Increasing attempts by independent institutions to obtain public funding on some proportionate basis in relation to public institutions;

17. Concern about the role of specialized licensing boards and professional organizations with particular interest that they do not prescribe certain actions that should be left to faculty and administrators, for example, curricula and course content, admissions policies, faculty salaries;

18. The issue of general liberal education versus specialized, vocational preprofessional education will continue to be debated with concern about truth in advertising in regard to what a particular institution truly offers;

19. Life learning and work experience credits, satellite and off-campus location students will be emphasized as areas for specific concern about quality control and standards of achievement, and performance equal to that of regularly matriculated students. Similarly, as those variations become more common it should be expected that support services, qualifications of staff, and caliber of instruction and facilities available to nontraditional students at nontraditional locations will be examined more critically to determine whether they are roughly equal to that normally provided by the institution;

20. In the face of decreasing resources and increasing competition, institutions must be ready to change organizational structures, courses, curricula, and teaching methods as appropriate to the mission of the institution;

21. Increased concern for care and accuracy in statements to students and prospective students in brochures, catalogues, recruitment materials in regard to courses, curricula, services, job prospects, job placement, services and facilities, participation of senior faculty;

22. Emphasis on faculty and staff professional development, midcareer retraining and early retirement;

23. Increasing demands upon institutions to provide full information in regard to finances, investment policies, enrollment, curriculum, facilities, percentage of tenured and full-time faculty, and to provide projections for the future;

24. Concern about productivity, workload, standards of performance, effectiveness, and efficiency;

25. Concern about the growth of programs for health professionals given projected needs for such staff in the future and also concern about the high cost of training health professionals. A review of cost would necessitate analysis and possible changes in regard to faculty-student ratios, use of time by faculty members, faculty compensation levels; and revenue generation and additional income of faculty members;

26. Increasing concern about the need for increased governmental and business support of basic and applied research at universities;

27. The need to develop a financial and management impact statement when planning for the possible introduction of new programs.

The picture of the future is not a euphoric one, but the educational enterprise can indeed be managed. The focus must be on increasing effectiveness and efficiency, on bringing to bear a managerial approach with an emphasis on planning, managing human resources, financing, innovation, successful representation of the institution to outside constituencies, organizing, coordination, and budgeting.

Marketing will become of increasing importance in terms of defining the institution's mission, improving or developing programs and approaches so that the "product" is appealing and sought after in a competitive world. It appears from several studies that where there is demonstrably evident academic quality, higher tuition rates are not necessarily an impediment. Tuition levels seem to become a major factor when one institution is basically indistinguishable from others.

A marketing approach will have to be concerned about advertising, publications, and responses to inquiries, but even more important will be the question of quality. How good are the programs, courses, and services, how profound is the concern for standards of quality, and how personal is the concern for students? Together with a marketing approach, the various innovation approaches outlined will be important: appealing to students other than the usual 18–21 year old group; changing the traditional time and place of teaching; emphasizing different teaching methods, technology, and programs; sharing of resources; community service programs; increasing services to students with emphasis on education as a life long process and continuing contacts between the institution and those who have attended or graduated.

An institution can indeed continue to thrive despite the more difficult climate, but success will require thoughtfulness, innovation, initiative, and adaptability. The institution that rests on its laurels and past accomplishments will be fortunate to maintain its standing and once an institution encounters severe financial problems, a snowball effect is likely to take place with cuts being made that in the long run can lead to further enrollment declines because of the impact on program quality.

The challenge and opportunity for educational managers will be to retain values, build upon strengths, reformulate when necessary, go on to different ways of thinking and serving, in order to meet changing times and needs.

CONCLUSION

It is difficult for those involved in or concerned about higher education to be totally objective about it. It is more natural to be either frustrated and hypercritical or passionately defensive.

A balanced view would suggest that higher education remains one of our most valued institutions, the strength and viability of which is clearly essential to our continued intellectual growth and material prosperity as a nation. It is at the same time one of our most complex institutions, attempting to confront a series of demanding problems, challenges, opportunities and constraints, with a number of profound ambivalences.

These ambivalences relate to such things as the fundamental mission of higher education and the appropriate mission for specific institutions (it is fair to say that many institutions are facing an identity crisis) and to the role, functions, and responsibilities of the faculty. For instance, do they participate in the management of the institution or do they bargain with it as employees?

The management of our higher education enterprise is a critical and demanding task. It requires, among other qualities, insight, imagination, thoughtfulness, and a heavy dose of patience, sensitivity, and dedication. Those who are involved in the management of our higher education enterprise—administrators, business managers, faculty, and others—merit our admiration, appreciation, *and* understanding. It was in part with a view toward contributing to that understanding that this book was written.

The authors started with two points of focus. The first was that higher education is indeed a major enterprise, albeit with its own important set of dynamics and complexities, and it is important in any discussion on higher education management to view it as an enterprise. The second point of focus was that in recent years the managerial affairs of higher education institutions have been subjected to a more intense scrutiny by their various constituencies (internal and external) than ever before experienced, and this creates an imperative for creating a context in which the issues and their interrelationships will be properly understood.

The forces of change that are buffeting our higher education institutions today cry out for all of the thinking, insights, perspectives, and understanding support that can be mustered. But it is essential that those who are directly involved in the management of higher education and those who would contribute to it have as full an understanding as possible of the nature of these institutions and the manner in which they function.

This was not intended to be a philosophic tract, nor is it a how to do it book. We have attempted to discuss some of the central issues involved in the management of higher education in the hope that this would broaden the understanding and perspective of those attempting to deal with specific problems.

We have attempted to strike an appropriate balance between the conceptual and the detailed. If we have not satisfied every reader in this regard, we hope that we have introduced some new perspectives or stimulated the raising of some questions.

In making our views known on the various issues, or at least not trying to hide them, the authors have, in particular, revealed one overriding bias, and that is a preference for action rather than inaction. There is a still widely cherished view of university administration which holds that that administration governs best that governs least. The authors do not share that view.

Moreover, we regard the issue of how active or aggressive university administrators should be as a pervasive one and, consequently, it has surfaced in many of the discussions on specific issues. We have no quarrel with the faculty member who asserts that we must never lose sight of the fact that the institution exists only as a vehicle or forum for faculty and students to engage in scholarly pursuits and that the role of the administrator is to facilitate that process as unobtrusively as possible. We *do* quarrel with the faculty member who, in a letter to the Editor, published in the *Chronicle of Higher Education* suggested that administrators could be dispensed with and faculty could run the institution in their spare time.

That kind of contention, made with no hint of facetiousness, suggests a continuing and compelling necessity to convey to faculty, students, and constituents, a broader understanding of the complexities and demands of higher education management in today's environment. We would further suggest that before they can persuasively assert a claim to participation in (much less dominance of) the governance process, faculty members need to resolve their critical ambivalence as to role. They cannot be part of the governance structure committed to sustaining a vibrant, viable institution while simultaneously, through the collective bargaining process, assuming an adversary posture that is essentially indifferent to what is necessary to sustain the institution. At the same time, job market concerns and the impact of inflation raise major personal concerns for faculty members that cannot be ignored. Many faculty members—perhaps most of them—who are passionately concerned about education are extremely concerned about this ambivalence.

The preference of the authors for an activist approach to managing the higher education enterprise is induced by the recognition that that management task is far more complex and demanding than it once was.

Passive stewardship as a concept of management and of accounting and management reporting is no longer a useful option when the continued viability of the institution over which stewardship is being exercised is threatened. A true fealty to the intent of those whose resources have helped to create and sustain the institution requires a recognition that they had in mind not only one or more specific purposes, but also the common and broader purpose that the institution be preserved. That task, in light of the difficulties confronting institutions today, demands enlightened, innovative, and aggressive leadership.

Appendix

A FIVE FOOT SHELF OF USEFUL MATERIAL

The listing below indicates sources of information as well as important books in two areas: I) General Management; II) University and College Management. The General Management section is included to provide the educational administrator with broad knowledge and reference material about the field of management which then serves as the foundation for his/her understanding of the particular areas, problems and concerns of university and college management. The second section also contains a listing of some NACUBO Professional Papers.

GENERAL MANAGEMENT

Ackoff, Russell L., *The Art of Problem Solving: Accompanied by Ackoff's Fables,* New York: Wiley, 1975.

Ackoff, Russell L. and Patrick Rivett, *A Manager's Guide to Operations Research,* New York: Wiley, 1963.

Allen, Louis A., *The Management Profession,* New York: McGraw-Hill, 1964.

Appleby, Paul H., *Big Democracy,* New York: Knopf, 1945.

———, *Policy and Administration,* University of Alabama Press, University of Alabama, 1949.

Appley, Lawrence, *Management in Action: The Art of Getting Things Done Through People,* New York: American Management Association, 1956.

Argyris, Chris, *Personality and Organization,* New York: Harper, 1957.

———, *Organization and Innovation,* Homewood, Ill.: R. D. Irwin, 1965.

———, *Integrating the Individual and the Organization,* New York: Wiley, 1964.

———, *Executive Leadership,* Hamden, Conn.: Archon Books, 1967.

———, *Management and Organizational Development,* New York: McGraw-Hill, 1971.

Argyris, Chris and Donald A. Schon, *Theory in Practice,* San Francisco: Jossey-Bass, 1974.

Barnard, Chester L., *The Functions of the Executive,* Cambridge: Harvard University Press, 1938.

————, *The Nature of Leadership,* Cambridge: Harvard University Press, 1940.

Bakke, E. Wight, *Bonds of Organization,* 2nd ed., Hamden, Conn.: Archon Books, 1966.

Beer, Stafford, *Cybernetics and Management,* London: English University Press, Ltd., 1968.

Bell, Daniel, *The Coming of Post-Industrial Society: A Venture in Social Forecasting,* New York: Basic Books, 1973.

Bennis, Warren G., *Changing Organizations,* New York: McGraw-Hill, 1966.

————, and others, *Interpersonal Dynamics,* 3rd ed., Homewood, Ill.: Dorsey Press, 1973.

————, *The Planning of Change,* 2nd ed., New York: Holt, Rinehart, Winston, 1964.

Bennis, Warren G. and Philip E. Slater, *The Temporary Society,* New York: Harper & Row, 1968.

Benton, Lewis (Ed.), *Management for the Future,* New York: McGraw-Hill, 1978.

————, *Private Management and Public Policy: Reciprocal Impacts,* Lexington, Mass.: D. C. Heath, 1980.

Blake, Robert R. and Jane S. Mouton, *The Managerial Grid,* Houston: The Gulf Publishing Co., 1964.

Blau, Peter M., *The Dynamics of Bureaucracy,* Rev. ed., Chicago: University of Chicago Press, 1963.

Boorstin, Daniel J., *The Republic of Technology: Reflections on Our Future Community,* New York: Harper & Row, 1978.

Bork, Robert H., *The Antitrust Paradox,* New York: Basic Books, 1978.

Burger, Chester, *The Chief Executive: Realities of Corporate Leadership,* Boston: CBI Publishing, 1978.

Burnham, James, *The Managerial Revolution,* New York: John Day, 1941.

Burns, James McGregor, *Leadership,* New York: Harper & Row, 1978.

Buskirk, Richard H., *Modern Management and Machiavelli,* Boston, Mass.: Cahners Books, 1974.

Carroll, Stephen T. F. and Henry L. F. Tosi, *Management By Objectives: Applications and Research,* New York: Macmillan, 1973.

Chamberlain, Neil W., *The Limits of Corporate Responsibility,* New York: Basic Books, 1973.

Chandler, Alfred D., Jr., *The Visible Hand,* Cambridge, Mass.: Belknap Press, 1977.

Churchman, C. West, *Challenge to Reason,* McGraw-Hill, 1968.

Cleveland, Harlan, *The Future Executive: A Guide for Tomorrow's Managers,* New York: Harper, 1972.

Cochran, Thomas C., *Business in American Life: A History,* New York: McGraw-Hill, 1972.

Cordiner, Ralph J., *New Frontiers for Professional Managers,* New York: McGraw-Hill, 1956.

Corson, John T., *Business in the Humane Society,* New York: McGraw-Hill, 1971.

Cyert, Richard M., *The Management of Nonprofit Organizations,* Lexington, Mass.: Lexington Books, D. C. Heath and Company, 1973.

Cyert, Richard M. and James G. March, *A Behaviorial Theory of the Firm*, Englewood Cliffs, N.J.: Prentice-Hall, 1963.

Dale, Ernest, *Management: Theory and Practice*, 3rd ed., New York: McGraw-Hill, 1973.

Dalton, Melville, *Men Who Manage*, New York: Wiley, 1959.

deMarc, George, *Corporate Lives*, New York: Van Nostrand Reinhold, 1976.

Diebold, John, *Man and the Computer*, New York: Praeger, 1967.

———, *The World of the Computer*, New York: Random House, 1973.

Dimoch, Marshall, *The Executive in Action*, New York: Harper, 1945.

Downs, Anthony, *Inside Bureaucracy*, New York: Little, Brown, 1967.

Drucker, Peter F., *Age of Discontinuity: Guidelines to Our Changing Society*, New York: Harper & Row, 1969.

———, *The Concept of the Corporation*, New York: John Day, 1972.

———, *Effective Executive*, New York: Harper & Row, 1967.

———, *Management: Tasks, Responsibilities, Practices*, New York: Harper & Row, 1974.

———, *Managing for Results*, New York: Harper & Row, 1964.

———, *The Unseen Revolution*, New York: Harper & Row, 1976.

Dunlop, John T. and Walter Galinson (Eds.), *Labor in the Twentieth Century*, New York: Academic Press, 1978.

Emerson, Harrington, *The Twelve Principles of Efficiency*, Ann Arbor, Mich.: University Microfilm, 1971.

Etzioni, Amitai, *Modern Organizations*, Englewood Cliffs, N.J.: Prentice-Hall, 1964.

Fayol, Henri, *General and Industrial Management*, Translated by Constance Stons, London: Pitman, 1949.

Forrester, Jay W., *Industrial Dynamics*, Cambridge, Mass.: M.I.T. Press, 1961.

Galbraith, John Kenneth, *The Affluent Society*, New York: Houghton Mifflin, 1971.

Gantt, Henry Laurence, in *Gantt on Management: Guidelines for Today's Executive*, Alex W. Rathe (Ed.), New York: American Management Association and American Society of Mechanical Engineers, 1961.

Gellerman, Saul W., *Management by Motivation*, New York: American Management Association, 1968.

———, *Motivation and Productivity*, New York: American Mannagement Association, 1963.

Gilbreth, Frank B., and Lillian Gilbreth, in *The Writings of the Gilbreths*, William R. Spreigel and Clark E. Meyers (Eds.), Homewood, Ill.: Irwin, 1953.

Greenwood, James W., Jr., and James W. Greenwood, *Managing Executive Stress: A System Approach*, New York: Wiley, 1979.

Gulick, Luther and Lyndall Fownes Urwick (Eds.), *Papers on the Science of Administration*, New York: Institute of Public Administration, 1937; reprinted in Reprints of Economic Classics Sciences, Clifton, N.J.: Kelley, 1969.

Heaton, Herbert, *Productivity in Service Organizations: Organizing for People*, New York: McGraw-Hill, 1977.

Hertz, David B., *New Power for Management*, New York: McGraw-Hill, 1969.

Herzberg, Frederick, Mausner, Bernard, and Synderman, Barbara Black, *The Motivation to Work*, 2nd ed., New York: Wiley, 1959.

Homans, George C., *The Homan Group*, New York: Harcourt, Brace, 1950.

Howe, Robert Franklin, *Scientific Management and Labor, Reprints of Economic Classics*, Clifton, N.J.: Kelley, 1966.

Heilbroner, Robert L., *Beyond Boom and Crash*, New York: W. W. Norton, 1978.

Jacoby, Neil H., *Corporate Power and Social Responsibility: A Blueprint for the Future*, New York: Macmillan, 1973.

Jacoby, Neil H., Peter Nehemkis, Richard Eells, *Bribery and Extortion in World Business*, New York: Macmillan, 1977.

Jay, Antony, *Management and Machiavelli*, New York: Holt, Rinehart & Winston, 1967.

———, *Corporation Man*, New York: Random House, 1971.

Joyles, Leonard and Margaret K. Chandler, *Merging Large Systems: Organizations for the Future*, New York: Harper & Row, 1971.

Kaufman, Herbert, *The Limits of Organizational Change*, University, Ala.: University of Alabama Press, 1971.

Kepner, Charles H., and Benjamin B. Tregoe, *The Rational Manager*, New York: McGraw-Hill, 1965.

Korda, Michael, *Power:How to Get It, How to Use It*, New York: Random House, 1975.

———, *Success*, New York: Random House, 1977.

Leavitt, Harold J., *Managerial Psychology*, Chicago: University of Chicago Press, 1972.

Leighton, Alexander, *The Governing of Men*, New York: S. J. R. Saunders, 1945.

Levinson, Harry, *Men, Management and Mental Health*, Cambridge: Harvard University Press, 1962.

Likert, Rensis, *New Patterns of Management*, New York: McGraw-Hill, 1961.

———, *The Human Organization*, New York: McGraw-Hill, 1967.

———, *New Ways of Managing Conflict*, New York: McGraw-Hill, 1967.

———, *Systems and Organizations*, Ann Arbor, Mich.: University of Michigan Press, 1976.

Lilienthal, David E., *TVA: Democracy on the March*, New York: Harper, 1944.

Lindblom, Charles E., *Politics and Markets: The World's Political-Economic Systems*, New York: Basic Books, 1977.

March, J. G. and H. A. Simon, *Organizations*, New York: Wiley, 1958.

Marrow, Alfred J., David G. Bowers, and Stanley E. Seashore, *Management by Participation: Creating a Climate for Personal and Organizational Development*, New York: Harper & Row, 1967.

Maslow, Abraham Harold, *Motivation and Personality*, 2nd ed., New York: Harper & Row, 1970.

Mason, Edward S., *The Corporation in Modern Society*, New York: Atheneum, 1966.

Mayo, George Elton, *The Human Problems of an Industrial Corporation*, Cambridge: Harvard Business School, 1933.

McGregor, Douglas, *The Human Side of Enterprise*, New York: McGraw-Hill, 1960.

Meadows, Dennis L. (Ed.), *Alternatives to Growth-1: A Search for Sustainable Futures*, Cambridge, Mass.: Ballinger Publishing, 1977.

Meadows, Donela, and others, *The Limits of Growth: A Report for the Club of Rome's Project on the Predicament of Mankind,* Secaucus, N.J.: University Books, 1972.

Metcalf, Henry C. and Lyndall Fownes Urwick, *Dynamic Administration—The Collected Papers of Mary Parker Follet,* New York: Harper, 1941.

Mintzberg, Henry, *The Nature of Managerial Work,* New York: Harper & Row, 1973.

———, *Structuring of Organizations,* Englewood Cliffs, N.J.: Prentice-Hall, 1979.

Mooney, James D., *The Principles of Organization,* New York: Harper, 1941.

Mooney, James D. and A. C. Reiley, *Onward Industry,* New York: Harper, 1931.

Nader, Ralph, *Whistle Blowing,* New York: Grossman Publishers, 1972.

Niles, Mary Cushing, *The Essence of Management,* New York: Harper, 1958.

Odiorne, George S., *Management by Objectives: A System of Managerial Leadership,* New York: Pitman, 1965.

Ogilvy, David, *Confessions of an Advertising Man,* New York: Atheneum, 1966.

Osborn, Alex F., *Management Decisions by Objectives,* Englewood Cliffs, N.J.: Prentice-Hall, 1969.

———, *Applied Imagination: Principles and Procedures of Creative Thinking,* Rev. ed., New York: Charles Scribner's Sons, 1957.

Paluszek, John L., *Will the Corporation Survive?,* Reston, Va.: Reston Publishing, 1977.

Parkinson, D. Northcote, *Parkinson's Law,* New York: Houghton Mifflin, 1957.

Peter, Laurence F. and Raymond Hull, *The Peter Principle,* New York: William Morrow, 1969.

Phyrr, Peter A., *Zero Base Budgeting—A Practical Management Tool for Evaluating Expenses,* New York: Wiley, 1973.

Randall, Clarence B., *The Folklore of Management,* Boston: Little, Brown, 1961.

Rock, Robert H., *The Chief Executive Officer: Managing the Human Resources of the Large, Diversified, Industrial Company,* Lexington, Mass.: D. C. Heath, 1977.

Roethlisberger, F. J., in *The Elusive Phenomena,* George F. F. Lombard (Ed.), Cambridge: Harvard University Press, 1977.

Roethlisberger, F. J., *Man-in-Organization,* Cambridge: Harvard University Press, 1968.

Roethlisberger, F. J. and W. Dickson, *Management and the Worker,* Cambridge: Harvard University Press, 1956.

Schultze, Charles L., *The Public Use of Private Interest,* Washington, D.C.: Brookings Institution, 1977.

Selznick, Phillip, *Leadership in Adminstration,* Evanston, Ill.: Row, Peterson & Co., 1957.

Sheldon, Oliver, *The Philosophy of Management,* London and New York: Pitman, 1924; Reprint, 1965.

Sherman, Harvey, *It All Depends,* University, Ala.: University of Alabama Press, 1966.

Simon, Herbert A., *Administrative Behavior: A Study of Decision-making Processes in Administrative Organization,* 2nd ed., New York: Macmillan, 1957.

———, *Models of Man,* New York: Wiley, 1957.

———, *The New Science of Management Decision,* New York: Harper, 1960.

———, *The Shape of Automation for Men and Management,* New York: Harper & Row, 1965.

Sloan, Alfred P., Jr., *My Years with General Motors,* New York: Doubleday, 1964.

Steiner, George A., *Top Management Planning: Studies of the Modern Corporation,* New York and London: Macmillan, 1969.

————, *Business and Society,* New York: Random House, 1971.

Taylor, Frederick Winslow, *Scientific Management,* New York: Harper, 1969; Reprint, Westport, Conn.: Greenwood Press, 1972.

Tead, Ordway, *The Art of Leadership,* New York: McGraw-Hill, 1935.

Toffler, Alvin, *Future Shock,* New York: Random House, 1970.

Townsend, Robert, *Up the Organization: How to Stop the Corporation from Stifling People and Strangling Profits,* New York: Knopf, 1970.

Urwick, Lyndall Fownes and E. F. L. Breck, *The Making of Scientific Management,* 3 Vols., London: Management Publications Trust and Pitman, 1946–48.

Urwick, Lyndall Fownes, *The Elements of Administration,* New York: Harper, 1944.

U.S. President's Committee on Administrative Management (Bramlow Committee) Report with Special Studies, Washington, D.C.: U.S. Government Printing Office, 1937.

Vogel, David, *Lobbying the Corporation: Citizen Challenges to Business Authority,* New York: Basic Books, 1978.

Waldo, Dwight, *The Administrative State,* New York: Ronald Press, 1948.

Walker, James W. and Harriet L. Lazer, *The End of Mandatory Retirement: Implications for Management,* New York: Wiley, 1978.

Walton, Clarence (Ed.), *The Ethics of Corporate Conduct,* Englewood Cliffs, N.J.: Prentice-Hall, 1977 (52nd American Assembly).

Ways, Max (Ed.), *The Future of Business: Global Issues in the 80's and 90's,* New York: Pergamon Press, 1979.

Webber, Ross A., *Time and Management,* New York: Van Nostrand Reinhold, 1972.

Weidenbaum, Murray L., *The Future of Business Regulation: Private Action and Public Demand,* New York: AMACOM, 1979.

Whyte, William, *The Organization Man,* New York: Simon & Schuster, 1956.

Work in America: A Report of a Special Task Force for the Secretary of Health, Education and Welfare, Cambridge, Mass.: M.I.T. Press, 1973.

Zolezwik, A., *Human Dilemmas of Leadership,* New York: Harper & Row, 1966.

COLLEGE AND UNIVERSITY MANAGEMENT

Educational Resources Information Center (ERIC) Clearinghouse on Higher Education, One Dupont Circle, Suite 630, Washington, D.C. 20036, provides information on educational literature. National Association of College and University Business Officers (NACUBO), National Center for Higher Education Management Systems (NCHEMS), National Center for the Study of Collective Bargaining in Higher Education all have various professional papers, reports, and so forth that provide very useful information on a variety of topics.

In addition, *Change Magazine, The Chronicle of Higher Education* and a variety of professional journals, a sample of which is listed below, provide current information and discussions of the field:

AAUP Bulletin
AGB Reports
American Education
College and University
Compact
Educational Administration Abstracts
Educational Record
A Fact Book on Higher Education
Higher Education Daily
Higher Education and National Affairs
Journal of Education Finance
The Journal of Higher Education
NACUBO Business Officer
New Directions for Higher Education
Research in Higher Education

Planning for Higher Education
EDUCOM Bulletin
College Law Bulletin
College Law Digest
Journal of College & University Law
The Journal of Student Financial Aid
The Journal of the College & University
  Personnel Association
American School and University
The Journal of College and University
  Student Housing
Campus Law Enforcement Journal
School Foodservice Journal
The Internal Auditor
The EDP Auditor
The College Store Journal

Books Dealing with Higher Education Administration

ACE/APPA/NACUBO Energy Task Force, *Energy Cost and Consumption Audit Program,* Washington, D.C.: Association of Physical Plant Administrators of Universities and Colleges, 1977.

ACE/APPA/NACUBO Energy Task Force, *Energy Management for Colleges and Universities,* Washington, D.C.: National Association of College and University Business Officers, 1977.

Aiken, Ray J., John F. Adams, and John W. Hall, *Liability: Legal Liabilities in Higher Education: Their Scope and Management,* Washington, D.C.: Association of American Colleges, 1976.

American Enterprise Institute for Public Policy Research, *Government and Academia: The Uneasy Bond,* 1978.

Anderson, Richard E., *Strategic Policy Changes at Private Colleges,* New York: Teachers College Press, 1978.

Anderson, Scarvia B. and Samuel Ball, *The Profession and Practice of Program Evaluation,* San Francisco, Jossey-Bass, 1978.

Angell, George W., Edward P. Keelye, Jr., et al., *Handbook of Faculty Collective Bargaining,* San Francisco, Jossey-Bass, 1977.

Anthony, Robert N. and Regina E. Herslinger, *Management Control in Non-Profit Organizations,* Homewood, Ill.: Richard D. Irwin, Inc., 1975.

Appleton, James R., Channing M. Briggs, and James J. Rhatigan, *Pieces of Eight: The Rites, Roles and Styles of the Dean by Eight Who Have Been There,* National Association of Student Personnel Administrators, 1978.

Association of Physical Plant Administrations of Universities and Colleges, *Comparative Costs and Staffing Report for Physical Plants of Colleges and Universities,* 1978.

Balderston, Frederick E., *Managing Today's University,* San Francisco: Jossey-Bass, 1974.

Barzun, Jacques, *The American University: How It Runs, Where It Is Going,* New York: Harper & Row, 1968.

Bender, Louis W., *Federal Regulation and Higher Education,* Washington, D.C.: American Association for Higher Education, 1977.

Benezet, Louis T., *Private Higher Education and Public Funding,* Washington, D.C.: American Association for Higher Education, 1976.

Biehl, Richard G., *Guide to the Section 504 Self-Evaluation for Colleges and Universities,* Washington, D.C.: National Association of College and University Business Officers, 1978.

Bird, Caroline, *The Case Against College,* New York: D. McKay Co., 1975.

Blackwell, Thomas E., *College and University Law for Administrators,* Monterey, Cal.: Herals Printers, 1977.

Breneman, David W. and Chester E. Finn, Jr., *Public Policy and Private Education,* Washington, D.C.: The Brookings Institution, 1978.

Brewster, Sam F., *Campus Planning and Construction,* Washington, D.C.: Association of Physical Plant Administrators of Universities and Colleges, 1977.

Bowen, Howard R. and Gordon K. Douglas, *Efficiency in Liberal Education: A Study of Comparative Instructional Costs for Different Ways of Organizing Teaching-Learning in a Liberal Arts College,* New York: McGraw-Hill, 1971.

————, *The Financing of Higher Education,* New York: McGraw-Hill, 1970.

Bowen, Howard R., Gordon K. Douglas, and John W. Minter, *Private Higher Education, Third Annual Report on Financial and Educational Trends in the Private Sector of American Higher Education,* Washington, D.C.: Assoc. of American Colleges, 1977.

Bowen, Howard R., Gordon K. Douglas, John W. Minter, and Lyman A. Glenny, *State Budgeting for Higher Education: State Fiscal Stringency and Public Higher Education,* Berkeley, Cal.: Center for Research and Development in Higher Education, University of California, 1976.

——, *Investment in Learning,* San Francisco: Jossey-Bass, 1977.

Boyer, Ernest L., and Martin Kaplan, *Educating for Survival,* New York: Change Magazine Press, 1977.

Brown, J. Douglas, *The Commonplace Book of an Academic Dean,* Industrial Relations Section, Princeton, N.J.: Princeton University, 1978.

Brown, Frank and Madelon D. Stent, *Minorities in U.S. Institutions of Higher Education,* New York: Praeger, 1977.

Cahn, Steven M., *Scholars Who Teach: The Art of College Teaching,* Chicago Ill.: Nelson-Hall, 1978.

Carnegie Commission on Higher Education, *Governance of Higher Education,* New York: McGraw-Hill, 1973.

——, *Higher Education: Who Pays? Who Benefits? Who Should Pay?,* New York: McGraw-Hill, 1973.

——, *Priorities for Action: Final Report of the Carnegie Commission on Higher Education,* New York: McGraw-Hill, 1973.

——, *The More Effective Use of Resources: An Imperative Need for Higher Education: A Report and Recommendation,* New York: McGraw-Hill, 1972.

——, *Models and Mavericks, A Profile of Private Liberal Arts Colleges,* San Francisco: Jossey-Bass, 1971.

Carnegie Council on Policy Studies in Higher Education, *Selective Admissions in Higher Education,* Comment and Recommendations and Two Reports, San Francisco: Jossey-Bass, 1978.

——, *The States and Private Higher Education: Problems and Policies in a New Era,* San Francisco: Jossey-Bass, 1977.

——, *Faculty Bargaining in Public Higher Education: A Report and Two Essays,* San Francisco: Jossey-Bass, 1978.

Carnegie Foundation for the Advancement of Teaching, *More Than Survival: Prospects of Higher Education in a Period of Uncertainty,* San Francisco: Jossey-Bass, 1975.

——, *The States and Higher Education,* San Francisco: Jossey-Bass, 1976.

————, *Missions of the College Curriculum: A Contemporary Review with Suggestions,* San Francisco: Jossey-Bass, 1978.

Carr, Robert K., and Daniel K. VanEyck, *Collective Bargaining Comes to the Campus,* Washington, D.C.: American Council on Education, 1973.

Change Magazine Press, *Faculty Development in a Time of Retrenchment,* New York, 1974.

————, *Colleges and Money: A Faculty Guide to Academic Economics,* New Rochelle, New York: Change Panel on Academic Economics, 1976.

————, *The Third Century,* New York, 1977.

Cheit, Earl F., *The New Depression in Higher Education: A Study of Financial Conditions at 41 Colleges and Universities,* New York: McGraw-Hill, 1971.

Cheit, Earl F., *The New Depression in Higher Education: Two Years Later,* New York: McGraw-Hill, 1973.

Commission on Private Philanthropy and Public Needs, *Giving in America: Toward a Stronger Voluntary Sector,* Washington, D.C.: The Commission, 1975.

Committee for Economic Development, *The Management and Financing of Colleges,* New York: The Committee, 1973.

Daedalus, Journal of the American Academy of Arts and Sciences, *American Higher Education: Toward an Uncertain Future,* Vol. I, 1974, Vol. II, 1975.

Dressel, Paul L., *Handbook of Academic Evaluation,* San Francisco: Jossey-Bass, 1976.

Duryea, E. C., *College Bargaining: Impact on Governance,* Washington, D.C.: Association of Governing Board of Universities and Colleges, 1977.

Eble, Kenneth E., *Professors as Teachers,* San Francisco: Jossey-Bass, 1972.

Ennis, Richard M. and J. Peter Williamson, *Spending Policy for Educational Endowments,* New York: The Common Fund, 1976.

Fellman, David (Ed.), *The Supreme Court and Education,* 3rd ed., New York: Teachers College Press, Columbia University, 1976.

Fife, Jonathan D., *Applying the Goals of Student Financial Aid,* Washington, D.C.: American Association for Higher Education, 1976.

Finkin, Matthew, Robert A. Goldstein, and Woodley B. Osborne, *A Primer on Collective Bargaining for College and University Faculty,* Washington, D.C.: American Association of University Professors, 1975.

Finn, Chester E. Jr., *Scholars, Dollars and Bureaucrats*, Washington, D.C.: Brookings Institute, 1979.

Froomkin, Joseph, *Trends in the Sources of Student Support for Post-secondary Education*, Iowa City: American College Testing, 1976.

Furniss, W. Todd and David P. Gardner (Eds.), *Higher Education & Government: An Uneasy Alliance*, Washington, D.C.: American Council on Education, 1979.

Garbarino, Joseph W., and Bill Aussieker, *Faculty Bargaining, Change and Conflict*, New York: McGraw-Hill, 1975.

Garms, Walter I., *Financing Community Colleges*, New York: Teachers College Press, Columbia University, 1976.

Glenny, Lyman A., Frank M. Bowen, Richard J. Meisinger, Anthony W. Morgan, Ralph A. Purves, and Frank A. Schmidtlein, *State Budgeting for Higher Education: Data Digest*, Berkeley, Cal.: Center for Research and Development in Higher Education, University of California.

Glenny, Lyman A., *State Budgeting for Higher Education: Interagency Conflict and Consensus*, Berkeley, Cal.: Center for Research and Development in Higher Education, University of California.

Griffin, Gerald, and David R. Burks, *Appraising Administrative Operations: A Guide for Universities and Colleges*, Washington, D.C.: American Council on Education, 1976.

Gross, Edward, Paul V. Grambsch, *Changes in University Organization*, New York: McGraw-Hill, 1974.

Haag, Leonard H., *Cash Management & Short-Term Investments for Colleges and Universities*, Washington, D.C.: National Association of College and University Business Officers, 1977.

Halstead, D. Kent, *Statewide Planning in Higher Education*, Washington, D.C.: U.S. Government Printing Office, 1975.

Harcleroad, Fred F., *Educational Auditing and Accountability*, Washington, D.C.: Council on Post-Secondary Accreditation, 1976.

Harrington, Fred Harvey, *The Future of Adult Education*, San Francisco: Jossey-Bass, 1977.

Harris, Norman C. and John F. Grede, *Career Education in Colleges*, San Francisco: Jossey-Bass, 1977.

Hartley, Harry J., *Educational Planning, Programming, Budgeting: A Systems Approach*, Englewood Cliffs, N.J.: Prentice-Hall, 1968.

Hesburgh, Theodore M., *The Hesburgh Papers: Higher Values in Higher Education,* Mission, Kansas: Andrews and McMeel, 1979.

Heyns, Roger W. (Ed.), *Leadership for Higher Education: The Campus View,* Washington, D.C.: American Council on Education, 1977.

Hook, Sidney, Paul Kurtz, and Miro Todorovich, *The University and the State: What Role for Government in Higher Education?,* Buffalo, N.Y.: Prometheus Books, 1978.

Houle, Cyril O., *The Design of Education,* San Francisco: Jossey-Bass, 1972.

Hughes, John F. (Ed.), *Education and the State,* Washington, D.C.: American Council on Education, 1975.

Hyman, Herbert H., Charles R. Wright, and John Shelton Reed, *The Enduring Effects of Education,* Chicago: University of Chicago Press, 1978.

James, Harvey L., *Managing Colleges and Universities by Objectives,* Wheaton, Ill.: Ireland Education Corp., 1976.

Jencks, Christopher and David Riesman, *The Academic Revolution,* New York: Doubleday, 1969.

Jenny, Hans H., *Higher Education and the Economy,* Washington, D.C.: American Association for Higher Education, 1976.

Kaplin, William A., *The Law of Higher Education: Legal Implications of Administrative Decision Making,* San Francisco: Jossey-Bass, 1979.

Kemerer, Frank R. and Ronald P. Satryb (Eds.), *Facing Financial Exigency: Strategies for Educational Administrators,* Lexington, Mass.: Lexington Books, D.C. Heath & Co., 1979.

Kirk, Russell, *Decadence and Renewal in the Higher Learning: An Episodic History of American University and College Since 1953,* South Bend, Indiana: Gateway Editions, 1979.

Knowles, Asa S. (Ed.), *Handbook of College and University Administration,* 2 Volumes, New York: McGraw-Hill, 1970.

Ladd, Everett Carll, Jr. and Seymour Martin Lipset, *Professors, Unions and American Higher Education,* New York: McGraw-Hill, 1973.

Lee, Eugene C. and Frank M. Bowen, *Managing Multicampus Systems: Effective Administration in an Unsteady State,* San Francisco: Jossey-Bass, 1975.

Lee, Robert D., Jr. and Ronald W. Johnson, *Public Budgeting Systems,* Baltimore: University Park Press, 1973.

Levine, Arthur, *Handbook on Undergraduate Curriculum,* San Francisco: Jossey-Bass, 1978.

March, James G., and Michael D. Cohen, *Leadership and Ambiguity: The American College President,* New York: McGraw-Hill, 1974.

Mauer, George J. (Ed.), *Crisis in Campus Management,* New York: Praeger, 1976.

Means, Howard B. and Philip W. Semos, *Faculty Collective Bargaining,* 2nd ed., Washington, D.C.: The Chronicle of Higher Education, 1977.

Meisinger, Richard J., Jr., *State Budgeting for Higher Education: The Uses of Formulas,* Berkeley, Cal.: University of California Center for Research and Development in Higher Education, 1976.

Millard, Richard M., *State Boards of Higher Education,* Washington, D.C.: American Association for Higher Education, 1976.

Miller, Jerry W. (Ed.), and Olive Mills, *Credentialing Educational Accomplishment,* Washington, D.C.: American Council on Education, 1979.

Miller, Richard I., *Evaluating Faculty Performance,* San Francisco: Jossey-Bass, 1972.

————, *The Assessment of College Performance: A Handbook of Techniques and Measures for Institutional Self Evaluation,* San Francisco: Jossey-Bass, 1979.

Millett, John D., *An Outline of Concepts of Organization, Operation and Administration for Colleges and Universities,* Washington, D.C.: Academy for Educational Development, Management Division, 1973.

————, *Allocation Decisions in Higher Education,* Washington, D.C.: Academy for Educational Development, 1975.

————, *Mergers in Higher Education: An Analysis of Ten Cases,* Washington, D.C.: American Council on Education, 1976.

————, *Higher Education and the 1980's,* Washington, D.C.: Academy for Educational Development, 1978.

————, *New Structures of Campus Power: Success and Failures of Emerging Forms of Institutional Governance,* San Francisco: Jossey-Bass, 1978.

Milton, Ohmer and Associates, *On College Teaching, A Guide to Contemporary Practices,* San Francisco: Jossey-Bass, 1978.

Moodies, Graeme C, and Rowland Eustare, *Power and Authority in British Universities,* Montreal: McGill-Queen's University Press, 1974.

Mortimer, Kenneth P. (Ed.), *Faculty Bargaining, State Government, and Campus Authority,* Denver: Education Commission of the States, 1976.

Mortimer, Kenneth P. and T. R. McConnell, *Sharing Authority Effectively: Participation, Interaction and Discretion,* San Francisco: Jossey-Bass, 1978.

National Association of College and University Business Officers, *A College Planning Cycle: People, Resources, Process,* Washington, D.C.: The Association, 1975.

————, *Procedures for Determining Historical Full Costs,* Washington, D.C.: NACUBO; Boulder, Colo.: NCHEMS, 1977.

————, *Management Reports: A System of Reporting and Accounting,* Washington, D.C.: The Association, 1975.

————, *Bond Valuation for Colleges and Universities,* Washington, D.C.: The Association, 1977.

————, *Investment Policies and Procedures at Selected Colleges and Universities,* Washington, D.C.: The Association, 1977.

————, *Results of the 1977 NACUBO Comparative Performance Study and Investment Questionnaire,* Washington, D.C.: The Association, 1978.

National Board on Graduate Education, *Minority Group Participation in Graduate Education,* Washington, D.C.: National Academy of Sciences, 1976.

National Center for Education Statistics, *The Condition of Education,* Washington, D.C.: U.S. Government Printing Office, 1977.

National Institute of Education, *Higher Education Planning: A Bibliographic Handbook,* D. Kent Halstead (Ed.), 1979.

Newman Commission, *Report on Higher Education,* Washington, D.C.: U.S. Government Printing Office, 1971.

Packwood, William T., *College Student Personnel Services,* Springfield, Ill.: Charles C. Thomas, 1978.

Patton, Carl V., *Academia in Transition: Mid-Career Change or Early Retirement,* Cambridge, Mass.: Abt Books, 1979.

Peltason, J. W. and Marcy V. Massengale, *Students and Their Institutions: A Changing Relationship,* American Council on Education, 1978.

Perkins, James A., *The University as an Organization,* New York: McGraw-Hill, 1973.

————, *Higher Education: From Autonomy to Systems,* New York: International Council for Educational Development, 1972.

————, *The University in Transition,* Princeton, N.J.: Princeton University Press, 1966.

Petersen, Richard E. and Associates, *Lifelong Learning in America: An Overview of Current Practices, Available Resources and Future Prospects,* San Francisco: Jossey-Bass, 1979.

Peterson, Marvin W., Robert T. Blackburn, Zelda F. Gamson, Carlos H. Arce, Roselle W. Davenport, and James R. Mingle, *Black Students on White Campuses: The Impacts of Increased Black Enrollments,* Ann Arbor, Mich.: Institute for Social Research, 1979.

Purves, Ralph A. and Lyman A. Glenny, *State Budgeting for Higher Education: Information Systems and Technical Analyses,* Berkeley Cal.: University of California, Center for Research and Development in Higher Education, 1976.

Riley, Gary L. and J. Victor Baldridge (Eds.), *Governing Academic Organizations: New Problems, New Perspectives,* Berkeley, Cal.: McCutchan Publishing Corporation, 1977.

Robertson, D. B., *Power and Empowerment in Higher Education,* Lexington, Ky.: The University Press of Kentucky, 1978.

Robinson, Daniel D. and Frederick J. Turk, *Cost Behavior Analysis for Planning in Higher Education,* Washington, D.C.: National Association of Colleges and University Business Officers, 1977.

Rudolph, Frederick, *Curriculum: A History of the American Undergraduate Course of Study Since 1636,* San Francisco: Jossey-Bass Publishers, 1979.

Sammartino, Peter, *Demanage Higher Education,* The Crispen Company, 1978.

Scheps, Clarence, and E. E. Davidson, *Accounting for Colleges and Universities,* Rev. ed, Baton Rouge, La.: Louisiana State University Press, 1978.

Schmidtlein, Frank A. and Lyman A. Glenny, *State Budgeting for Higher Education: The Political Economy of the Process,* Berkeley, Cal.: University of California, Center for Research and Development in Higher Education, 1976.

Schwab, Joseph J., in *Science Curriculum and Liberal Education, Selected Essays,* Ian Westbury and Neil J. Wilkof (Eds.), University of Chicago Press, 1978.

Scurlock, Reagan A., *Government Contracts and Grants for Research: A Guide for Colleges and Universities,* Washington, D.C.: The Association, 1975 (and revision one, 1976, supplementary update to the analyses).

Sindler, Allan P., *Bakke, DeFunis, and Minority Admissions: The Quest for Equal Opportunity,* Longman, 1979.

Smith, Bruce L. and Joseph J. Karlesky, *Background Papers,* New Rochelle, New York: Change Magazine Press, Vol. 2, 1978.

————,*The State of Academic Science, Vol. 1, The Universities in the Nation's Research Effort,* New Rochelle, New York: Change Magazine Press, 1977.

Walker, Donald E., *The Effective Administrator: A Practical Approach to Problem Solving, Decision Making, and Campus Leadership,* San Francisco: Jossey-Bass, 1979.

Wegener, Charles, *Liberal Education and the Modern University,* Chicago: University of Chicago Press, 1979.

Weinschrott, David J., *Demand for Higher Education in the United States: A Critical Review of the ˙Empirical Literature,* Report R-2195-LE, Rand Corporation, Santa Monica, California, 1977.

Wilkinson, J. Harvie III, *From Brown to Bakke,* Oxford, England: Oxford University Press, 1979.

Woodrow, Raymond J., *Management for Research in U.S. Universities,* Washington, D.C.: National Association of College and University Business Officers, 1978.

NACUBO PROFESSIONAL PAPERS

"Business-Education: Parallels in Management," Edgar B. Speer (September 1976).

"External Forces Affecting Higher Education," Stephen K. Bailey (August 1975).

"Financing Instruction in Public Higher Education," John D. Millett (July 1977).

"Legislative Financial Issues in Higher Education: 1976 and Beyond," A. Alan Post, (December 1976).

"Performance Management in Higher Education," Elmer B. Staats (August 1976).

"Resource Management and Financial Equilibrium," William F. Massy (October 1975).

"Systems Theory, Excellence, and Values: Will They Mix?" Howard R. Bowen (February 1977).

"Reduction Planning: Managing in an Era of Decline," Harvey H. Kaiser (September 1976).

"Management Data Base Development," Robert L. Dan (July 1975).

"Management Reporting: Who Really Needs What?" Jerry Dermer (March 1974).

"Management Systems and Budgeting Methodology: Do They Meet the Needs and Will They Work?" Peggy Heim (September 1972).

"The Governing Board's Role in Risk Management and Insurance for Higher Education," by the Insurance and Risk Management Committee, NACUBO (March 1973).

"Student Financial Aid: True Costs?" William T. Haywood (July 1976).

"A Comprehensive Personnel System for Colleges and Universities," Owen R. Houghton (January 1974).

"On the Management of People," John D. R. Cole (September 1975).

"Personnel Management: Stewardship of Human Resources," Douglas G. MacLean (October 1976).

"The National Labor Relations Act and Higher Education: Prospects and Problems," Robert E. Doherty (June 1973).

"Energy Planning: A Total Concept," Stephen S. J. Hall (November 1975).

"Budget Control and Analysis in the Small College," A. Dean Buchanan (August 1977).

"State Budgeting for Higher Education," Lyman A. Glenny (January 1976).

"Cost Behavior Analysis for Planning in Higher Education," Daniel D. Robinson, Howard W. Ray, and Frederick J. Turk (May 1977).

"Cost Benefit Analysis in Non-traditional Education," Charles A. Parker (April 1975).

"Educational Policy Analysis—A Long Way to Go," John A. Bielec (March 1975).

"Inflation in the Higher Education Industry," G. Richard Wynn (January 1975).

"Accounting Principles and Financial Statements," Daniel D. Robinson (May 1973).

"Analysis and Interpretation of Financial Data," Daniel D. Robinson (June 1975).

"Meeting the Demand for Accountability," Clarence Scheps (March 1976).

Index

Index